TRADITIONS IN SOCIAL THEORY

Founding Editor: Ian Craib

Series Editor: Rob Stones

This series offers a selection of concise introductions to particular traditions in sociological thought. It aims to deepen the reader's knowledge of particular theoretical approaches and at the same time to enhance their wider understanding of sociological theorising. Each book will offer: a history of the chosen approach and the debates that have driven it forward; a discussion of the current state of the debates within the approach (or debates with other approaches); and an argument for the distinctive contribution of the approach and its likely future value. The series is a companion to the *Themes in Social Theory* series, edited by Rob Stones.

Published

PHILOSOPHY OF SOCIAL SCIENCE (*Second Edition*)
Ted Benton and Ian Craib

CRITICAL THEORY
Alan How

STRUCTURATION THEORY
Rob Stones

MARXISM AND SOCIAL THEORY
Jonathon Joseph

MICRO SOCIAL THEORY
Brian Roberts

Forthcoming

THE DURKHEIMIAN QUEST
David Howarth

POST-STRUCTURALISM AND AFTER
Willie Watts Miller and Susan Stedman Jones

THEMES IN SOCIAL THEORY

This series explores how cutting-edge research within the social sciences relies on combinations of social theory and empirical evidence. Different books examine how this relationship works in particular subject areas, from technology and health to politics and human rights. Giving the reader a brief overview of the major theoretical approaches used in an area, the books then describe their application in a range of empirical projects. Each text looks at contemporary and classical theories, provides a map of primary research carried out in the subject area and highlights advances in the field. The series is a companion to the *Traditions in Social Theory* series, founded by Ian Craib and edited by Rob Stones.

Published

HEALTH AND SOCIAL THEORY
Fernando De Maio

Forthcoming

CRIME AND SOCIAL THEORY
Eammon Carrabine

POLITICS AND SOCIAL THEORY
Will Leggett

TECHNOLOGY AND SOCIAL THEORY
Steve Matthewman

HUMAN RIGHTS AND SOCIAL THEORY
Lydia Morris

INTERNATIONAL MIGRATION AND SOCIAL THEORY
Karen O'Reilly

ENVIRONMENT, NATURE AND SOCIAL THEORY
Damian White, Alan Rudy and Brian Gareau

Further titles in preparation

Philosophy of Social Science

*The Philosophical Foundations of
Social Thought*

2nd Edition

Ted Benton
and
Ian Craib

First edition 2001
Second edition 2011
Published by PALGRAVE MACMILLAN

Palgrave Macmillan in the UK is an imprint of Macmillan Publishers Limited, registered in England, company number 785998, of Houndmills, Basingstoke, Hampshire RG21 6XS.

Palgrave Macmillan in the US is a division of St Martin's Press LLC, 175 Fifth Avenue, New York, NY 10010.

Palgrave Macmillan is the global academic imprint of the above companies and has companies and representatives throughout the world.

Palgrave® and Macmillan® are registered trademarks in the United States, the United Kingdom, Europe and other countries.

ISBN 978–0–230–24259–3 hardback
ISBN 978–0–230–24260–9 paperback

This book is printed on paper suitable for recycling and made from fully managed and sustained forest sources. Logging, pulping and manufacturing processes are expected to conform to the environmental regulations of the country of origin.

A catalogue record for this book is available from the British Library.

A catalog record for this book is available from the Library of Congress.

10   9   8   7   6   5   4   3   2   1
20   19   18   17   16   15   14   13   12   11

Printed in China

Contents

v

Preface to the Second Edition

The death of my co-author, Ian Craib, on the 22 December 2002 has made the preparation of this second edition both poignant and somewhat awesome. Although, rather to the surprise of both of us, we were able to co-write a book with little or no discomfort, there were quite deep differences of philosophical orientation between us (see Appendix I – originally intended to be included as Chapter 11 of the first edition). I have therefore refrained from any attempt at revision of Ian's chapters and, as a consequence, have left my own as they were However, in the 10 years or so since we wrote our respective sections of the book, the literature of the philosophy of social science has grown. As the rate of change in philosophy and its sub-disciplines is usually quite slow – even 'glacial' – it is unlikely that a topic such as ours will have been transformed in so short a time-span. Where new developments have seemed to me of particular significance, in clarifying, developing or calling into question our lines of argument in the first edition, I have added a short post-script to the relevant chapter. In most cases, this will refer the reader to a more detailed treatment in the new chapter 'Commentary on Recent Developments', written specifically for this edition. Again, published work that has appeared since the first edition has been added to the bibliography. Inevitably, the selection of new work for discussion in this edition would have been different if I had been sharing the task with Ian. Almost certainly significant new thinking has appeared but no one volume could cover all materials. Partly this is because the world of academic publishing has escalated in sheer volume to the point where any claim to 'completeness' must be treated with scepticism.

But also, some of the developments that have taken place more recently bear upon topics and traditions of thought that belong to Ian's share in the division of labour between us. As well as being less familiar with those topics than was Ian, I also have a somewhat different 'take' on the issues. So, where I comment on some of this literature (especially in relation to Chapter 6), I have taken the opportunity to include some thoughts of my own that open up differences with Ian's arguments. In fact, this was part of our original intention for the book – Ian and I had conducted one very long discussion, often including other colleagues and students, through the quarter-century that we worked together. Our initial thought was that we might actually emphasize our differences in this book and continue the debate in print. In the end, the book took the form of something closer to a conventional textbook than either of us had intended. If this new edition takes us back in this respect to something more like the original intentions of its authors, then the only sadness is that Ian is no longer around to add his characteristically pithy and insightful rejoinders. That said, enough of Ian remains in my head for me to hear him chortle a witty demolition.

I have also taken the liberty of responding to one of the reviewers of the first edition. Garry Potter (2002), in a very generous set of comments, argues for a rather different pedagogy. Maybe Ian and I were too scrupulous in being fair to the various positions we discussed – perhaps we should have made it clearer where we thought the arguments were more convincing? Should we have 'come out' more with our own (albeit provisional) intellectual positions? Of course, I cannot speak for Ian (though his contribution to Appendix I should give some illumination), but hopefully my own sympathies will be more evident in the new 'Commentary on Recent Developments'. However, despite their more 'committed' character, these notes are intended to retain the careful and respectful attitude to alternative points of view which (I hope) were a feature of the first edition. Partly because of its more committed nature, the new 'commentary' section will probably be experienced as more demanding in its level. New readers might be advised to read the relevant sections of the main text before turning to the new material.

In sum, this new edition includes brief updates on the state of debate on the topics covered in most chapters. These updates are added as post-scripts to the relevant chapters. There is a more extended review and critical commentary on what has seemed to me the more significant of the additions to the literature since Ian and I wrote the book. This new 'Commentary on Recent Developments' includes a detailed engagement with a recent book staunchly defending the work of Peter Winch that allows me to take the discussion of Winch's work rather further than Ian does in his Chapter 6. It also includes a discussion of an important development among the 'posts' in the shape of post-Marxist discourse theory, together with an overview of the great recent proliferation of work in the critical realist tradition.

This new edition also includes a slightly modified version of an obituary for Ian that I wrote for publication in the journal *Radical Philosophy*. Finally, I have included a chapter originally prepared for, but not published in, the first edition. Ian and I both felt that it would help readers to make sense of the selection of topics and arguments used in the book if we owned up to our own personal intellectual (and political) journeys. We accepted the advice of readers not to include it at that time, but the lapse of time since we wrote it has made it seem more appropriate for this second edition. The insights Ian gave into his own intellectual biography may be of particular interest.

Finally, many new works are included in the updated bibliography.

Ted Benton

1

Introduction to the First Edition

Philosophy and the Social Sciences

Philosophy and the social sciences are usually seen to be separate subjects, so why should students of the social sciences be interested in philosophy? We hope that this question will have answered itself by the end of our book, but we can make a start with it right away. At the time when modern science was in the process of emergence in the sixteenth and seventeenth centuries, it was very difficult to say where the boundary between philosophy and science should be placed. It was only later that it became more conventional to see a separation between the two. As this separation took place, there were two basic models of the relationship. In one view, philosophy could arrive at certain knowledge by rational argument. The most fundamental truths about ourselves and the nature of the world we live in, as well as the rules for arriving at such knowledge, could be established by philosophers. In this way, philosophy provided 'foundations' for the research done in the particular scientific specialisms. This is sometimes called the 'masterbuilder' or 'master-scientist' view of philosophy, and it is associated with an approach to philosophy called 'metaphysics'. In metaphysics, philosophers try to give an account of the universe, the world and everything in it. Nowadays philosophers tend to be a bit more modest.

The alternative view of the relation between philosophy and the sciences is sometimes called the 'underlabourer' view. On this view, it is accepted that armchair speculation about the nature of the world cannot give us certain or reliable knowledge. Knowledge can come only from practical experience, observation and systematic experimentation. So, the special sciences don't need to wait for philosophers to provide them with foundations, or to tell them what they should think. On the underlabourer view, philosophy should be there to provide help and support to the work of the scientists, as they get on with the job of discovering how nature works. But what sort of help can philosophy give?

There are various different views on this. One view is that in our common-sense thinking there are prejudices, superstitions and unquestioned assumptions which are obstacles to scientific progress. Philosophy can perhaps play a part in exposing these and criticizing them, so as to set science free. This is a bit like clearing away the dead leaves on the railway line to let the trains run on.

1

Another sort of help might be to provide a map of the pattern of existing scientific knowledge, so that scientific specialists can get some idea about where they are in the wider field of knowledge. A third possibility is that the philosophers can use their expertise in logic and argumentation in refining the methods of investigation which scientists use.

In this book, philosophy will be used in all these ways, but most importantly it will be used to provide underlabouring in yet another way. To see what this sort of help might be, we can remind ourselves that philosophy is not just an academic discipline. In everyday life people use the word to mean something rather different from its use in academic contexts. We sometimes say that someone who has had to face up to very distressing circumstances, such as a job loss, or bereavement, that they were 'philosophical' about it. Certainly, most of us do not spend a great deal of time soul-searching about the meaning of life, or the ultimate basis of our values and attitudes. However, there are moments in everyone's life when we are faced with serious moral dilemmas, or with such life-challenging events as losing a job, or a loved one, or being diagnosed with a serious illness. It is at times like these when we are forced to reflect on these questions of fundamental meaning and value in our lives. It is in this sense that, as the Italian Marxist philosopher, Antonio Gramsci (Gramsci 1971) said, 'Everyone is a philosopher.' But if we are philosophers at these times of crisis, it is also true that in the way we interact with each other in our everyday lives, in the way we choose to spend our free time, in the jobs we choose (if we are lucky enough to have that choice) and so on, we are still *implicitly* philosophers. Our lives display or represent, whether we are generally self-conscious about it or not, a philosophical orientation to the world. We can think of this as a tacit or practical philosophy of life.

So, how does this relate to the question we started out with – the relationship between philosophy and social science? If we go back to the map analogy, it is obvious that people don't usually refer to a map if they are confident they already know where they are going, and how to get there. In everyday life, when things are going on smoothly, with no major problems, we aren't forced to question our basic attitudes and priorities in life. But in the social sciences, things do not run along smoothly. (As we will see, the natural sciences don't run along smoothly either, but most of the time this fact is less obvious.) The social sciences are often derided by public figures and in the media, and social scientists themselves tend to be less confident about their achievements than are natural scientists: they can't prove their success by generating new and impressive technologies, for example. Moreover, social scientists are themselves divided about what is the nature of their disciplines. Many, for example, would not agree that their work is scientific in the same sense as the natural sciences are. Even the ones who do will often disagree about what science is. For this reason, social scientists, and sociologists in particular, tend to be more reflexive about their subjects than natural scientists – that is, they are more likely to spend time thinking about just what kind of activity sociology (or political science or anthropology or any other such subject) is, what sort of methods it should use, what sort of relationship it should have with its subject-matter and so on. The kinds of questions we ask when we are being reflexive in this way about our own disciplines are philosophical questions. They are not imposed on us from outside, as in the masterbuilder view, but they arise from within our subjects, as a result of the special difficulties and deep disagreements that we find there. So, the main job of underlabouring we will be doing in this book will be an attempt to address the question: 'What are we doing when we attempt to study human social life in a systematic way?' Depending on how we answer that question, further questions arise: what are the proper methods of investigation of social processes? Can there be objective knowledge of society when the investigators as well as the subject-matter are all part of society? What role do moral and political values play in our work? How should we view the fact of continuing disagreement among social scientists about basics? Is this perhaps a sign of the immaturity of the social sciences, or is it something we should expect as a permanent fact of life, and even welcome? And so on.

A Philosophical Toolkit

To help us be more systematic in our reflexive investigation, we can call in the help of the academic discipline of philosophy. There are some very valuable ideas and arguments we can draw upon, but always, of course, to answer questions posed by the problems we face as would-be social scientists. There are four sub-disciplines, or fields, within philosophy from which we can most usefully draw. These are:

Theory of knowledge

The technical term for this is 'epistemology'. In the seventeenth-century disputes about philosophy and science there were two main alternative views, in opposition to each other. Generally, the masterbuilders had a 'rationalist' view of the nature of knowledge. They were very impressed by mathematics, which seemed to arrive at absolutely certain conclusions by formal reasoning. The seventeenth-century French philosopher Descartes (1641, 1931) is perhaps the best known of the rationalists. His method of systematically doubting everything that could be doubted led him to the conclusion that even as he doubted he must at least be thinking. So what could not be doubted was his own existence as a thinking being. This provided the certain foundation from which he was able (at least to his own satisfaction!) to begin the task of reconstructing the whole edifice of knowledge.

The rival theory of knowledge, generally associated with the underlabourer view, was 'empiricism'. For the empiricist philosophers (see Honderich 1999), the sole source of knowledge about the world was the evidence of our senses. At birth, they held, the human mind is a blank sheet, as it were, and our knowledge is acquired subsequently, through learning to recognize recurrent patterns in our experience, and attaching general ideas to them. Genuine knowledge (as distinct from mere belief, or prejudice) is limited to the statement of these patterns in experience, and what can be inferred from them. The apparent certainty of the conclusions of mathematical and logical arguments, which the rationalists were so impressed by, is due to the fact that they are true by definition. So the certainty of such statements as 'All bachelors are male', or '$2 + 2 = 4$', tells us nothing we didn't already know about the world. They are statements in which we make explicit the implications of the way we define certain words, or mathematical operations.

As we will see, the empiricist view of knowledge has been the one that most natural and social scientists have appealed to when making out their claims to provide genuine or authoritative knowledge. It is also the view of knowledge which is closest to most people's common-sense intuitions: 'Seeing is believing,' 'I saw it with my own eyes.'

Ontology

This is a technical term in philosophy, and unfortunately it is used in very different ways in different traditions of philosophical thinking. In the sense we use the term here, an 'ontology' is the answer one would give to the question: 'What kinds of things are there in the world?' In the history of philosophy the many different ways of answering this question can be loosely divided into four main traditions. 'Materialists' have argued that the world is made up entirely of matter (or 'matter in motion'), and the different characteristics of material objects, living things, people, societies and so on can in principle be explained in terms of the greater or lesser complexity of the organization of matter. By contrast, 'idealists' have argued that the ultimate reality is mental, or spiritual. This may be because they, like Descartes, think that their experience of their own inner, conscious life is the thing they can be most certain of. If one begins with this, then it can seem reasonable to think of the material objects and other bodies one encounters as constructs of one's own inner thought processes. As we will see, 'constructivist' views of the external world, with historical roots in Descartes's philosophy, have become fashionable in sociology and related disciplines.

But idealists do have difficulty in being fully convincing when they deny the independent materiality of the external world, and, similarly, materialists have difficulty being fully convincing in explaining away the distinctive character of subjective experience. This is why a third option has been quite popular in the history of philosophy. This is referred to as 'dualism'. Again, Descartes is a convenient and well-known example. Having convinced himself of his own existence as a thinking being, it seemed to him that there was a further question as to whether he existed as an embodied, material being. Eventually, he was able to be certain of that, but in the process came to see body and mind as two quite different kinds of thing, or 'substance'. So human individuals were, for him, a rather mysterious and contingent combination of a mechanical body with a ghostly mind, or soul (see Ryle 1976).

In Descartes especially we see a close connection between epistemology, or theory of knowledge, on the one hand, and ontology, on the other: what is accepted as *existing* depends on how confident we can be about our *knowledge* of it. For some philosophers, the apparent difficulty of being sure about the nature of anything beyond the limits of our own conscious experience leads them to 'agnosticism'. This is not just the don't-know option in the philosophers' public opinion poll. Rather, it is the positive doctrine that the nature of the world as it exists independently of our subjective experience just cannot be known.

This rather crude division of philosophers into rival materialist, idealist, dualist and agnostic traditions does have some relevance to debates in the social sciences, and we can find many echoes of the debates among philosophers here. However, the disputes in the social sciences tend to be more localized in character. They usually concern not philosophical ontology, but what we might call regional or special ontology. So, instead of asking 'What kinds of things are there in the world?', we might, as biologists, ask 'What kinds of things are living organisms made up of, and how are they put together?' As chemists, we might ask: 'How many elements are there, what are their properties, how do they interact, and so on?' Each discipline has its own regional ontology, its own way of listing, describing and classifying the range of things, relations or processes it deals with; this is the range of things which it claims to give us knowledge of.

In the case of the social sciences, there are deep, on-going controversies about what the constituents of the social world are. One of the most basic disputes has to do with whether society itself is an independent reality in its own right (a 'reality *sui generis*', as Durkheim put it). So-called 'methodological individualists' argue against this. For them, society is nothing over and above the collection of individual people who make it up. Another ontological dispute concerns whether sociologists are justified in referring to social and economic structures and processes which exist independently of the symbolic or cultural meanings of social actors. Are we justified, for example, in talking sociologically about social classes and class interests in societies where individual social actors have no concept of themselves as belonging to social classes?

Logic

So far we've often referred to the disputes, disagreements, arguments and so on which go on among philosophers and social scientists. If we examine the texts in which these disputes are conducted, we will often find stereotyping and caricaturing of one another's views, outright misrepresentation, questioning of political motives, allegations of bias and so on. While these tactics might have a lot of rhetorical and persuasive force, they are not the same thing as good arguments. The discipline of logic is an attempt to set down in a systematic way what makes the difference between a good and a bad argument. When we construct an argument we are usually attempting to show why a particular statement (our 'conclusion') should be accepted as true. In order to do this, we bring together other statements, which give an account of the relevant evidence, or other considerations, which provide the grounds for believing the truth of the conclusions. These statements are the 'premisses' of the argument. A 'valid argument' is one in which the conclusion follows from the premisses. It is one in which anyone who accepts the premisses *must* accept the conclusion. This does not mean that the conclusion itself must be true, only that it is as reliable or as well established as the premisses from which it is derived. For example:

> If there is a peace settlement in Ireland, this government has at least one great achievement to its credit.
>   There is a peace settlement in Ireland.
>   ————
> Therefore: This government has at least one great achievement to its credit.

This is a valid argument, because the conclusion does follow from the premisses.

However, the conclusion could still be false, because there might turn out not to be a peace settlement in Ireland, or because even if there is, it might not be an achievement of the government. Interestingly, the conclusion could also turn out to be true, even though the premisses turned out to be false, because the government might, for example, have failed to settle the Irish question, but have found a permanent solution to the problem of unemployment instead. What the validity of the argument *does* rule out is the possibility that both premisses could be true and the conclusion false.

However, this is not a book on formal logic, and most of the time we will have to rely on our intuitive sense of when an argument is or is not valid. The important thing to keep in mind is that the validity of an argument is a matter of the logical relationship between sets of statements. It is not a matter of how good or bad the evidence is for or against any particular factual claim (though, confusingly, in research methods courses, there is a completely different use of the term 'validity' to refer to the adequacy of a measure to quantify the thing it is supposed to be measuring).

Ethics and Moral Philosophy

Ethical questions arise at many points in the course of social scientific research. Sociologists are often involved in uncovering information about the beliefs and practices of the people they study which might put those people at risk. Some-times this might be because the practices concerned are socially stigmatized, and the researcher might be concerned not to jeopardize the anonymity of her or his informants. Alternatively, the researcher might well feel that her dis-covery of corrupt or unjustly discriminatory practices in official organizations ought to be made public. But doing so would at the same time be a betrayal of trust, and might also jeopardize the possibility of further research. Often, too, researchers may be employed to carry out research for projects they did not design, or for organizations whose aims they might not sympathize with. To what extent should they keep quiet about their reservations in order to keep their career prospects open?

These are moral quandaries which frequently arise in the course of research practice. There are other ethical questions which are intrinsic to the research process itself. These have to do with the power relations between researcher and researched. In most social research there is inequality of social status between the two, and even where there is not, the social scientist is implicitly claiming the authority to interpret and represent the beliefs or attitudes of those who are the objects of study. Where there are class, gender, ethnic or other social differences between researcher and researched, such ethical issues necessarily arise.

Finally, sociologists and anthropologists, especially, are constantly confronted by the enormous diversity of human cultures and subcultures. Part of this diversity is diversity in moral values. Because of the ethnographic requirement to interpret other cultures in terms available to the participants in those cultures, these social scientists must be able to suspend their own judgements. The ethical sensitivity which goes along with this, and reflexivity about the power relations between researcher and researched, leads many sociologists and anthropologists towards a position of 'moral relativism'. That is to say, they tend to resist the idea that there are universally obligatory moral values, applicable across all cultures. Morality comes to be seen as a matter of what participants in each culture take to be acceptable or unacceptable. No one culture has a right to dictate to any other what rules it should live by.

On the other hand, closer examination shows that cultures themselves tend not to be so consensual internally as this picture assumes. If there are ethical conflicts *within* a culture, the relativist view is not much help. Also, it can be argued that the relativist position itself rests on a universal principle – that all cultures have a right to their own autonomy and integrity. Finally, it is much easier to adopt the stance of a moral relativist in the abstract than when confronted with a real moral issue. When they encounter cultures in which systematic torture, female circumcision, endemic racism or capital punishment is accepted as morally proper, most social scientists are liable to find their capacity to suspend judgement sorely tested.

So, there seems to be plenty of room for the help of moral philosophy in the work of the social sciences!

Politics and Political Philosophy

These moral issues that might be faced by the researcher have wider implications. Whether we are thinking about female circumcision, capital punishment or social stratification, we are implicitly or explicitly taking a stand on what sort of society we want to live in, and what the 'good' society might look like. Some social sciences and social scientists have been intimately involved with political arguments and processes – from Marx's leading role in the foundation of the International Working Men's Association to Anthony Giddens's involvement with New Labour and the 'Third Way' (from the sublime to the ridiculous?). Government advisers include economists, political scientists, social policy and other experts (although interestingly not many psychologists and historians), all of whom would regard themselves as in some sense or another social scientists. It is not just in the social sciences that we find this connection, since modern governments have teams of natural science advisers. The main difference is that in the latter case, scientific advice is commonly treated as a clear warrant for or legitimation of action.

Be that as it may, the social sciences raise issues about the desirability and possibility of different types of society, and this takes us into issues of political philosophy. This will become most apparent when we discuss the idea of an 'emancipatory' science – a science whose aim is human liberation – and theories of feminist epistemology, developed from Marxism, that suggest that an oppressed group has access to knowledge in a way that other groups do not. Politics will, however, always be close to the surface.

The Book and Its Arguments

It is important to emphasize that this is going to be a book of arguments – arguments about the nature of the social sciences that are not settled, and perhaps by their nature cannot be. Each science, each type of science, changes and is affected by changes in related disciplines as researchers and thinkers learn from each other. We will be discussing the issues in fairly general terms – our aim is to introduce the student to the most general issues, and at this level the development of the field is comparatively slow. There are two ways in the which the reader can approach this book, the first being to see it as a high-altitude photograph or a small-scale map of a particular terrain in which he or she can situate a particular discipline or approach even if we do not mention it directly. It should be possible to situate every social science and every variation somewhere in the picture or on the map. The arguments we explore in relation to one science can certainly be discovered in others.

The second way to approach the book is as a sort of language primer, an introduction to often difficult ideas and arguments which take time to learn and which are best learnt through participating in the arguments. In an everyday sense we are all philosophers, and as you read you should reflect on your own ideas about the subject you are studying: for example, does the way in which you think about your subject, whether it be geography, sociology, economics, psychology, history or whatever, place it near to or far away from the natural sciences?

We will in fact start by examining the philosophy of natural science. The natural sciences are not as monolithic or simplistic in their approach as critics often seem to assume. Even within the most influential philosophy of natural science, known as 'empiricism', we can find a number of different approaches, and there has been a serious questioning of principles and accepted views of scientific progress from within the philosophy of natural science and the natural sciences themselves. We will be discussing arguments that the social sciences, if they are to be 'real sciences', should model themselves on the empiricist account of science, and we will be discussing where this might or might not be appropriate. We will also be looking at developments in the history and social study of the natural sciences that raise important questions about the nature and status of the knowledge produced by those disciplines.

It might seem strange to start a book on the philosophy of the social sciences with three chapters on the natural sciences, but the two are intimately related. It is not possible to grasp the development of philosophical debates in the social sciences or indeed the development of the social sciences themselves without a knowledge of the way in which the natural sciences have thought about themselves, and the way philosophers have thought about them, as they have developed. These chapters are centrally concerned with empiricist views of natural science, and with the critics of empiricism. The most telling criticisms of empiricism as an account of natural scientific knowledge have come from approaches which recognize the sciences as historically and socially located practices. However, sociological and historical approaches to the understanding of science themselves make knowledge-claims, use empirical methods of research and so on. So to treat their findings about science as authoritatively true would beg the central questions of this book. As we will see in Chapter 4, attempts to construct sociological and historical accounts of science as alternatives to the empiricist view remain controversial. The divisions and debates in the field of social studies of science, or science studies, have many connections with, and often directly reflect, the more general debates about the nature of social scientific knowledge which make up our theme in this book. The main approaches we will introduce in Chapter 4 are selected partly by virtue of the influence they have had on debates in the philosophy of social science, and partly because of their importance as background to the discussion in later chapters. In most cases, we have had space to provide only a brief introductory outline, and you are advised to follow up approaches which interest you with further reading.

We will move from this discussion to an examination of those positions and writers that argue that the social sciences, or some social sciences, *are* scientific but not in the same way as the natural sciences. The social sciences study human beings, and human beings are different from the objects of physics or chemistry – they know they are being studied, they can understand what is said about them and they can take the scientists' findings into account and act differently.

This approach is more closely linked to the rationalist tradition, although in the social sciences it is often referred to as 'interpretivist'. There are in fact several such interpretivist positions and several different conceptions of rationality to be found in the social sciences: the simple instrumental rationality of rational choice theory to be found in some forms of economics and some forms of sociology; the more complicated instrumental rationality of Weberian sociology and the descendants of G. H. Mead's pragmatism; the idea of rationality as rule-following, stemming from anthropology and the philosophy of Wittgenstein and Peter Winch; and the notion of dialectical or critical rationality developed from the Marxist interpretation of the German idealist philosopher G. W. F. Hegel. We will be exploring and comparing all of these approaches.

This will take us on to more recent developments, which move in two directions. One development of some of the arguments about positivism in the natural and social sciences has been the development of modern critical realism, particularly in such disciplines as geography, sociology, politics, economics and psychology. Whereas positivism is primarily concerned with epistemology, the theory of knowledge, realism is primarily concerned with *ontology*, the theory of what exists in the world. This enables a reopening of the debate about the relationship between the social and natural sciences, in a way which suggests that there are both similarities and differences between the two – a more sophisticated view than we will have come across before.

The second development has been towards a systematic relativism. In this book we will trace this through the development of identity politics and in particular feminism. Some feminists have tried to develop a feminist epistemology, basing their arguments on the work of the early twentieth-century Marxist philosopher George Lukács, who argued that the proletariat, the working class, had a privileged position as far as knowledge of the social world was concerned precisely because of their underprivileged position in that world. To put it very crudely, they had nothing to lose by acknowledging the truth. Lukács was of course more sophisticated than this might suggest, as are the feminist philosophers who tried to develop his ideas to argue the same point about women. There is a continuing debate between advocates of various versions of this 'standpoint' epistemology and their post-modernist critics.

We will follow this first through the development of post-structuralism. The first generation of structuralist theorists developed the idea of underlying structures in society and social life, using a linguistic analogy. Realism developed the idea further, but post-structuralism has moved away from this concern to become part of what is now known as the 'linguistic turn' in twentieth-century philosophy. This approach sees the social world as constituted in and by language, or different 'discourses'. In much post-structuralist philosophy we find the development of a relativist position – the idea that no one discourse is more right, or scientific, than another. This approach has been particularly influential in sociology, cultural studies and social psychology and the study of literature, but it can also be found in history. Post-modernism takes this move-ment even further, almost to the point of abandoning philosophy altogether – or more accurately using philosophical arguments against philosophy.

How to Read the Book

To repeat: this is a book of arguments not of conclusions. It should perhaps be read as a primer in constructing arguments. Most students should find them-selves intuitively sympathetic to one position or another. If you do, you should first try to work out the reasons for and the implications of holding a particular position, and then try to argue against yourself from alternative points of view and see what happens. You should be asking questions about how these ideas apply to your particular discipline: Are some of them irrelevant to the pursuit of knowledge or understanding in your area? Are they mutually exclusive? Whatever you do, don't stop asking questions about these ideas.

As well as being a book of arguments and about arguments, it is a book which has grown out of arguments between the authors, who have taught a course together in the University of Essex sociology department for the last twenty-five years. We think that the ideas and arguments presented here have a life of their own, independently of the biographies of their authors. They can be evaluated, criticized, tested for their wider applicability, accepted, rejected, played with or developed according to the interests of the reader. On the other hand, the biographies of the authors do have a bearing on the pattern of inclu-sions and exclusions, emphases and omissions you will find in the book. Ideas don't drop from the sky (to quote an eminent philosopher), and it will help you to situate yourself in relation to our arguments to know something of where they came from. Both authors could be described as of the generation of the sixties. We both started out with a strong sense of the political and moral significance of social scientific work. As philosophically informed social scien-tists, we were engaged through our careers with attempting to make sense of our work as would-be social scientists in a historical context which has changed enormously during that period, and in ways which have repeatedly called into question our favourite assumptions. Our initial commitments to Marxism (though on opposite sides of the debate then raging about how to understand and develop that tradition) were called into question by proliferating social movements and issues which could not be readily addressed without deep revision of basic assumptions. Black power, gay rights and liberation, feminism in its many forms and, more recently, the green movement provided intellectual challenges with which we are still trying to grapple, with effects noticeable throughout this book. Given our different starting-points in the discipline, we have addressed these challenges in rather different ways. I. C. has focused on the problematic relationship between social scientific approaches and the understanding of subjective life and personal agency. Meanwhile, T. B. has been concerned with the no less problematic relationship between the social sciences and the understanding of non-human nature – a concern prompted by both green and feminist thought. These differences in biography go a long way to explaining the differences of emphasis you will find in the different parts of the book, and also the division of labour we have adopted in the allocation of the chapters.

Although we have worked together on all chapters, we should plead guilty to those parts of the book for which we carry prime responsibility: Ted Benton for Chapters 2, 3, 4, 8 and 9, Ian Craib for Chapters 5, 6, 7 and 10. We both contributed to the introduction and conclusion. All mistakes are of course the responsibility of the other author!

2

Empiricism and Positivism
in Science

Introduction

In this chapter we will discuss the main outlines of the empiricist account of natural science, and then go on to consider why and how the positivist tradition has tried to apply it to social scientific explanation.

Empiricism and the Theory of Knowledge

As we mentioned in Chapter 1, the history of modern science and the history of theories of knowledge have been closely bound up with each other. Sciences such as physics and chemistry, which rely a great deal on observation and experiment, have tended to justify their methods and knowledge-claims in terms of the empiricist view of knowledge. Empiricist philosophers have tended to return the compliment, by treating science as the highest form of genuine knowledge, or often even the only one. In the twentieth century, empiricist philosophers (particularly those, such as R. Carnap (1966), and the British philosopher A. J. Ayer (1946), who are known as the 'logical positivists') have been especially concerned to draw a clear dividing line between science, as genuine knowledge, and various belief-systems such as religion, metaphysics, psychoanalysis and Marxism. In the empiricist view, these belief-systems, which sometimes present themselves as scientific, can be shown to be 'pseudo-sciences' (though it is a bit more complicated than this – one of the leading logical positivists, Otto Neurath, was also a Marxist). One of the difficulties they have encountered in trying to do this is that a very strict criterion of scientific status, which is adequate to the job of keeping out Marxism, psychoanalysis and the rest, generally also rules out a great deal of established science!

Although empiricist philosophy is concerned with the nature and scope of knowledge in general, our concern is more narrowly with its account of natural science. We will also be working with an 'ideal-typical' construct of empiricist

13

philosophy, which does not take much notice of the many different versions of empiricism. Anyone who wants to take these debates further will need to read more widely to get an idea of the more sophisticated variants of empiricism. For our purposes, the empiricist view of science can be characterized in terms of seven basic doctrines:

1. The individual human mind starts out as a 'blank sheet'. We acquire our knowledge from our sensory experience of the world and our interaction with it.
2. Any genuine knowledge-claim is testable by experience (observation or experiment).
3. This rules out knowledge-claims about beings or entities which cannot be observed.
4. Scientific laws are statements about general, recurring patterns of experience.
5. To explain a phenomenon scientifically is to show that it is an instance of a scientific law. This is sometimes referred to as the 'covering law' model of scientific explanation.
6. If explaining a phenomenon is a matter of showing that it is an example or 'instance' of a general law, then knowing the law should enable us to predict future occurrences of phenomena of that type. The logic of prediction and explanation is the same. This is sometimes known as the thesis of the 'symmetry of explanation and prediction'.
7. Scientific objectivity rests on a clear separation of (testable) factual statements from (subjective) value judgements.

We can now put some flesh on these bare bones. The first doctrine of empiricism is associated with it historically, but it is not essential. In the seventeenth and eighteenth centuries, empiricists tended to accept some version of the association of ideas as their theory of how the mind works, and how learning takes place. This governed their view of how individuals acquire their knowledge (that is, from experience, and not from the inheritance of innate ideas, or instinct). Today's empiricists are not bound to accept this, and they generally make an important distinction between the process of gaining or acquiring knowledge (a matter for psychology) and the process of testing whether beliefs or hypotheses (however we acquired them) are true. In the terminology of Karl Popper, this is the distinction between the 'context of discovery' and the 'context of justification'.

The second doctrine of empiricism is at the core of this philosophical approach. The basic point the empiricists are making is that if you want us to accept any claim as true, you should be able to state what the evidence for it is. If you can go on claiming it is true whatever evidence turns up, then you are not making a factual statement at all. If the manufacturer of a food additive claims that it is safe for human consumption, but cannot give evidence that anyone has yet consumed it, we would expect the official body concerned with food safety standards to refuse to accept their assurances. If they then provide results of tests on animal and subsequently human consumers of the product which show unexpected instances of symptoms of food-poisoning, but continue to insist the product is safe, we might start to suspect that they are not interested in the truth, but solely in selling the product. Thus far, this doctrine of empiricism accords very closely with widely held (and very reasonable!) intuitions.

It is important to note that our statement of the second doctrine of empiricism could be misleading. For empiricism, a statement can be accepted in this sense as genuine knowledge, or as scientific, without being true. The important point is that statements must be capable of being shown to be true *or false*, by referring to actual or possible sources of evidence. On this criterion, 'The moon is made of green cheese' is acceptable, because it can be made clear what evidence of the senses will count for it, and what evidence will count against it. A statement such as 'God will reward the faithful' is ruled out because it cannot be made clear what evidence would count for or against it, or because believers continue to believe in it whatever evidence turns up. This latter possibility is significant, since for some empiricists the testability of a statement is not so much a matter of the properties of the statement as of the way believers in it respond to experiences which appear to count against it.

But once we recognize that there might be a choice about whether to give up our beliefs when we face evidence which seems to count against them, this raises problems about what it is to test a belief, or knowledge-claim. In a recently reported case, it was claimed by a group of researchers that rates of recovery of patients suffering from a potentially fatal disease who were undergoing additional treatment at a complementary clinic were actually worse than those of patients not undergoing this treatment. This appeared to be strong evidence that the treatment was ineffective, if not actually harmful. Would it have been right for the clinic to have accepted these findings, and to have closed down forthwith? In the event, subsequent analysis of the data suggested that patients selected for the additional treatment had, on average, poorer prognoses than those who were not. They were, in any case, less likely to recover, so that the research did not, after all, show the treatment to be ineffective or even harmful. Even had advocates of the 'complementary' treatment not been able to show this weakness in the research design, they might well have argued that a more prolonged investigation, or one which included the results of a number of different clinics offering the same sort of treatment, might have come up with more favourable evidence.

In this case, a potentially beneficial treatment might have been abandoned if its advocates had been too ready to accept apparent evidence against it. On the other hand, to keep hanging on to a belief against repeated failure of test-expectations starts to look suspicious. However, because tests rarely, if ever, provide conclusive proof or disproof of a knowledge-claim, judgement is generally involved in deciding how to weigh the significance of new evidence.

In practice it can be very difficult to see where to draw the line between someone who is being reasonably cautious in not abandoning their beliefs, and someone who is dogmatically hanging on to them come what may.

This is a big problem for the empiricist philosophers of science who want a sharp dividing line between science and pseudo-science, and want to base it on the criterion of 'testability' by observation or experiment. To preserve the distinctive status of scientific knowledge-claims they need to reduce the scope for legitimate disagreement about how to weigh evidence for or against a hypothesis. There are two obvious ways of doing this. One is to be very strict about what can count as a hypothesis, or scientific statement, so that the knowledge-claims it makes are very closely tied to the evidence for or against it. A general statement which just summarizes descriptions of direct observations might satisfy this requirement. A standard textbook example is 'All swans are white.' This is supported by every observation of a white swan, and actually disproved by any single observation of a non-white swan.

This example can also be used to illustrate the second way of tightening up on testability. If we consider the implications of the claim that all swans are white, it is clear that it is about an indefinitely large class of possible observations. Someone interested in testing it could go out and observe large numbers of swans of different species, in different habitats and in different countries. The more swans observed without encountering a non-white one, the more confidence the researcher is likely to have that the universal statement is true: each successive observation will tend to add to this confidence, and be counted as confirmation. This seems to be common sense, but, as we will see, there are serious problems with it. However, for empiricist philosophers of science, the issue is seen as one of finding a set of rules which will enable us to measure the degree of confidence we are entitled to have in the truth of a knowledge-claim (the degree of confirmation it has) on the basis of any given finite set of observations. A great deal of ingenuity has gone into applying mathematical probability theory to this problem.

The third doctrine of empiricism was initially meant to rule out as unscientific appeals to God's intentions, or nature's purposes, as explanatory principles. Darwin's explanation of the adaptive character of many features of living organisms in terms of differential reproduction rates of random individual variations over many generations made it possible to explain the *appearance* of design in nature without reference to God, the designer. But in many scientific, or would-be scientific, disciplines, researchers appeal to entities or forces which are not observable. Newton's famous law of universal gravitation, for example, has been used to explain the rotation of the earth around the sun, the orbit of the moon, the motion of the tides, the path of projectiles, the acceleration of freely falling bodies near the earth's surface and many other things. However, no one has ever seen gravity. It has been similar with the theory that matter is made up of minute particles, or atoms. This theory was accepted as scientific long before instruments were developed to detect atomic- and molecular-level processes. And even now that such instruments have been developed, the interpretation of observations and measurements made with them depends on theoretical assumptions – including the assumption that the atomic view of matter is true!

Other appeals to unobservable entities and forces have not been accepted. These include the view, widely held among biologists until the middle of the last century, that there were fundamental differences between living and non-living things. Living things displayed 'spontaneity', in the sense that they did not behave predictably in response to external influences, and they also showed something like 'purposiveness' in the way individuals develop from single cells to adult organisms. These distinctive features of living things were attributed, by 'vitalist' biologists, to an additional force, the 'vital force'. The opponents of this view had several different criticisms of it. Some were philosophical materialists in their ontology, and were committed to finding explanations in terms of the chemistry of living things. But the vitalists were also criticized in empiricist terms for believing in unobservable forces and 'essences'. More recently, the empiricists have directed their attention to psychoanalysis as a pseudo-science which postulates unobservable entities such as the unconscious, the superego and so on (Cioffi 1970; Craib 1989).

The fourth doctrine of empiricism is its account of the nature of scientific laws. It is acknowledged that a very large part of the achievement of modern science is its accumulation of general statements about regularities in nature. These are termed 'scientific laws', or 'laws of nature'. We have already mentioned Newton's law of gravitation. Put simply, this states that all bodies in the universe attract each other with a force that is proportional to their masses, but also gets weaker the further they are apart. Not all laws are obviously universal in this way. For example, some naturally occurring materials are unstable and give off radiation. The elements concerned (such as uranium, radium and plutonium) exist in more than one form. The unstable form (or 'isotope') tends to emit radiation as its atoms 'decay'. Depending on the isotope concerned, a constant proportion of its atoms will decay over a given time period. The law governing radioactive decay for each isotope is therefore statistical, or probabilistic, like a lot of the generalizations that are familiar in the social sciences. A common way of representing this is to state the time period over which, for each isotope, half of its atoms undergo decay. So, the half-life of uranium-235 is 700 million years, that of radon-220 a mere 52 seconds. Of course, this can also be represented as a universal law in the sense that each and every sample of radon-220 will show the same statistical pattern.

In biology, it is harder to find generalizations which can count as universal in the same way. One of the best-known examples is provided by the work of the nineteenth-century Augustinian monk Gregor Mendel. He was interested in explaining how the characteristics of organisms get passed on from generation to generation. He did breeding experiments on different varieties of pea plants, using pairs of contrasting characteristics, or 'traits', such as round- versus wrinkled-seed shapes, and yellow versus green colour. He showed that the off-spring of cross-breedings did not, as might be expected, show blending of these characters. On the contrary, the offspring in successive generations showed definite statistical patterns of occurrence of each of the parental traits. These statistical patterns are Mendel's laws, and Mendel is generally acknowledged as the founder of modern genetics.

However, Mendel did not stop at simply making these statistical general-izations. He reasoned back from them to their implications for the nature of the process of biological inheritance itself. His results showed that some factor in the reproductive cells of the pea plants is responsible for each of the traits, that this factor remains constant through the generations, and that when two dif-ferent factors are present in the same cell (as must be the case for at least some of the offspring of cross-breeding), only one of them is active in producing the observed trait. Subsequently, it became conventional to refer to these factors as 'genes', and to distinguish between 'dominant' and 'recessive' genes according to which trait was produced when the genes for both were present together. This way of thinking also led to an important distinction between two different ways of describing the nature of an organism: in terms of its observable charac-teristics or traits (the phenotype), and in terms of its genetic constitution (the genotype).

With these examples of scientific generalizations in mind, we can see how well or badly the empiricist view fits them. As we saw above, empiricists are committed to accepting as scientific only those statements which are testable by observation or experiment. The most straightforward way to meet this requirement, we saw, was to limit scientific generalizations to mere summaries of observations. But it would be hard to represent Newton's law of universal gravitation in this way. For one thing, the rotation of the earth and planets around the sun is affected to some degree by the gravitational forces of bodies outside the solar system. These forces have to be treated as constant, or for practical purposes as irrelevant, if the pattern of motions within the solar sys-tem is to be analyzed as the outcome of gravitational attractions operating between the sun and the planets, and among the planets themselves. The law of universal gravitation is therefore not a summary of observations, but the outcome of quite complex calculations on the basis of both empirical obser-vations and theoretical assumptions. Moreover, it could be arrived at only by virtue of the fact that the solar system exists as a naturally occurring closed system, in the sense that the gravitational forces operating between the sun and planets are very large compared with external influences.

But Newton's law cannot be treated as a mere summary of observations for another reason, namely that it applies to the relationship between any bodies in the universe. The scope of the law, and so the range of possible observations required to conclusively establish its truth, is indefinitely large. No matter how many observations have been made, it is always possible that the next one will show that the law is false. It is, of course, also the case that we cannot go back in time to carry out the necessary measurements to find out if the law held throughout the past history of the universe. Nor will we ever know whether it holds in parts of the universe beyond the reach of measuring instruments. In fact, subsequent scientific developments have modified the status of Newton's law to an approximation with restricted scope. However, it is arguable that if the law had not made a *claim* to universality, then the subsequent progress of science in testing its limitations and so revising it could not have taken place.

This suggests that it is in the nature of scientific laws that they make claims which go beyond the necessarily limited set of observations or experimental results upon which they are based. Having established that the half-life of radon is 52 seconds from a small number of samples, scientists simply assume that this will be true of any other sample. As we will see, this has been regarded as a fundamental flaw in scientific reasoning. It simply does not follow logically, from the fact that some regularity has been observed repeatedly and without exception so far, that it will continue into the future. The leap that scientific laws make from the observation of a finite number of examples to a universal claim that 'always' this will happen cannot be justified by logic. This problem was made famous by the eighteenth-century Scottish philosopher David Hume, and it is known as the problem of 'induction'. A common illustration (not unconnected with Newton's law) is that we all expect the sun to rise tomorrow because it has always been observed to do so in the past, but we have no logical justification for expecting the future to be like the past. In fact, our past observations are simply a limited series, and so the logic is the same as if we were to say 'It has been sunny every day this week, so it will be sunny tomorrow,' or 'Stock markets have risen constantly for the last ten years, so they will carry on doing so.'

As we saw above, a possible response to this problem for empiricists is to resort to a relatively weak criterion of testability, such that statements can be accepted as testable if they can be confirmed *to a greater or lesser degree* by accumulated observations. Intuitively, it seems that the more observations we have which support a universal law, without encountering any disconfirming instances, the more likely it is that the law is true. Unfortunately, this does not affect the logic of the problem of induction. No matter how many confirming instances we have, they remain an infinitesimally small proportion of the indefinitely large set of possible observations implied by a universal claim. So, in the terms allowed by empiricism, it seems that we are faced with a dilemma: either scientific laws must be excluded as unscientific, or it has to be accepted that science rests on an untestable and metaphysical faith in the uniformity and regularity of nature.

This brings us to the empiricist account of what it is to explain something scientifically. Let us take a biological example. Some species of dragonfly emerge early in the spring. Unlike later-emerging species, they generally exhibit what is called 'synchronized emergence'. The immature stages or 'nymphs' live underwater, but when they are ready to emerge they climb out of the water and shed their outer 'skin' to become air-breathing, flying, adult dragonflies. In these species, local populations will emerge together over a few days, even in some cases in one night. How can this be explained? The current view is that larval development ceases over the winter (a phenomenon known as 'diapause'), leaving only the final stage of metamorphosis to be completed in the spring. A combination of increasing day length and reaching a certain temperature threshold switches on metamorphosis so that each individual emerges at more or less the same time. To explain why a particular population of a particular species emerged on a particular night would involve a pattern of reasoning somewhat like this:

Emergence is determined by day length d plus, combined with temperature t.
  On 17 April, population p was exposed to temperature t, and day length d had already been passed.

———————

Therefore: population p emerged on 17 April.

This could fairly easily be stated more formally as a logically valid argument, in which the premises include the statement of a general law linking temperature and day length with emergence and particular statements specifying actual day lengths and temperatures. The conclusion is the statement describing the emergence of the dragonflies – the event we are trying to explain. The 'covering law', combined with the particular conditions, shows that the event to be explained was to be expected.

This analysis of the logic of scientific explanation also enables us to see why there is a close connection between scientific explanation and prediction. If we know an event has happened (for example, the dragonflies emerged on 17 April), then the law plus the statement of the particular circumstances (day length and temperature in this case) explains it. If, on the other hand, the emergence has not yet happened, we can use our knowledge of the law to predict that it will happen when the appropriate 'initial conditions' are satisfied. Knowledge of a scientific law can also be used to justify what are called 'counterfactual' statements. For example, we can say that the dragonflies would not have emerged if the temperature had not reached the threshold, or if they had been kept under artificial conditions with day length kept constant below d. And these counterfactuals can then be used in experimental tests of the law.

Again, what is clear from these examples is that a scientific law makes claims which go beyond the mere summary of past observations. If the event to be explained was already part of the observational evidence upon which the law was based, then the 'explanation' of the event would add nothing to what was already known. Similarly, if the law were treated simply as a summary of past observations, it would not provide us with any grounds for prediction. This point can be made clear by distinguishing between scientific laws, on the one hand, and mere 'contingent' or 'accidental' generalizations, on the other. The standard example, 'All swans are white,' is just such a 'contingent generalization'. It just so happened that until Western observers encountered Australian swans they had only seen white ones. There was no scientific reason – only habit or prejudice – for expecting swans in another part of the world to be white. To call a generalization a law is to say that it encapsulates a regularity which is more than just coincidence: exceptions are ruled out as impossible, events 'must' obey the law and so on.

As we have seen, this presents problems for a thoroughgoing empiricist, since claims as strong and as wide in scope as those made by scientific laws cannot be conclusively tested by observation and experiment. One way out of this was recognized by the philosopher Karl Popper, and it formed the basis for a quite different approach to the nature of science (see Popper 1963, 1968). Popper pointed out the fundamental difference between confirming, or proving, the truth of a scientific law, on the one hand, and disproving or 'falsifying' it, on the other. Any number of observations of dragonfly emergence which were consistent with the law would still not prove it to be true, but a single case of dragonflies emerging at lower temperatures, or during shorter day lengths, would be enough to conclusively disprove the law. On this basis, Popper argued that we should not see science as an attempt to establish the truth of laws, since this can never be done. Instead, we should see science as a process whereby researchers use their creative imaginations to suggest explanations – the more implausible the better – and then set out systematically to prove them false. The best that can be said of current scientific beliefs is that they have so far not been falsified. So, for Popper, the testability of a statement is a matter of whether it is open to falsification.

Unfortunately, as Popper himself acknowledged, this doesn't solve all the problems. As we saw above, evidence which appears to count against a belief or even to disprove it may itself be open to question. Countless experiments conducted in school science labs 'disprove' basic laws of electricity, magnetism, chemistry and so on, but scientists don't see this as a reason for abandoning them. The assumption is that there were technical defects in the way the experiments were set up, instruments were misread or results were wrongly interpreted. Whether we view testability as a matter of verification or falsification, it cannot be avoided that *judgements* have to be made about whether any particular piece of evidence justifies abandonment or retention of existing beliefs. For this reason, Popper argued that in the end the distinguishing feature of science was not so much a matter of the logical relation between hypotheses and evidence as one of the normative commitment of researchers to the fallibility of their own knowledge-claims.

The empiricist aim of establishing the distinctive character and status of science implies separating out types of statements which can be scientific from those which cannot. We already saw that this means excluding statements which *look* like factual statements, but in the empiricist view are not, because they are not testable by experience (for example, statements of religious belief, utopian political programmes and so on). Moral or ethical judgements pose special problems for empiricists. They are not obviously factual, but when someone says that torture is evil, for example, they do seem to be making a substantive statement about something in the world.

Empiricists have tended to adopt one or another of two alternative approaches to moral judgements. One is to accept them as a special kind of factual judgement, by defining moral concepts in terms of observable properties. Utilitarian moral theory is the best-known example. In its classical form, utilitarianism defines 'good' in terms of 'happiness', which is defined, in turn, in terms of the favourable balance of pleasure over pain. So, an action (or rule) is morally right if it (tends) to optimize the balance of pleasure over pain across all sentient beings.

However, in more recent empiricist philosophy of science it has been much more common to adopt the alternative approach to moral judgements. This is to say that they get their rhetorical or persuasive force from having a grammatical form which makes us think they are saying something factual. However, this is misleading, as all we are really doing when we make a moral judgement is expressing our subjective attitude to it, or feelings about it. This, interestingly, implies that there are no generally obligatory moral principles, and so leads to the position referred to in Chapter 1 as moral relativism.

Positivism and Sociology

The nineteenth-century French philosopher Auguste Comte is generally credited with inventing both of the terms 'positivism' and 'sociology' (see Andreski 1974; Keat and Urry 1975; Benton 1977; Halfpenny 1982). Comte was very much influenced in his early days by the utopian socialist Saint Simon, and he went on to develop his own view of history as governed by a progressive shift from one type of knowledge, or belief-system, to another. There are three basic stages in this developmental process. The initial, theological stage gives way to the metaphysical, in which events are explained in terms of abstract entities. This, in turn, is surpassed by the scientific stage, in which knowledge is based on observation and experiment. Writing in the wake of the French Revolution, and desiring the return of normality and social stability, Comte was inclined to explain continuing conflict and disorder in terms of the persistence of outdated metaphysical principles such as the rights of man. Such concepts and principles were effective for the 'negative' task of criticizing and opposing the old order of society, but in the post-revolutionary period what was needed was 'positive' knowledge for rebuilding social harmony.

This positive knowledge was, of course, science. However, the problem as Comte saw it was that each branch of knowledge goes through the three stages, but that they don't all reach scientific maturity at the same time.

Astronomy, physics, chemistry and biology had all, Comte argued, arrived at the scientific stage, but accounts of human mental and social life were still languishing in the pre-scientific, metaphysical stage. The time was now ripe for setting the study of human social life on scientific foundations, and Comte set out to establish 'social physics', or 'sociology', as a scientific discipline. Since Comte's day the term 'positivism' has been used extensively to characterize (often with derogatory connotations) approaches to social science which have made use of large data sets, quantitative measurement and statistical methods of analysis. We will try to use the term in a more precise and narrow sense than this, to describe those approaches which share the following four features:

1. The empiricist account of the natural sciences is accepted.
2. Science is valued as the highest or even the only genuine form of knowledge (since this is the view of most modern empiricists, it could conveniently be included under 1).
3. Scientific method, as represented by the empiricists, can and should be extended to the study of human mental and social life, to establish these disciplines as social *sciences.*
4. Once reliable social scientific knowledge has been established, it will be possible to apply it to control, or regulate the behaviour of individuals or groups in society. Social problems and conflicts can be identified and resolved one by one on the basis of expert knowledge offered by social scientists, in much the same way as natural scientific expertise is involved in solving practical problems in engineering and technology. This approach to the role of social science in projects for social reform is sometimes called 'social engineering'.

There are several reasons why positivists might want to use the natural sciences as the model for work in the social sciences. The most obvious one is the enormous cultural authority possessed by the natural sciences. Governments routinely take advice on difficult matters of technical policy-making, from food safety to animal welfare and building standards, from committees largely composed of scientific experts. In public debate (until quite recently – see Beck 1992) scientists have had a largely unchallenged role in media discussions of such issues. Social scientists might well want to present their disciplines as sufficiently well established for them to be accorded this sort of authority. Not unconnected with this is the still controversial status of the social sciences within academic institutions. Strong claims made by social scientists about the reliability, objectivity and usefulness of the knowledge they have to offer may be used to support their claim to be well represented in university staffing and research council funding for their research. This was, of course, of particular significance in the nineteenth-century heyday of positivism when the newly emerging social sciences were still struggling for recognition.

Table 1 Suicides in different countries per million persons of each confession

		Protestants	Catholics	Jews	Names of Observers
Austria	(1852–59)	79.5	51.3	20.7	Wagner
Prussia	(1849–55)	159.9	49.6	46.4	Id.
Prussia	(1869–72)	187	69	96	Morselli
Prussia	(1890)	240	100	180	Prinzing
Baden	(1852–62)	139	117	87	Legoyt
Baden	(1870–74)	171	136.7	124	Morselli
Baden	(1878–88)	242	170	210	Prinzing
Bavaria	(1844–56)	135.4	49.1	105.9	Morselli
Bavaria	(1884–91)	224	94	193	Prinzing
Wurttemberg	(1846–60)	113.5	77.9	65.6	Wagner
Wurttemberg	(1873–76)	190	120	60	Durkheim
Wurttemberg	(1881–90)	170	119	142	Id.

Source: Durkheim (1952: 154).

That positivists should have accepted the empiricist account of science is not surprising, given the pre-eminence of this view of science until relatively recent times, and given its clear justification for science's superiority over other forms of belief-system. However, the positivist commitment to extending scientific method to the human sciences is more obviously contestable. In later chapters (particularly 5, 6 and 7) we will consider in detail some of the most powerful arguments against this positivist doctrine, but for now we will just consider the case for it. We will use some of the work of Durkheim as our example here, but it is important to note that we are not claiming that Durkheim was himself a positivist (see Lukes 1973; Pearce 1989; Craib 1997). For our purposes in this book, he shares some important features in common with positivists, and this is what we will focus on.

In his classic work on suicide (Durkheim 1896, 1952), Durkheim drew on a vast array of statistical sources to show that there were consistent patterns in suicide rates. He showed that these patterns could not be accounted for in terms of a series of non-social factors, such as race, heredity, psychological disorder, climate, season and so on. He then went on to show that they *could* be accounted for in terms of variations in religious faith, marital status, employment in civilian or military occupations, sudden changes in income (in either direction) and so on. Table 1 shows the pattern for religious faith.

Although there are variations in suicide rates over time in each country, comparison between countries shows remarkable constancy – some countries having consistently higher or lower rates than others. Similarly with religious confession: though absolute rates vary a great deal for the same faith in different countries, there is constancy in that in each country Protestants have higher rates than Catholics, and Catholics higher rates than Jews. Durkheim argues that this pattern cannot be explained in terms of doctrinal differences between the religions, but, rather, is a consequence of the different ways the churches relate to individual followers:

> If religion protects a man from the desire for self-destruction, it is not that it preaches the respect for his own person to him . . . but because it is a society. What constitutes this society is the existence of a certain number of beliefs and practices common to all the faithful, traditional and thus obligatory. The more numerous and strong these collective states of mind are, the stronger the integration of the religious community, and also the greater its preservative value. The details of dogmas and rites are secondary. The essential thing is that they be capable of supporting a sufficiently intense collective life. And because the Protestant church has less consistency than the others it has less moderating effect upon suicide. (Durkheim 1952:170)

In his book on suicide, and his methodological classic *The Rules of Sociological Method* (1895, 1982), Durkheim uses a series of arguments to establish that society is a reality in its own right. The facts, 'social facts', of which this reality is made up exist independently of each individual, and exert what he calls a 'coercive power' over us. For example, each individual is born into a society whose institutions and practices are already in existence. Each of us, if we are to participate in our society, communicate with others and so on, must learn the necessary skills, including those involved in speaking and understanding the local language. In this sense, as well as in more obvious respects, we are coerced into following the established rules of our 'social environment', or 'milieu'. There is a particularly powerful statement of this towards the end of *Suicide*:

> [I]t is not true that society is made up only of individuals; it also includes material things, which play an essential role in the common life. The social fact is sometimes so far materialized as to become an element of the external world. For instance, a definite type of architecture is a social phenomenon; but it is partially embodied in houses and buildings of all sorts which, once constructed, become autonomous realities, independent of individuals. It is the same with avenues of communication and transportation, with instruments and machines used in industry or private life which express the state of technology at any moment in history, of written language, and so on. Social life, which is thus crystallized, as it were, and fixed on material supports, is by just so much externalized, and acts upon us from without. Avenues of communication which have been constructed before our time give a definite direction to our activities. (Durkheim 1952: 314)

This is enough for Durkheim to show that there is an order of facts, social facts, which are distinct from facts about individual people and their mental states, or biological characteristics. This class of facts, most obviously detected through the analysis of statistical patterns, justifies the existence of a distinct science – sociology – which takes it for its subject-matter. This science, having its own distinct subject-matter, will not be reducible to biology, or to psychology.

However, a further step in the argument is required. As practising participants in social life, it could be argued that all of us possess knowledge of it –
this seems to be implied in Durkheim's own argument. If this is so, why do we
need a specialist science to tell us what we already know? In answer to this
Durkheim could point out that his analysis of statistical patterns in the occurrence of suicide had come up with results which most people would find surprising. This apparently most individual and lonely of acts, when studied
sociologically, turns out to be determined by variable features of the social
environment. In the *Rules of Sociological Method* he offers us a more general
argument. As the facts of social life exist prior to each individual, are independent of their will, and exert a coercive power, they resemble facts of nature.
We all interact with natural materials and objects, and we do so through 'lay'
or common-sense understandings of their properties, but just because of this
we would not generally claim that there was no need for natural science. The
history of the natural sciences shows innumerable instances of common-sense
beliefs being corrected in the face of new scientific evidence and theory. So
why should we assume that common-sense assumptions and prejudices give us
reliable knowledge of the *social* world? If, in general, science progresses by
increasingly distancing itself from common-sense assumptions, and gaining
deeper understanding of its subject-matter, we should expect this to be true of
the social sciences too.

Finally, some brief comments are due on the fourth doctrine of positivism –
the proposal to apply social scientific knowledge in social policy-making. This
view of the public role of social science has continued to be very widely held,
and it provides yet another justification for extending the methods of the natural sciences into the study of society. Only on the basis of the sorts of claims to
quantitative reliability, objectivity and general applicability already made by the
natural sciences could the social sciences expect to be taken seriously by policy-
makers. Today in most countries official statistics are collected on virtually all
aspects of social and economic life – on patterns of ill-health and death, on
marriage and divorce, on unemployment, income differentials, attitudes and
values, consumption patterns and so on – and social scientists are employed to
collect and interpret these, as well as to give advice on policy implications
(in the UK, such publications as *Social Trends* and *British Social Attitudes*
contain selections from such statistical surveys).

The logical form of a scientific explanation as represented in the empiricist
'covering law' model shows how the link between such knowledge and policy
might be made. To oversimplify considerably, the statistics might show that
criminal behaviour by juveniles was more common among the children of
divorced parents. This is not a universal law, but a statistical generalization
(though the required element of universality might be present, if it is held that
this statistical generalization holds across different cultures and historical
periods). However, the basic structure of a scientific explanation can be
maintained:

If there are high divorce rates then there will be high rates of juvenile crime.
Divorce rates are high.

Therefore: There are high rates of juvenile crime.

If policy-makers are convinced by public opinion that high rates of juvenile crime are a bad thing, and are charged with coming up with policies to reduce them, then this piece of scientific explanation will yield the policy recommendation to take action to reduce divorce rates. Of course, there are some obvious complications here. One is that a mere statistical association between divorce rates and juvenile crime does not show that one causes the other. It could be that some third social fact, such as unemployment rates, causes both high rates of divorce and juvenile crime. A policy of dealing with unemployment therefore might be more effective than trying to do something about divorce. But there might be more subtle problems with the statistical association. It might, for example, be that the association of juvenile crime with divorce holds only where divorce is stigmatized by prevailing values. If this were so, then the appropriate policy might be to work for a cultural shift in favour of more liberal social values. However, none of this counts against the positivist notion of 'social engineering' as such. Each of these possibilities can in principle be addressed by more exact data-gathering, and more sophisticated analytical methods. There are, however, other lines of criticism, which we will explore in the next chapter.

Further Reading

Auguste Comte (see Andreski 1974) is widely credited as the originator of positivism, and is still worth reading, if only to see that he was a much more sophisticated thinker than he is often made out to be. Durkheim's *Rules of Sociological Method* (1895, 1982) presents a very powerful case for a naturalistic approach to social science. Ayer (1946) is a classic statement of the logical positivist philosophy, while Hempel (1966) is still unsurpassed as a clear, introductory statement of a more moderate, empiricist view of natural science. Good critical accounts of empiricist philosophy of science are to be found in Harré (1970, 1972), Keat and Urry (1975), Benton (1977), Newton-Smith (1981) and Chalmers (1999).

3

Some Problems of Empiricism and Positivism

Introduction: Two Ways to Criticize Positivism

So far, we have discussed the broad outlines of the empiricist view of human knowledge, and of scientific explanation. We have seen that 'positivism' in social science can be seen as an attempt to put the study of human social life on a scientific footing by extending the methods and forms of explanation which have been successful in the natural sciences. In doing this, positivists have generally relied on some version of the empiricist theory of knowledge, and have been committed to the application of social scientific knowledge in programmes of social reform.

We now come to our consideration of some of the criticisms which have been made of positivism in social science. These criticisms are of two main kinds, and we will be dealing with them in separate chapters. The criticisms which have been most widely made and accepted among social scientists themselves concern the extension of scientific methods to the domain of human social life. Anti-positivists who take this line of argument point out that there are fundamental differences between human social life and the facts of nature which are the subject-matter of the natural sciences. These differences include the alleged unpredictability of human behaviour, which stems from our unique possession of free will; the 'rule-governed', as distinct from law-governed, character of social life; and the role of consciousness and meaning in human society. Connected with these ontological differences between the natural and the social worlds, it is argued, the relations between social scientists and their subject-matter are very different from those between natural scientists and the things and processes they study. One such difference has to do with the way moral or political values enter into the selection of topics for investigation. Social scientists will be guided by value orientations to seek explanations of particular social phenomena or historical processes, so that social explanation will be 'value-relevant', and concerned with particulars. By contrast, natural scientists are concerned with discovery of general laws by methods which exclude value judgements. Another difference derives directly from a recognition of the role of consciousness and meaning in social life. When social scientists come to the systematic study of social life, they encounter a subject-matter which already has an understanding of itself! Moreover, the social scientist will often herself be part of that social life, and will in any case have to learn to communicate with it in its own terms in order to gain understanding of it. This, again, is very different from the external relation between natural scientists and their subject-matters.

These arguments are, of course, very persuasive, and we will return to investigate them and their implications in more depth (especially in Chapters 5, 6 and 7). However, for the moment we will be considering a quite different line of criticism of positivism. The key point here is not so much whether it makes sense to extend the methods of science to the study of society, but *what account of science* one draws on in doing that. As we saw, the empiricist account of science is broadly accepted by positivists as the model for a scientific approach to society. But there are some serious and unresolved difficulties in the empiricist account of science (see especially Keat and Urry 1975, Benton 1977, Quine 1980, Halfpenny 1982, Chalmers 1999), and there are now, in addition, some quite well-established *alternative* accounts of science. These are based more on historical studies, and on sociological investigation of science in action, and we will discuss some of these in Chapter 4. It is very important to explore these further because they open up more possibilities for thinking about what the social sciences are or could be. In particular, it has been (and still is) very common for philosophers of social science to contrast positivist with interpretivist views, as if this exhausted all the alternatives. But there *are* other alternatives. For example, it is possible to reject positivism because of its empiricist account of science, but still keep open the possibility that society might be studied scientifically, drawing on an alternative account of what *natural* science is like. Of course, even with an alternative view of what science is, it may still be held that human society cannot be studied scientifically. But to ask this question with alternative models of science in mind is likely to raise new and interesting issues about just where the differences and similarities lie between natural science and the study of society.

Some Problems of Empiricism

Concepts and Experience

The empiricist view that all knowledge is acquired by experience, and that there are no innate ideas, has been called into question by developments in a number of disciplines. Noam Chomsky, widely regarded as the founder of contemporary scientific approaches to language, has argued that the child's experience of language is far too limited and fragmentary for us to explain language acquisition in empiricist terms (see Lyons 1977). Our ability to produce an indefinite number of well-formed sentences presupposes not just an innate disposition to learn language, but also innate knowledge of the 'depth grammar' common to all languages. Much more controversially, self-styled 'evolutionary psychologists' and sociobiologists argue that many of our basic thought processes and behaviours are expressions of our genetic inheritance (see Pinker 1997; also the criticisms of this approach in Rose and Rose 2000). However, even if we are sceptical of claims such as these, there are other sources of evidence which suggest that knowledge acquisition can't just be a matter of recognizing patterns of regularity in the flow of sensory experience. One very telling illustration is given by the case-studies reported by Oliver Sacks, a neurologist whose work was concerned with helping people who suffer from various kinds of brain damage. One of his patients ('the man who mistook his wife for a hat') was referred to him by an ophthalmologist:

> Dr P. was a musician of distinction, well-known for many years as a singer, and then, at the local School of Music, as a teacher. It was here, in relation to his students, that certain strange problems were first observed. Sometimes a student would present himself, and Dr P. would not recognise him; or, specifically, would not recognise his face. The moment the student spoke, he would be recognised by his voice. Such incidents multiplied, causing embarrassment, perplexity, fear – and, sometimes, comedy. For not only did Dr P. increasingly fail to see faces, but he saw faces when there were no faces to see: genially, Magoo-like, when in the street, he might pat the heads of water-hydrants and parking meters, taking these to be the heads of children. (Sacks 1986: 7)

Sacks continued his examination: 'His visual acuity was good: he had no difficulty seeing a pin on the floor, though sometimes he missed it if it was placed to his left. He saw all right, but what did he see?' (p. 9). Sacks's unfortunate patient was someone who, though he had good eyesight, had lost the ability to make sense of the flow of visual impressions he was undoubtedly receiving. This sort of case illustrates the complex and pre-conscious mental activity of selecting and interpreting sensory inputs which goes into 'normal' visual experience. Our ability to identify people, recognize faces, interpret a landscape and so on is not just a matter of having sense-organs which are in good order, but it also involves active processes of conceptual ordering and interpretation of which we are mostly unaware. As the philosopher of science N. R. Hanson once put it: 'There is more to seeing than meets the eyeball' (Hanson 1965: 7).

On this view, then, experience is a complex synthesis of sensory impressions and conceptual ordering and selection. All experience is to some extent shaped by our previously acquired conceptual map of the world. As far as scientific observation is concerned, this is even more clearly the case. For an experience to count as a scientific observation it must be put into language, as a statement which can be understood and tested by other scientists. The activity of putting an experience into language is, precisely, to give conceptual order to it. An elementary statement, such as 'The litmus paper turned from blue to red,' implies ability to recognize a physical object, to classify it as litmus paper, and to deploy the vocabulary of colour terms.

But, of course, this only shows that any *particular* statement of an experience, or factual statement, must presuppose an ability to conceptually order experience. It does not demonstrate the existence of innate knowledge, in the sense of knowledge prior to and independent of *all* experience. It still remains an open question how we acquired the concepts through which we interpret our experiences. Given the great diversity across cultures and through historical time in ways of interpreting experience (Durkheim 1912, 1982), it seems obvious that a large part of the conceptual apparatus each of us brings to bear must be learnt.

On the other hand, some very basic capacities for conceptual ordering do seem to be presupposed for learning itself to be possible. The eighteenth-century German philosopher Immanuel Kant developed some of the most powerful arguments for this view (see Kant 1953; Körner 1990; Hoffe 1994: esp. part 2). On his account, the ordering of the flow of our sensory experience in terms of sequences through time and locations in space was necessary to the making of all 'judgements of experience'. It is similar with the ability to judge identity and difference, to distinguish between things and their characteristics, and to think in terms of cause and effect. So, for example, we can learn from experience that touching a piece of burning wood causes pain, but the concept of 'cause' could not *itself* be derived from experience. In Kant's view, these very basic organizing concepts (the 'forms of intuition' and 'categories of the understanding') are presupposed in all experiential judgements, and so must be considered both innate, and universal to humankind. Ever since Kant, the main alternative approaches to empiricism have taken his work as their point of departure.

Scientific Laws, Testability and Interpretation

We have already explored some of the difficulties with the empiricist demand that scientific statements must be empirically testable. If this demand is made very strictly, then it would require scientists to be much more restrictive in the nature of the hypotheses they advance than they generally are. In particular, scientific laws would have to be treated as mere summaries of observations, as empirical generalizations. But if this were done, scientific explanations would loose their explanatory power, scientific prediction would be impossible, science would be deprived of an important stimulus to further research and so on. These features of scientific statements depend on an interpretation of scientific laws such that they make claims which go beyond what is strictly implied by the existing evidence. To preserve this feature of scientific laws it is necessary to adopt a looser criterion of testability, which acknowledges that new observations may count for or against a hypothesis, but can never conclusively prove or disprove it.

As we saw in Chapter 2, attempts to develop a rigorous quantitative measure of the degree to which hypotheses are supported, or confirmed, by the available evidence fall foul of the fact that any finite set of evidence will be vanishingly small compared with the indefinitely large class of *possible* evidence which may be relevant. In addition, the more relaxed empiricists become in loosening the requirement of testability (for example, some *possible* observation must be *relevant* to the truth or falsity of the hypothesis), the more difficult it becomes to make clear and defensible distinctions between genuine science and the non-scientific belief-systems which empiricists are generally committed to excluding.

But there is a further difficulty with testability which relates more closely to what was said above about the relationship between experience and interpretation. If every statement of experience is at the same time an interpretation, then in principle every factual statement is open to *re*interpretation. As we saw in Chapter 2, with the example of the apparent evidence against the effectiveness of a complementary medical practice, whether to accept a piece of evidence as confirming or refuting our existing beliefs will always involve making judgements. In part, these judgements will concern how to interpret both one's existing beliefs, or hypotheses, and the new piece of evidence. Ambiguous figures are the most commonly used illustration of this. The pattern in Figure 1, the famous 'duck-rabbit', can be seen either as the head of a duck (facing left, the two projections forming the beak) or as the head of a rabbit (facing right, the projections representing the long ears).

In such cases as this, the same patterns of markings on paper are interpreted in radically different ways by different observers, and by the same observer at different times. The possibility of different interpretations of the same body of evidence raises serious problems for the empiricist account of scientific practice. Apparently conflicting evidence can always be rendered consistent with a favourite hypothesis by reinterpreting either the hypothesis or the new evidence. Though such 'conventionalist' tactics tend to be disapproved of by empiricists, it is hard to show that they are never justified. But the most important problem posed by ambiguity and interpretation is at the level of rivalry between major theoretical orientations. So, for example, in the controversy between the proponents of Darwinian evolutionary theory and its theologically oriented opponents, fossil evidence which favoured the view that there was historical change in organic forms was contested as a temptation laid by the devil. The remarkable adaptations of organisms to the requirements of their conditions of life, again, was interpreted as the result of design by the theological tradition, but as the result of natural selection by Darwinians. In this way, rival theories are able to offer alternative interpretations of the

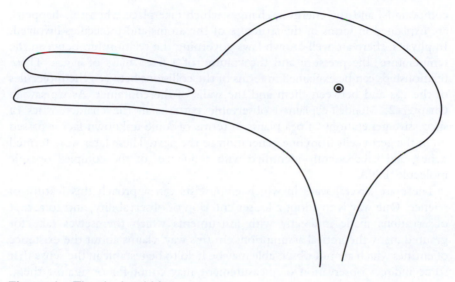

Figure 1 The duck-rabbit

available evidence in such a way that whatever the evidence, each can with logical consistency maintain its own account of things.

This situation of systematic disparities of interpretation between two (or more) theoretical perspectives implies debate which is invariably at cross-purposes, and the absence of anything that will serve as a crucial experiment, or decisive test-case. When rival theories have this sort of relation to one another they are said to be 'incommensurable'. A great deal depends on how far this concept accurately captures situations of theoretical rivalry in science, and on how common such rivalry is. Empiricists and others who seek to defend the rationality of science will tend to regard incommensurability as rarely if ever complete, so that there is generally the possibility of resolving scientific disputes through rational argument about the evidence. Those who adopt a *relativist* view of science (such that science is no more and no less reliable as a source of knowledge than any other belief-system) will tend to emphasize the importance of incommensurability as a common feature of theoretical controversy in science.

Theoretical Entities in Science

A very strict version of empiricism will rule out any reference to theoretical entities which cannot be directly observed. However, a great part of the explanatory work of the natural science involves inventing classes of entities which, if they exist, and behave as described, can explain observed phenomena. In chemistry, the ways in which elements combine with others to form compounds, and the energy exchanges which take place when this happens, are explained in terms of the structure of the atoms and molecules involved. In physics, there are well-known laws governing the relationship between the temperature, the pressure and the volume of a fixed mass of a gas. These relationships can be explained in terms of the collisions between the molecules of the gas and between them and the walls of the container. As we saw in Chapter 2, Mendel explained observable patterns in the characteristics of successive generations of pea plants in terms of some unknown factor passed on in the germ cells from one generation to the next. These later were termed genes, and subsequently identified with sequences of the complex organic molecule 'DNA'.

There are several ways in which empiricists can approach this feature of science. One way is to adopt a looser criterion of observability, and to accept observations made indirectly with instruments which themselves take for granted many theoretical assumptions. In this way, claims about the existence of entities which are not observable may be held to be testable in the sense that some indirect observation or measurement may count for or against them. Again, however, these concessions on the part of empiricists make it harder for them to maintain the special and superior status of science compared with other sorts of knowledge-claims. Another empiricist approach to the problem of theoretical entities is to treat statements about them as useful fictions, which enable scientific prediction in virtue of their formal (mathematical) content. No claim as to the real, physical existence of atoms, molecules and the like need be involved. This sort of approach is called 'instrumentalism'.

The Role of Theories in Scientific Explanation

But this rather grudging approach on the part of empiricism to the issue of theoretical entities seems at odds with the huge proliferation of new classes of entity with which modern science has filled the world as we now know it (Latour 1987: 93). From quarks, quasars and black holes, through bacilli, retroviruses and prions to protons, neutrinos and photons, the very content of scientific advance seems to consist in the progressive uncovering of hitherto unimagined complexity in the macro- and microstructures of the world we inhabit.

At issue here is the view we take of the nature and role of theories in scientific explanation. The 'covering law' model of scientific explanation (see Chapter 2) is an attempt to show the logic of a simple explanation at the level of observable patterns of phenomena. However, if we return to our example of the simultaneous spring emergence of some species of dragonfly, this sort of explanation clearly does not exhaust the possible roles for science. Indeed, on some accounts, the gathering of evidence for observational generalizations (such as, in this case, linking emergence with temperature and day length) belongs to an early, 'natural history' phase of science. The properly scientific work only begins when such observational generalizations have been acquired, and scientific theory is required to explain them.

There are (at least) three further sets of questions that might be asked once such observational generalizations are established. One set has to do with the part played by simultaneous emergence in the mode of life of the dragonfly species concerned. One plausible answer is that when populations have relatively short flight periods, simultaneous emergence maximizes the chances that members of the opposite sex find each other and successfully reproduce. This is recognizable as a 'functional' explanation: it purports to tell us what part the piece of behaviour concerned plays in the wider whole constituted by the mode of life of the population and its reproduction.

The second set of questions has to do with the 'historical narrative' whereby this pattern of dragonfly behaviour itself emerged, and became established in the population. Most biologists today would draw on some version of Darwinian natural selection to answer this set of questions, though in fact the currently most favoured version of this theory has difficulty in explaining the establishment of mutual adaptations of this kind. The third set of questions has to do with the internal structures and processes whereby external stimuli such as temperature and day length switch on metamorphic change in the dragonfly larva. This entails research into the anatomy and physiology of growth and development in the relevant species. In turn, this may lead to further questions about the interaction between the physiological processes (such as hormone secretion, cell division and differentiation) involved in growth and development, and the genetic mechanisms which regulate and are in turn regulated by them. Through this route, the genetic aspects of larval development may be linked back to the Darwinian narrative account of the evolution of the relevant population-level adaptations, and that in turn to the functional explanation. Through linkages such as these, research in answer to one sort of question can produce findings relevant to explanations proposed in response to others. This example illustrates two further features of the role of theory in science.

Reasoning and Creativity in the Invention of Theories

Theories are invented as plausible answers to questions posed by reflection on already-acquired observational generalizations. The process whereby such answers are invented involves scientific imagination and creativity. For this reason, empiricist philosophers of science tend to treat it as outside their sphere of concern, relegating it to psychology. For them, philosophy of science is concerned only with such matters as the logical structure and openness to empirical testing of scientific theories once they have been invented (the 'context of justification'). However, it is clear that something more can be said about the logic and, more broadly, the sorts of reasoning involved in the *invention* of theories. For one thing, not just anything will count as a *plausible* candidate for an explanation. It might be proposed, for example, that our dragonfly larvae note the appropriate temperature rise, and signal to each other that it is time to get on with their metamorphosis. However, what is known about the nervous system of dragonflies, and more generally about the physiology of insect metamorphosis makes it unlikely that this sort of conscious regulation of activity is available to dragonfly larvae. In this way both background knowledge and experimental intervention can narrow down the range of plausible explanations of the phenomenon.

Moreover, even if plausible, a potential explanation would still have to satisfy a criterion of *relevance*. So, for example, someone might give the functional explanation of the role of simultaneous emergence of dragonflies in their reproductive activity in answer to the historical-narrative question about how this behaviour pattern became established in the population. However, this might be quite irrelevant. It could, for example, be that the particular combination of day length and temperature in the course of evolution of this population provided optimal chances for meeting nutritional needs and avoiding predation. Selective pressures operating at the level of individual dragonflies would, if this were true, be likely to result in ever-closer approximation to emergence under these conditions across the whole population over a number of generations. The observed phenomenon of simultaneous emergence would thus be a contingent outcome of the spread through the population of an individual adaptation to environmental conditions. So, there are constraints on the range of inventions that can count as plausible candidates for theoretical explanations. In particular, the proposed explanation must refer to something which, *if* true, *would* account for the observed pattern, and something which, given background knowledge, *could well be* true. The philosopher N. R. Hanson has referred to the logic of this sort of creative work in science as 'a conclusion in search of premises': we know what the observed pattern of phenomena is, and what we are searching for is something that could have brought it about. Hanson (following Peirce) calls this sort of reasoning 'retroduction' (as distinct from 'induction' and 'deduction') (Hanson 1965: 85ff.).

So, we can see a certain logical pattern and an associated set of constraints on the invention of theoretical explanations in science. Also, there are features of scientific reasoning which link it closely with creativity in other areas of life. The most discussed of these is the use of metaphor and analogy (see, especially, Hesse 1963). We are all familiar with the textbook diagrams of atoms as miniature solar systems, with a nucleus and orbiting electrons. Darwin's theory of evolution makes use of an analogy between the practices whereby the breeders of domesticated animals and plants bring about changes by 'selective breeding', and the action of environmental conditions in 'selecting' which variants in a population in the wild survive and reproduce. The term 'natural selection' embodies this metaphor. The explanation of the role of DNA in the development of organisms involves thinking of the sequencing of molecular units on strings of DNA as a code carrying instructions for making different protein molecules. Much more controversially, practitioners of 'cognitive science' commonly use the operation of computers as their model for thinking about human cognitive processes (see, for example, Pinker 1997, and the criticisms in Greenfield 1997).

This feature of scientific creativity is also difficult to square with any strict version of empiricism. An imaginative leap is required to recognize that the observed pattern of phenomena would be produced if some process analogous to one already understood in another field were at work. Since the source of the metaphor may be a mechanism or process outside science, as, for example with the idea of a genetic code, or of natural selection, the use of metaphors in the construction of scientific theories is an important link between science and the wider cultural context to which it belongs. This link is an important starting-point for sociologists of science (see Chapter 4) and others (such as advocates of 'standpoint' epistemologies – see Chapter 9) who argue that seemingly universal and objective scientific knowledge contains unacknowledged value commitments and culturally specific assumptions. This aspect of science tells against the empiricist tendency to claim that science is objective because it is exclusively the result of applying formal logical rules to factual evidence.

On the other hand, the use of metaphors in science does not necessarily justify the 'reduction' of science to its cultural context (see, for example, Beer 1983 and the criticisms in Benton 1995). Though it is important to recognize what other creative activities, such as the writing of fiction, have in common with scientific theorizing, it is also important to understand the different constraints involved in the development of analogical reasoning in science. To be acceptable, scientific analogies have to satisfy requirements imposed by the field of phenomena which they have been invented to explain, and the further elaboration of a metaphor as it is subjected to experimental and observational testing may take it progressively further from its original formulation (see Lopez 1999).

Types of Theoretical Explanation

Scientific theorizing may be invoked to answer a number of different kinds of question. In the case of the simultaneous emergence of dragonflies, we noted three sorts of answer which could reasonably be called 'theoretical'. One of these is *functional explanation*, and it answers questions about the relationship between elements, or parts, and the wholes to which they belong. Often functional explanations will be concerned with the way in which specific properties or activities of elements enable the continued existence or reproduction of the more complex totalities, or systems, to which they belong. So, for example, the heart functions to circulate the blood round the body, and the circulation of the blood, in turn, functions to deliver oxygen and nutrients to tissues, and carbon dioxide and other waste products of metabolism to the lungs and kidneys, which, in turn, function to – and so on. Functional explanations are extensively used in both the biological and the social sciences, and remain controversial.

The second sort of explanation involving theory is *historical-narrative* explanation. It is frequently confused with functional explanation, but is really quite distinct. The question of how an object, class of beings, or pattern of phenomena came into being is distinct from the question of how it now sustains itself or is sustained (the functional question). The former question requires the construction of a historical narrative – the characterization of a particular sequence of events or processes through time. For this to be more than description of 'one damn thing after another', and even for the narrative to work with criteria of what is relevant, what irrelevant to the telling of the story, some reference, implicit or explicit, has to be made to causal mechanisms. Generally, the story will make reference to numerous, interacting causal mechanisms which are at work, and coming into play at different points in the narrative. Here, the role of theory is to provide accounts of the key causal mechanisms at work, and, perhaps, some characterization of typical patterns of interaction. An example here is the relationship between Darwinian evolutionary theory, on the one hand, and a genealogical account of the emergence of a particular species or lineage through time, on the other.

The third sort of theoretical explanation in science is the one foregrounded in most philosophical accounts of science, and we will devote more detailed discussion to it here, returning in the next section to a further consideration of narrative explanation in relation to the issue of explanation and prediction. This third sort of theoretical explanation begins with patterns of observable phenomena (such as the characteristics of successive generations of pea plants, or the relationships between day length, temperature and emergence in dragonflies) and proceeds to investigate the causal relations involved by analysis of the microstructure underlying the observations. In the case of these biological examples, this will involve analysis of the formation of tissues and organs, of cell division and differentiation, and, at a still more fundamental level of analysis, of the activity of genes in the cell nuclei. The basic idea here is that to find out how a thing works one should take it to pieces, and study its components. The deeper one searches for an explanation, the more one will need to divide up the pieces into their components and so on. At a certain point, of course, this will lead to the making of hypotheses about parts that are so small as to be unobservable, and we are returned to our old problem of the legitimacy of appeals to unobservable entities in science.

This sort of role for theory in scientific explanation is represented in the 'hypothetico-deductive' model (see Hempel 1966). In this model, a 'microstructure' of theoretical entities and their relationships is invented to account for observable, macrolevel patterns. The statements describing the microlevel entities and processes are the 'hypothetical' aspect of the theory. As we saw, empiricists tend to see the process of invention as beyond rational analysis. However, once the theoretical hypothesis has been arrived at, statements

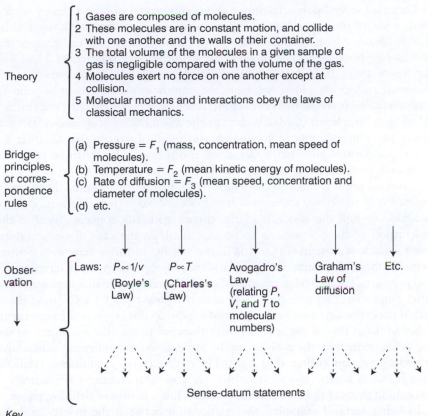

Key

'*F*' means 'function of', in the sense that terms so related have a definite quantitative relationship to one another such that from known values of one, corresponding values of the other can be calculated.

'*P*' is short for 'pressure', '*T*' for 'temperature', '*V*' for 'volume', and '∝' for 'is proportional to'. Arrows represent the direction of deductive inferences. Arrows drawn with broken lines indicate a further set of inferences which are insisted upon by strict positivists and phenomenalists.

Figure 2   The Hypothetico-Deductive account of scientific theories: the kinetic theory of gases as an example

Source: Benton (1977: 64).

describing the phenomena to be explained by the theory can be deduced from the theoretical statements. This is the 'deductive' aspect of the theory. If the theory is true, then the truth of statements describing the phenomena to be explained follows with necessity. Figure 2, a diagram of the kinetic theory of gases, represents a simplified version of the physical theory which uses certain hypotheses about the molecular microstructure of gases to explain observed patterns in their behaviour at the macrolevel.

There are several points to notice about this model of how a theory works. First, some of the statements which go to make up a theory are known to be strictly speaking false, but represent an 'idealization', to which real entities and processes approximate more or less closely (in this case, statements 3 and 4 in the figure are of this kind). Many scientific laws are idealized abstractions of this sort, and so are a long way from the empiricist view of them as generalizations from observation. There are interesting parallels here with the abstract 'ideal types' employed by Max Weber, or the assumptions made about 'rational actors', in some theories in economics and political science (see Chapter 5). Such idealizations give rise to questions about how they are to be tested or evaluated, given that they are intended to be counterfactual.

A second point is that, on the hypothetico-deductive account, theories can be used only to deduce statements about observable patterns if definitions are provided to link the concepts in the theory with the concepts used in the description of the phenomena to be explained. In the case of our example, these include statements (a) to (d) in the figure, and they state connections between the microstructure of gases and macroproperties such as temperature and pressure. These 'bridge principles' can be interpreted in different ways. For strict empiricists they may be seen as merely formal rules for translating theoretical concepts into empirical ones, and which do not commit the scientist to belief in the reality of the 'entities' hypothesized in the theory. Alternatively, the bridge principles themselves may be understood as containing substantive knowledge-claims in their own right. The nature of the quantitative relationship between kinetic energy of molecules and temperature, for example, is something that has to be discovered – it isn't just a matter of defining terms.

In other sorts of examples, the relationship between the macro- and the microlevel is more complex. In developmental biology, for example, there are assumed to be links between genetic constitution (genotype) and the characteristics of the developing organism (phenotype), but extremely complex interactions between these two levels of biological organization are involved, such that the representation of the links between them in terms of 'correspondence rules' would be inappropriate. In part, the difference between the two sorts of case is that processes at the macrolevel are active in modifying the behaviour of entities at the microlevel (that is, the genetic level), as well as *vice versa*. In part, the difference has to do with 'emergent properties' or power which living organisms have which are not possessed by genes or genomes.

In general, the relationship between theoretical statements and descriptions of the observations the theories are attempting to explain is a controversial area in the philosophy of science. What is at stake is the relationship between different *levels of analysis*, and therefore the status of the different disciplinary specialisms which focus on each level. Empiricists tend, as we have seen, to be resistant to any scientific theorizing which gets very far from what can be directly observed. They are thus committed to a rather flat ontology, in which the world consists essentially of the sorts of things and patterns which can be observed. In opposition to this tendency of thought are various sorts of 'realists' who are prepared to accept that one of the achievements of science is to discover whole categories of entities and processes not available to ordinary observation. We will return to this topic later (Chapter 8), but for now it is worth making a distinction between two sorts of realist. The first sort sees scientific explanation as moving always from the macro to the micro. Things are to be explained in terms of the parts of which they are made, and the parts in terms of *their* parts and so on. This suggests that there might be an ultimate stopping-point when we get to the most fundamental particles and the laws governing their behaviour. In principle, the behaviour of all the higher levels of complexity in organization would be explicable in terms of these basic building blocks of the universe. This is a kind of scientific metaphysics, sometimes called 'physicalism', and is an example of 'reductionism': the attempt to 'reduce' phenomena of belonging to different levels to a single, fundamental level.

However, another sort of realism can accept that science does, indeed, reveal ever more fundamental layers in the physical structure of the world. But once this has been done, it does not at all follow that everything about the higher levels of organization can be explained in terms of the lower. On this view, each level has its own particular features and can be studied to some extent independently of theories about levels 'above' or 'below' it (see Rose 1997 for an example of this sort of realism in opposition to genetic reductionism in biology). So, for example, it might be argued that chemists can get a long way in studying the ratios in which different elements combine to form compounds, and the properties which result without referring much or at all to molecular and atomic theory. Similarly, students of animal behaviour can develop their science without knowing much, or anything, about the ways in which genes are involved in the regulation of behaviour.

One way of grounding this claim for the (relative) autonomy of the different sciences is to argue for the existence of emergent properties or powers which are possessed by higher levels of organization but are not deducible from the lower. So, for example, birds indulge in courtship behaviour, make nests and lay eggs. Theories about their genetic constitution may play a part in our explanations of how and why they do this, but genes themselves don't court, make nests or mate. No amount of study of the genetic makeup of a bird would give you any idea what it was to build a nest or lay an egg unless you already knew. Such arguments are used to maintain 'anti-reductionist' forms of realism, which respect the *specificity* of each level. The dispute between reductionist and anti-reductionist approaches to the relationship between levels is of great importance for the social sciences. It separates sociological realists such as Durkheim and Marx from individualists such as Weber. The recurrent attempts by ultra-Darwinists to explain human social life in terms of the genetic constitution of individuals (as in sociobiology and, more recently, 'evolutionary psychology') are a version of reductionism designed to replace the social science disciplines altogether.

One further feature of theories can be illustrated by the hypothetico-deductive model. This is that the potential scope of the theoretical statements is far wider than the specific pattern of observations they are designed to explain. In our example, a whole series of patterns can be predicted from the statements which make up the kinetic theory. For empiricists, the explanatory power of the theory is a matter of the range of such predictions which can be deduced from it, and the theory is confirmed to the extent that these predictions turn out to be correct.

Explanation and Prediction

This takes us on to the question of the relationship between theoretical explanation and prediction. As we saw in Chapter 2, the symmetry of explanation and prediction is a tenet of the empiricist view of science. The hypothetico-deductive model of scientific theories displays this relationship very clearly. However, what is much less clear is whether this model applies to *all* sorts of scientific explanation. As we saw, the phenomenon of simultaneous emergence in populations of dragonflies could pose questions of a historical-narrative kind about how and why it came about in the course of the evolution of the species concerned. A relevant theory (but not the only relevant one) in this case would be some version of Darwinian evolution. Darwin's specific achievement was to arrive at a plausible hypothesis about the mechanism which brought about organic change in the direction of closer adaptation of organisms to their environments. To simplify somewhat, his theory consisted of the following statements:

1. In any population of animals or plants, there are many individual variations.
2. At least some of these are inherited from one generation to the next.
3. In any generation, many more offspring are produced than will survive to reproduce themselves.
4. Depending on the nature of the environment in which they live, some variations will be more likely to survive and reproduce than others ('natural selection').

These four propositions, appropriately formally stated, combined with the assumption that the environment remains stable in the relevant respects, yield the conclusion that those variations which confer enhanced survival and reproductive chances on their bearers will become progressively more common in the population over a series of generations. Cumulative change over numerous generations will eventually yield sufficiently different features for the population to be designated a new species. Darwin's hypothesis is generally recognized as a theory, but it does not hypothesize any theoretical entities. Moreover, it does not lead to any specific predictions about the formation of any particular species, or what its characteristics will be. The widespread acceptance of the theory must be based on something other than successful predictions.

There are several reasons why Darwin's theory cannot be used to predict the formation of particular new species. One is that nature only 'selects' from among the available variant forms which happen to exist in a population. The processes of genetic mutation and recombination which give rise to these variant forms are not explained in the theory, which simply works on the assumption that they are random with respect to any adaptive function which they may contingently turn out to have. Another reason is that the theory has nothing to tell us about the precise environmental pressures and affordances which may be operating on any particular population at any particular time. In several places, Darwin emphasized the immense diversity of ways in which survival chances are affected by environmental pressures, referring to the face of nature as like 'a hundred thousand wedges'. He noted that almost nothing was known about this complexity in particular cases.

So, in the case of Darwinian evolutionism, applying the theory to the explanation of a particular case is not merely a matter of applying a law to a description of existing 'initial conditions' and deducing the phenomenon to be explained. In fact, all the theory does is to provide some heuristic indications to guide substantive research towards an adequate historical narrative in each case. In part, this much more modest (but still indispensable) role for theory in what might be called 'historical sciences' is a consequence of the fact that the mechanism specified by the theory (in this example, natural selection) is only one of a number of mechanisms (for example, mutation, recombination, predation, climate, food supply, parasitism, disease, reproductive isolation, molecular drive, genetic drift and so on), each of which may partially constitute, interact with, determine or modify the effects of natural selection. These other mechanisms may be topics for other, related sciences, requiring complex forms of interdisciplinary collaboration in relation to empirical study for the production of plausible explanatory narratives. In sciences where explanation and prediction are closely related, this is usually because particular mechanisms are naturally isolated from such interactions (as, for example, with the gravitational fields of the bodies making up the solar system) or because they can be artificially isolated by experimental practice. This is usually impossible in the case of historical natural sciences and most social sciences, which is one of the main reasons why explanation in these disciplines is not generally matched by predictive power. We will return to the problems posed by this feature of social scientific explanation in Chapter 8.

Values in Science

As we saw in Chapter 2, empiricists have two basic options for thinking about the nature of value judgements. These can be treated either as disguised factual statements, about, for example, the consequences of actions for the balance of pleasure and pain in the world, or as mere subjective expressions of feeling or preference. The latter, 'subjectivist', view of value judgements has been the most widespread among empiricists in the twentieth century, and empiricists accordingly tend to argue for the exclusion of value judgements from science. For them, science is a rigorous attempt to represent the world as it is, using observation, experiment and formal reasoning. The intrusion of the personal values of the scientist would clearly undermine this objective. However, as we saw above, science necessarily involves more than experiment, observation and formal logic. Active processes of conceptual interpretation are involved in all observation; theory construction is an imaginative, creative activity; and the role of metaphor in science commonly involves drawing ideas from the wider culture. If all this is so, how could science fail to incorporate value commitments? One empiricist response to this relies on distinguishing between the creative activity of *inventing* theories, on the one hand, and the processes of critically evaluating and empirically *testing* them, on the other. These latter processes are governed by formal rules of logic and methodological rigour which can be expected to iron out biases deriving from value preferences of individual scientists.

The core intuition of the empiricist view is that science should not be about how we would *like* the world to be. On the contrary, science can make progress only if scientists are prepared to abandon their cherished hypotheses in the face of evidence about the way things *really are*. Indeed, were science merely a matter of advancing our own wishes and preferences about nature, then there would be no point in doing any experimentation or observation at all.

We can distinguish three different sorts of criticism of the empiricist distinction between facts and values, one of which, however, still preserves what we have called this 'core intuition'. One line of criticism is to dispute the 'subjectivity' of value judgements, and to argue that at least in some cases successful explanation implies moral values. On this view, '*moral realism*', values are themselves independently real, like the entities and processes studied by science. A second line of criticism insists that cultural norms and values cannot be disentangled from scientific knowledge-claims. Therefore the empiricist image of science as above conflict about moral and political values is an ideology which gives science a spurious social authority. Instead of trying to make science value-free, or pretending that it already is, we should demand that scientists make their value commitments explicit, so that rival values and related knowledge-claims can be openly debated in the context of more democratic institutions for decision-making about technical matters (see Wynne 1996, and subsequent debate in the journal *Social Studies of Science*).

A third line of criticism, which, unlike the first two, still preserves the core intuition of empiricism, recognizes that the view of science as the pursuit of objective knowledge about the world itself implies value commitments – namely, not to misrepresent the results of experiments, to give serious consideration to arguments against one's own views (no matter what the status of the person who advocates them), to abandon one's prejudices when it becomes clear that

that is what they are and so on. At a deeper level, many scientists are motivated by respect for and wonderment at the integrity, otherness and intrinsic beauty of the objects of their investigation. This is a dimension of scientific culture which is often missed in much of the social scientific literature on science, but is, as we will see in Chapter 4, emphasized in some feminist approaches to science.

On this third view, then, it is argued against empiricism that values are intrinsically and indispensably involved in science. However, a distinction can still be made between those norms and values which are necessary to and supportive of science, considered as a practice which aims at the production of objective knowledge of its subject-matter, and those values which either are obstructive of this aim or are simply extraneous, and so irrelevant. In the case of Darwin, for example, he was inspired in his student days by the harmonious vision of nature portrayed in the work of the theologian W. Paley. However, his growing recognition of the 'struggle for existence' through which natural selection operated led to his reluctant abandonment of this vision: 'What a book a Devil's Chaplain might write on the clumsy, wasteful, blundering low and horridly cruel works of nature!' (quoted in Desmond and Moore 1992: 449). Clearly, Darwin would have wished living nature to have been kinder and more harmonious than it was, but it is arguable that his commitment to the values of scientific investigation required him to give up such comforting images (note that Desmond and Moore take the more conventional view that Darwin's ideas were shaped by wider Victorian cultural values).

Of course, this distinction between those values which are intrinsic to scientific practice, and those which are not is a controversial one, and it is very much an open question whether it can be applied in a defensible way when we come to consider the role of value commitments in the human social sciences.

Further Problems of Positivism

The Failings of the Empiricist Model of Science

So far we have considered at length some of the difficulties involved in the empiricist view of natural scientific knowledge. Since, as we saw in Chapter 2, this is a key tenet of positivism, positivism itself falls if the empiricist view of the natural sciences cannot be supported. However, it is still worth thinking further about other elements in the positivist approach.

The Superiority of Science

The second tenet, it may be remembered, was the notion that science is the highest, most authoritative, even the sole source of genuine knowledge.

According to Comte's three-stage 'law' of social development, theological modes of thought give way to metaphysical ones, and these, in turn, to scientific ones. There are two claims distinguishable, here. One, the claim of 'functional equivalence', is that science, metaphysics and theology are competitors, in the sense that they are alternative modes of thought, covering the full range of purposes for which human societies require knowledge, so that it makes sense to think of each as replacing the others. The second claim is that the scientific mode of thought is superior to the others, and so represents progress in the sphere of thought to match (and, indeed, contribute to) industrial and social progress.

The first claim, of functional equivalence, is open to two sorts of objection. First, theology and metaphysics are not solely concerned with giving accounts of the nature of the world – they also attempt to derive authoritative norms for human conduct. They provide their adherents with reasons for obedience to certain rules of conduct, and for accepting some kinds of institutional arrangements rather than others. By contrast, the exclusion of values in the empiricist view of science restricts science to the narrow task of predicting what *would* be the consequence *if* such and such policy were to be implemented. Science, on this view, cannot pronounce on the desirability or otherwise of either the policy or its predicted consequence. If this is so, then science cannot replace the functions performed by theology and metaphysics. If people are to have means of orienting themselves to the ethical dilemmas and challenges of modern life then they have need of specifically moral and political sources of guidance which science alone cannot deliver – though, of course, the sources they draw on may be other than religion or metaphysics!

However, Max Weber (Chapter 5), and some of those influenced by his ideas in the Frankfurt School of Critical Theory (Chapter 7), argue that the spread of scientific modes of thought into public administration, business and everyday life does, indeed, undermine our ability to confront questions of basic value and meaning. As they see it, modern society becomes pervaded by a narrow rationality, consisting of matching the most efficient means to 'given' ends, which services an increasingly self-legitimating and totalitarian control over both society and nature. This bleak pessimism is the opposite side of the coin from Comte's utopian vision of a new social order bound together by scientific and technical progress.

The second sort of objection to the claim of functional equivalence is closely connected to the first. What Comte and, arguably, empiricists more generally neglect is the extent to which social life depends on knowledge which cannot be put into the form of statements or propositions: what is sometimes called 'know-how', as distinct from 'knowledge that'. In every context of social interaction we respond to cues and act according to implicit rules and shared understandings which none of us could fully articulate. Language itself is constituted by rules which are learned and deployed tacitly, without our ability or any need to render them explicit for everyday conversational purposes.

Specific skills, such as those involved in cooking, sports and games, maintaining relationships, parenting and so on, are learned through practice, in which trial and error, intuition and imitation are at least as important as following explicit rules. The role of *tacit knowledge* in social life is arguably both centrally important and also irreplaceable. Practical know-how may be informed by scientific insights, but never replaced by it (the literature on this is enormous, but see especially Hayek 1949; O'Neill 1998: ch. 10; Wainwright 1994).

This leads on to a consideration of the claim that science is superior to other sources of knowledge and understanding. Both the above lines of argument suggest that science is not strictly comparable with other sorts of knowledge. It makes no sense to say that science is superior to tacit knowledge, for example, since they are not alternative ways of doing the same sort of thing, or achieving the same sort of purpose. One could argue that buses are superior to cars as environmentally sustainable modes of transport, but what could be meant by saying that buses are superior to fridge-freezers?

On the other hand, it is clear that there is, at least, some overlap between theology, metaphysics, magical and witchcraft beliefs and so on, on the one hand, and science, on the other. The resistance of the church to the new mechanical science in the seventeenth century, and the opposition of theologians to Darwin and Wallace's theory of evolution by natural selection from the 1860s onwards, was not mere coincidence. The church and the emerging scientific establishment were rival institutional locations for authorizing knowledge-claims about the nature of our world. Among other things, a struggle for cultural power was being waged. The empiricist view of science can be seen as providing clear justification for the claims of science: its objectivity is underwritten by its observational basis and its openness to empirical testing. However, if this claim about science is itself open to question, then perhaps we should give equal credence to religious, metaphysical, magical and other non-scientific ways of understanding the world? Why should science be accorded exclusive privilege? The 'anarchist' philosopher of science Paul Feyerabend (see Chapter 4) was one of the most forceful advocates of this view, and he has been followed in the same direction by a number of post-modernist writers (Chapter10).

A Natural Science of Society?

The third tenet of positivism is its advocacy of extending the methods of the natural sciences (as represented in the empiricist view of knowledge) to the study of human social life. In Chapters 5, 6 and 7 we will be considering the arguments of those, such as Max Weber, Peter Winch and Jürgen Habermas, who have offered strong arguments against this. The view that there is, or could be, such a thing as a scientific study of society, in the same sense (but not necessarily using the same methods) as natural processes can be studied scientifically is often termed '*naturalism*'. Weber, Winch and Habermas are, in this sense, anti-naturalists, and positivists such as Comte are naturalists. However, the criticisms of the empiricist view of science, and the fact that we now have quite well-worked-out alternatives to empiricism open up the possibility of forms of naturalism which are not positivist. It may be that there cannot be an *empiricist* science of social life, but the social sciences might count as scientific from the point of view of alternative, non-empiricist models of science. Chapter 4 provides a review of at least some of the main alternative views of science which have been developed so far. The question, 'What might a social science modelled on natural science might be like?' could be asked on the basis of any of these alternatives. The answers would not be positivist in our strict sense of the term, and would no doubt raise interesting philosophical issues. We do not have the space to explore all of these possibilities, but we do give more detailed consideration to the implications of two non-empiricist understandings of science for the practice of social science. These are feminist approaches (Chapter 9) and critical realism (Chapter 8). The issue of epistemological relativism, a feature of several non-empiricist approaches, also has its counterpart in the philosophy of social science, and we will return to it, in particular in Chapters 6 and 10.

Social Science and Social Engineering

The fourth tenet of positivism is its view of social scientific knowledge as useful knowledge, in the sense that it can be fed into the process of social policy-making in the form of projects of social engineering. Despite his differences with positivism in other respects, Popper endorsed this view of the role of social scientific knowledge, so long as it was confined to small-scale reforms 'piece-meal' social engineering) rather than revolutionary attempts at wholescale social transformation, what he called 'utopian' social engineering (see his *Poverty of Historicism*, 1961). However, it is not clear that, in the absence of the symmetry of explanation and prediction which (on the empiricist view) characterizes natural scientific knowledge, the social sciences can provide the right sort of knowledge for this reformist project of social engineering. Any particular policy intervention is likely to be modified in its effects by complex interactions between social processes, and unless there is some means of taking these into account, reform strategies are liable to generate unintended and possibly unwanted consequences.

A more practical problem has to do with the institutional power required to implement reforms. The underlying assumption of most social policy is that government, acting through state institutions, will be the agent of change. But it is at least arguable that there are economic and socio-cultural sources of social power which are able to resist or modify reform strategies, or obstruct their implementation. The institutions of the state, itself, are also heterogeneous, and can by no means be assumed to offer a smooth transmission belt for the application of social science in social policy. Having noted all of this, however, it would be hard to deny the considerable achievements of the link between social science and policy in the formation of the post-war welfare state, in expanding opportunities for women in social and economic life, and in providing social-ized health care in response to need rather than ability to pay. Though achieve-ments such as these remain fragile and open to reversal, and in many countries are heavily compromised, they are a significant testimony to the strengths of policy-oriented research generated on broadly positivist assumptions.

But the issue of power in relation to social engineering also raises ethical questions. The post-structuralist writer Michel Foucault, for example (Chapter 10), has argued that forms of knowledge in the human sciences are indissolubly linked to strategies of power, whereby human subjects (such as the mad, the sexually deviant, or the criminal) are classified and subjected to regimes of sur-veillance and regulation in institutions such as the asylum, clinic and prison. This reveals a much more sinister dimension of social engineering than would be accepted by its positivist advocates. At least part of the reason why social engineering seems so sinister to Foucault is his view of human agency and sub-jectivity as constituted and manipulated by relations of power. So there is little space in his account for agents to acquire and exercise autonomous agency. By contrast, the critical theorist Habermas (Chapter 7) would share Foucault's opposition to manipulation and incarceration, while arguing for an enlarged and democratic public sphere, in which *emancipatory* forms of understanding could be effective.

So far, then, we have considered some of the possible lines of criticism of the positivist tradition, focusing especially on the problems of the empiricist account of science upon which it relies. In the next chapter we will take a necessarily rather selective look at some of the alternative views of science, most of them closely related to the sociological or historical study of science in action, but in each case posing important philosophical issues.

Further Reading

Chalmers (1999) provides an excellent contemporary introduction to the philosophy of science. Older texts which are still of great value include Harré (1972), and the relevant chapters in Keat and Urry (1975) and Oldroyd (1986). Non-empiricist attempts to defend the rationality of science include Newton-Smith (1981), Brown (1994), Hacking (1983), Longino (1990) and Laudan (1996). For alternative accounts of science, see Chapter 4. For hermeneutic criticisms of positivism in the social sciences, see Chapters 5, 6 and 7.

4

Science, Nature and Society: Some Alternatives to Empiricism

Until the early 1960s philosophical thinking about natural science in the English-speaking countries was dominated by the various forms of empiricism, together with Popper's 'falsificationist' approach. Both these traditions were committed to a view of science as radically distinct from other forms of knowledge or belief. It was held that the rules governing collection and analysis of empirical evidence, admitting only testable (or falsifiable) statements into the corpus of scientific knowledge, separating fact from value and so on, made scientific knowledge-claims especially reliable. The whole cumulative exercise of science was leading to an ever-closer approximation to a true account of the natural world.

However, as the arguments we reviewed in Chapter 3 became more widely accepted, alternatives to the optimistic view of the rationality and objectivity of science were developed. Indeed, that such alternatives were available was an important condition for loosening the hold of the orthodox empiricist accounts of science. The existence and plausibility of these alternatives to empiricism makes it necessary for philosophy of social science to ask new questions about the relationship between natural and social science. The choice is no longer simply between the positivist approach discussed in the previous two chapters, on the one hand, or an anti-naturalistic hermeneutic or interpretivist approach (Chapters 5 and 6) on the other. This chapter reviews and offers also some limited evaluations of a selection of the non-empiricist accounts of science. As we will see, despite their important differences, these are generally united in their emphasis on the socially and historically located character of scientific practice. One such alternative view, critical realism, was devised precisely with the relation of the natural to social sciences in mind, and for this reason we deal with it only very briefly in this chapter, but return to it later (in Chapter 8).

Marxism and Science

In the traditional view, the exclusion of moral, social and political influences from the sphere of scientific discovery and debate was necessary to its objectivity.

To a considerable extent this philosophical view of science was shared by the historians and sociologists of knowledge. One tradition stemmed from Marx and Engels. In his early writings (see Marx and Engels 1975: vol. 3; esp. the *Economic and Philosophical Manuscripts* of 1844), Marx proposed a philosophical view of history according to which private property was viewed as a symptom of human alienation from nature, as well as giving rise to alienation between classes in capitalist society. At that stage in his thinking, Marx's vision of the future good society was one in which alienation among humans themselves and between them and nature would be overcome. In this future society, humans would come to realize their oneness with nature, and the artificial split between social and natural sciences would be overcome. Science would be transformed from a means of domination of both humans and nature into a new kind of expression of the spiritual and aesthetic appreciation of nature, and the various sciences would be reunified.

This critique of science as an expression of the alienated relationship between modern capitalism and nature was continued and developed by later social theorists, most especially by the 'first generation' of the Frankfurt School of Critical Theory (see Chapter 7). These writers were associated with an institute of social research which was attached to Frankfurt University until the Nazi takeover in 1933, and was subsequently re-formed at Columbia University in the USA. Adorno, Horkheimer and Marcuse, especially, retained the early Marx's vision of an unalienated relation to the rest of nature, and the associated critique of the existing natural sciences as a mere instrument of human domination of nature.

However, Marx's later work seemed to fit more easily with the orthodox nineteenth-century view of science as providing objective and useful knowledge of the world, in contrast to earlier superstitious and religious world-views. The view of history advanced by Marx and Engels from the late 1840s onwards is one in which advances in human freedom and self-determination are to be won through a two-fold struggle: against limits imposed by nature, and against class oppression. The former struggle was being progressively won by the application of scientific knowledge in agricultural and industrial technologies, so harnessing the forces of nature to human purposes, and vastly increasing the social wealth. Indeed, the great achievement of modern capitalism was its power the revolutionize the 'forces of production' at a rate and on a scale never before seen.

The downside of capitalism, though, was that this vast, constantly advancing apparatus of technical mastery of nature was under the control of one class in society only, so that its direction and the benefits deriving from it served only the interests of this one, dominant class – the owners of capital. Increasingly, the scale of social coordination required by the new technologies of production pointed to the need for spreading control to the whole of society, and giving the benefits of ever-increasing wealth production to everyone.

In this approach, the objectivity of scientific knowledge is not questioned. Nor is the power of science to harness the forces of nature through technology.

Science and technology have the potential to liberate all humanity from disease, poverty and external risk, but this potential is not being realized because of the class monopoly over the wealth needed to finance and apply scientific knowledge. On the contrary, under capitalism, science and technology is a massively powerful weapon through which the exploitation and control of the labour force is maintained.

Despite all this, Marx and Engels (especially the latter) were great enthusiasts for the scientific advances of their day, and declared their own view of history to be 'scientific', in contrast to the 'ideologies' peddled by other economists and social theorists, which mostly presented a distorted account of the social world favourable to the dominant class. To the extent that many people, including members of the working class, lived according to such beliefs, and did not question the existing system of class rule, there was an opposition between the distorted, or false, consciousness of 'common sense', on the one hand, and the scientific knowledge claimed by Marx and Engels, on the other.

These contrasts between 'science', as objective and interest-free, and 'ideology', or 'common sense', as distorted, or false because of the influence on it of practical interests and values were carried forward by the later Marxist sociology of knowledge. The focus in this tradition was on explaining distorted or false beliefs in terms of the social position of the group whose beliefs they were, in terms of the misleading appearance presented by social relations, or in terms of the cultural power of the economically dominant class and its allies in educational institutions or the media.

So far as the natural sciences are concerned, Marxist approaches have tended to follow Marx himself in focusing on the role of science in the invention of technologies which enhance employer control over the labour force, and enable the replacement of workers by machines. In Britain during the 1930s there emerged a radical movement of scientists, part of which was greatly influenced by Marxist ideas. One focus of this movement was resistance to the eugenics movement and its proposals for forced sterilization of the 'unfit'. This campaign won growing support as eugenics became increasingly identified with the Nazi regime in Germany and with the influential fascist movement in Britain. But the radical scientists were also concerned with the poor working conditions and 'proletarianization' of technical and support workers in research institutions, and the exclusion of scientists from areas of public policy-making. As Werskey (1978) has argued, however, the movement was by no means united, and the shared concern for the 'social relations' of science covered rather different political positions. For some, the main aim was to increase the public standing and funding of science, whereas for the more radical figures the potential of science to serve universal human need was obstructed by its increasing incorporation into industrial capitalism. Nothing less than a socialist revolution was required for science to be opened to wider participation and social accountability. Key representatives of this radical perspective were J. D. Bernal (see Bernal 1939), J. B. S. Haldane, J. Needham, L. Hogben, H. Levy and C. H. Waddington.

There remained ambiguity about what a socialist approach to science meant. Did it mean enabling the further development of science and technology in response to people's needs, as against priorities determined by profit and control, or would 'socialist science' be different in *content* from existing 'bourgeois' science? At the time, Soviet scientists and philosophers were arguing for this latter position, and the mainly pro-Soviet radical scientists in Britain tended to adopt it until the notorious Lysenko episode in Soviet biology (see Lenin Academy 1949; Lewontin and Levins in Rose and Rose 1976b; Lecourt 1977; Benton 1980). In the name of 'proletarian science', Soviet geneticists were denounced as 'bourgeois' and 'idealist'. Many were arrested, some died, Soviet genetics was destroyed, and great damage was done to Soviet agriculture. This disaster divided the radical scientists in Britain, and took radical visions of an alternative science off the agenda until the resurgence of scientific radicalism in the context of the US war against Vietnam and the broad political radicalization of the late 1960s.

At the start of the 1970s, many scientists involved in the newly formed British Society for Social Responsibility in Science were concerned about abuses of science in the massive application of chemical weapons in Vietnam, in research on biological, chemical and nuclear weaponry, in the use of CS gas in maintaining public order, in hazardous conditions of work, in surveillance technologies, in pollution and so on. But, again, a radical wing of the movement, influenced by Marxism, but also by the New Left's critique of Soviet state socialism, by the women's movement and by anti-racist concerns, wanted to go further than denouncing individual abuses. For them, what was needed was an analysis of the institutional nexus of science, capitalist industry and the state, and an integration of the radical science movement with a wider struggle for socialist transformation (see Rose and Rose 1969, 1976a, 1976b). One legacy of that period was the *Radical Science Journal* (later *Science as Culture*) which was, arguably, influential in the academic development of the new sociology of science (see below).

Weber, Merton and the Sociology of Science

Max Weber may be taken as the starting-point for an alternative tradition of social thinking about science. Weber linked the growth of science with the increasingly pervasive 'rationalization' and 'disenchantment' of life under modern capitalist civilization (see Chapter 5). The norms of science demanded intellectual integrity, and a value-free commitment to empirical truth. Paradoxically, however, this meant that the attitude of the scientist to 'his' (Weber doesn't discuss science as a possible vocation for women!) vocation was one which could be understood only as a species of value-oriented rationality (Weber 1948; see also Chapter 5). Science was to be viewed as a distinct value sphere, independent of the various instrumental purposes to which its findings might be put. Weber adds to this account of the normative character of science some brief but suggestive remarks about its institutional character. The dependence of scientific professions on public funding allows Weber to describe scientific practice as a form of 'state capitalism', the general trend in which will be (as with industrial capitalism) a growing separation of scientific workers from ownership and control of their means of production. The craft character of much research, especially in the humanities and social sciences, would eventually be displaced in favour of large institutional research bureaucracies and an associated proletarianization of research.

However, at the level of the normative ethos of science, Weber merely reflected the view that scientists themselves have tended to project: disinterested pursuit of the truth through obedience to rational rules for collecting and analysing evidence and so on. As in the Marxist approaches to the sociology of knowledge, and the empiricist philosophy of science, science was held to be objective to the extent that it held external social interests and influences at bay. Only distorted beliefs and falsehoods stood in need of explanation in terms of social (or psychological) factors.

The autonomy of science from external pressures was also emphasized in the most influential sociological approach to science prior to the 1960s. This was the functionalist approach, developed by R. K. Merton. Merton authored a classic study (Merton 1938, 1970) of the seventeenth-century establishment and legitimization of modern physical science which closely paralleled Weber's study of the relationship between the Protestant sects and modern capitalism (see Chapter 5). His interest in the distinctive normative character of science persisted in his general sociology of modern science. For Merton, science is characterized by adherence to a set of technical and moral norms which are peculiar to it, and which insulate its key processes from external distorting or constraining influences. The technical norms are those of logical inference and adequate, reliable and valid empirical evidence.

So far, Merton simply accepts without question the empiricist account of scientific knowledge, and the accounts scientists tend to give of their own practice. However, ensuring conformity to these technical norms, and achieving the goal of ever-expanding 'certified knowledge', requires institutionally sanctioned (and preferably psychologically internalized) moral norms, or 'institutional imperatives'. Merton identifies four of these. First, *universalism* – 'The acceptance or rejection of claims entering the lists of science is not to depend on the personal or social attributes of their protagonists; his race, nationality, religion, class and personal qualities are as such irrelevant' (Merton 1967: p. 55). The second institutional imperative is *communism*: scientific knowledge doesn't belong to its inventor or discoverer, in the sense that it can be bought and sold. The only benefit a scientist may legitimately claim is recognition and esteem from his peers. This is why there is a strong emphasis on publication, and also explains the importance of priority disputes. The third norm is that of *disinterestedness*, and the fourth *organized scepticism*. Both norms require suspension of judgement, and obedience to the dictates of evidence and logic. As Merton points out, this is liable to give rise to conflict with non-scientific institutions (such as religious ones) which treat as sacred sets of beliefs which science subjects to empirical and rational evaluation.

Merton's sociology of science was subsequently criticized for its failure to empirically investigate the practice of scientists, as distinct from taking on trust their accounts of it. Later sociology of science, as we will see, claimed that in practice the lofty norms described by Merton have little purchase on the way science is actually conducted. However, Merton's account can be understood as an 'ideal type' in the Weberian sense (see Chapter 5), not describing the actual practice of science but rather providing a conceptual model with which to study the extent of empirical deviation. Taken in this spirit, Merton's model of the normative structure of science can provide a basis for a critical under-standing of the extent to which today's institutionalization of science around commercial and military objectives contradicts the professed values of science. However, Merton's sociology of science is self-limiting in ways which later developments were to override. He, like most of his Marxist and Weberian pre-decessors, thought that the sociology of (successful) science must be confined to the study of how a particular institutionalized practice for the pursuit of knowledge could arise and be sustained. So far as the natural sciences were concerned, there could be no question of a sociological explanation of their *content*: this was determined entirely by evidence and logic.

Historical Epistemology and Structural Marxism

However, a quite different approach to understanding the nature of the sciences was emerging in France. In the empiricist tradition, debate about science tended to be carried on as if some abstract criteria for distinguishing science from non-science could be established independently of historical or social context. Science was also believed to be uniquely cumulative and progressive in its gathering of more and more factual knowledge and its increasing approxi-mation to the truth. The French tradition, whose best-known exponents have been Alexandre Koyré, Gaston Bachelard and Georges Canguilhem, based its view of science on close study of its history. This led to posing questions of the philosophy of science differently, and in particular required a much greater sensitivity to historical and social processes both within science and in its contextual conditions.

Despite these differences, the French tradition of 'historical epistemology' (see Lecourt 1975; Gutting 1989) shared with the other approaches so far mentioned a strong commitment to the distinction between science and non-scientific patterns of belief. Their historical studies focused on the processes of formation of scientific disciplines through a struggle against the networks of error and delusion which precede them. Common-sense and pre-scientific thought is not mere ignorance, or absence of knowledge, but, rather a tenacious and powerful source of resistance to genuine science. Even after the establishment of a science, this tissue of errors continues to exist and threatens to invade the tentative achievements of a new science in the shape of 'epistemological obstacles'.

As the notion of a tissue of errors suggests, this approach recognizes the ways in which particular concepts are bound together through mutual definition into a systematic network. Scientific ideas are not invented one by one, but coexist in theoretical 'problematics'. That is to say, the network of concepts forming the new science enables the posing of a certain set of questions, and provides solutions to them. However, the other side of this coin is that each network of concepts, each problematic also *excludes* the posing of other questions. The problematic can thus be compared to the beam of a torch: it casts a clear light on those objects within its frame, but leaves all else in darkness. This calls into question any view of science as somehow 'complete' knowledge, and also illustrates the relation between scientific knowledge and some specific set of theoretical questions. Other questions might give us a different science.

Another consequence of the concept of the problematic is that scientific change must necessarily be discontinuous, and non-cumulative. For a new science to be born, a whole interconnected mesh of falsehood has to be overthrown. This moment is termed an 'epistemological break'. Similarly, subsequent scientific change has to take place, not through the steady accumulation of facts (as in the empiricist picture) but by way of wholesale restructuring of the problematic. In this process, previous assumptions are called into question, and science advances not so much by adding to its past achievements as by overthrowing and replacing them.

Key features of this approach were carried forward in France by Louis Althusser and structural Marxism, and by the post-structuralist Michel Foucault (see Chapter 10 for more on Foucault). In a series of articles written during the 1960s (collected in English translation as Althusser 1969), Althusser made use of the concepts of problematic and epistemological break in an attempt to relaunch Marxism as a creative scientific research programme, after decades of orthodox subservience to the policy requirements of Communist Party leaders (see Benton 1984; Elliott 1994). He and his collaborators provided close textual readings designed to show the emergence of a new 'scientific' problematic in the study of history in Marx's works after 1845. This implied that the 'humanist' Marx of the early texts, which were currently influential in Communist Party circles, belonged to the ideological prehistory of Marxism. Then began an extensive work of defining and elaborating the concepts of the 'scientific' Marx, and making use of these ideas in the analysis of media communications, youth culture, education, anthropological studies, Third World 'development', gender divisions and so on.

But Althusser and the structural Marxists faced a particularly difficult problem. Like their predecessors, the historical epistemologists, they emphasized the gap between ordinary, common-sense thought, or 'ideology', and genuine science. The radically egalitarian student movement of the 1960s was quick to point out the potentially elitist and undemocratic implications of this insistence on the distance between 'science' – the possession of a small coterie of self-styled intellectuals on the left – and 'ideology' – the allegedly inadequate and defective beliefs of the 'masses' whose benefit the science was supposed to serve.

Though he radically revised his views, Althusser never resolved this problem in a satisfactory way. However, his earlier writings were significant for his distinctive way of thinking about science as a social practice of a quite special kind. For Althusser, science was a practice of social production of knowledge, in which the key role was played by the theoretical problematic of the science concerned. On this model of science, the theoretical concepts making up the problematic are employed as 'means of production' of new theoretical concepts by transforming conceptual 'raw materials' (which might be ideas produced by prior 'theoretical practice', or drawn from the wider culture, and so on). This model opens up the possibility of sociological explanation of the content of scientific knowledge, but without giving up the notion of scientific objectivity (unlike most other 'constructionist' sociological approaches – see Glossary, p. 179).

In effect, Althusser's approach welds the insights of the historical epistemologists together with the realist and materialist legacy of the Marxist tradition. In his terms, theoretical practice produces knowledge in the form of 'thought-objects', which, in the case of science, correspond to 'real objects', whose existence is independent of and external to the process of producing knowledge of them. However, Althusser never succeeded in solving the problem of how, in science, it is ensured that this correspondence really does hold. Unless this could be done, the crucial distinction between science and ideology could not be sustained.

Post-Althusserian sociology of knowledge and culture tended to accept that this problem was insoluble and as a consequence moved towards analyses of language and cultural processes in abstraction from epistemological questions of truth, falsity or reference to a real world independent of people's beliefs. As we will see (Chapter 10), much of the work of Michel Foucault takes this form, as does the work of 'post-Marxists' such as Ernesto Laclau and Chantal Mouffe (1985). However, there were some who attempted to hold onto Althusser's project: to combine together the model of science as a social practice of production of knowledge with a realist understanding of knowledge as *about* something independent of itself.

The critical realist approach, first developed in the early 1970s, tried to do just this, and to find ways of solving the problem Althusser had powerfully posed. Central to the critical realist case was the use of 'transcendental arguments' in relation to a range of scientific practices. A transcendental argument is one which takes as its premiss an uncontroversial or undisputed description of something actual (for example, scientific experiment), and then poses the question, 'What must be true for this to be possible?' In the case of scientific experiments, Roy Bhaskar, the most influential critical realist philosopher of science (see Bhaskar 1975, 1997 and 1979, 1998), demonstrated that only if the external world existed and had certain properties, and only if human agents had certain abilities to intervene in that world and monitor the consequences of doing so, could there be anything recognizable as experimentation.

These arguments offer a convincing way of combining together an under-standing of science as a historically changing and socially situated human practice with an acknowledgement of it as, distinctively, a social practice whose aim is the production of knowledge about objects, relations, processes and so on which exist and act independently of our knowledge of them. However, Althusser's own search for guarantees that our knowledge corresponds to its external objects is decisively abandoned: science is displayed as rational enquiry into the nature of an independently existing reality, but also as one whose products (currently accepted scientific knowledge-claims) are always provisional and subject to modification or rejection in the face of future evidence and argument. It is only, realists argue, if we recognize science as making knowledge-claims about independently existing realities that we can make any sense of what it is for a belief to be shown to be wrong. While appearing to be more modest in its claims, relativism turns out to be a way of insulating beliefs from refutation. Some of the most basic intuitions underlying realist approaches are derived from the experience of getting things wrong, of making mistakes and being – sometimes painfully – reminded of this by reality. We'll return to a discussion of this approach and its implications for the practice of social science in Chapter 8.

Revolutions and Relativism: From Kuhn to the 'Strong Programme'

Meanwhile, the historical approach to philosophy of science which had been pioneered by the French tradition found its way into the English-language debate through the work of the American historian and philosopher of science, Thomas Kuhn. Kuhn's study of the Copernican revolution in astronomy (Kuhn 1959) exemplified this approach, but it was not until his later, thorough-going conceptualization of his understanding of the history of science in *The Structure of Scientific Revolutions* (Kuhn 1970) that his ideas began to have their profound effect. In this work, Kuhn set out to use histori-cal evidence to undermine the prevailing view of science as involving a progres-sive accumulation of knowledge towards a greater approximation to the truth, and of the scientific community rationally and disinterestedly fitting fact with theory, rejecting the latter when the facts did not fit and so on. But in the process Kuhn also developed his own *alternative* account of the nature of scientific activity, with a focus on processes of historical change in scientific understanding.

Kuhn uses examples taken from the history of several natural sciences to construct a typical pattern of change. The period prior to the establishment of a scientific approach to any topic is characterized by a plurality of competing approaches. One of these eventually acquires the adherence of the emergent scientific community, and is from then onwards the basis for further research. Once consensus has been reached, the approach which governs subsequent research is called by Kuhn the 'paradigm'. Research carried out according to a paradigm is generally regarded as 'routine puzzle-solving', and Kuhn calls it 'normal science'. It is taken for granted within the scientific community that problems can be solved in the terms provided by the currently accepted paradigm, so that failure is seen a failure on the part of researchers, rather than as grounds for rejecting the paradigm (the opposite of what should be happening, according to both the empiricist and the Popperian accounts of scientific rationality). In Kuhn's view, paradigms are necessary for scientists to define problems and select methods in their research. To reject the prevailing paradigm just because of a little local difficulty in fitting together facts and theory would leave the scientists without any guidelines for further research (note the parallel here with Kant's criticism of the empiricist view of experience – see Chapter 3). In fact, there are always problems which have so far defied solution within the prevailing paradigm – this is what keeps scientists busy.

However, there are some problems which, either because they come to be seen as particularly persistent and challenging for the paradigm, or because they are posed by external demands on science, do eventually lead to a loss of confidence in the paradigm itself. Kuhn terms these problems 'anomalies', and an accumulation of them can lead to a period of 'crisis' in the science concerned. In the context of such a crisis, a plurality of alternative and conflicting approaches again emerges. Crises are only resolved when a consensus forms around one of these competing approaches, and normal science can resume, but now under the guidance of a new and different paradigm. Kuhn likens the whole process to a social revolution.

Kuhn's concept of a paradigm is central to his model of science, and it has generated a huge critical literature. For him, the key point is that it is a source of guidance for conducting and evaluating research which is consensual within a particular scientific discipline. It may take the form of a set of shared theoretical assumptions, a commonly accepted view of the subject-matter (ontology), an accepted set of standards for evaluating explanations, a metaphysical view of the world, or merely a generally acknowledged past scientific achievement (an 'exemplar') which provides rules for subsequent practice. Of course, it can be, and often is, all of these things.

The shift of paradigms which occurs through scientific revolutions involves far more than a mere accumulation of new factual knowledge. The appropriate analogy, in Kuhn's account, would be the shift of perspective one experiences when viewing an ambiguous figure, such as the famous 'duck-rabbit' (see Chapter 3, p. 33). There is a sense (just *what* this sense is has, of course, been very controversial!) in which scientists after a scientific revolution inhabit a different world: everything in their field is redescribed, and interpreted through different theoretical concepts. The new paradigm does not in any straightforward sense build on the past achievements of the science, but, rather, involves rejection of what had previously been accepted. The history of science is, thus, a 'discontinuous' process, periods of cumulative and consensual 'normal' science alternating with periods of crisis, 'revolution' and 'paradigm shift'.

The peculiar character of paradigm shifts in Kuhn's account is what makes his model of science so challenging to earlier views of scientific rationality. The all-embracing character of paradigms is such that they carry with them their own standards for evaluating explanations and judging between rival theories, as well as their own ways of interpreting new evidence. There are, in short, no standards for judging rival candidates to become the new paradigm which are neutral as between the contenders. It is as if there are two political parties, one offering a way of keeping inflation down, the other a way of reducing unemployment, but with no way of deciding which achievement would be the more desirable. The problem may go even deeper than this. Even where, as in the paradigm shift from Newtonian mechanics to the relativistic physics developed by Einstein, there are terms that the rival theories have in common, such as 'mass' and 'time', they are defined in different ways. The consequence of this 'meaning variance' is that dialogue between advocates of the rival theories is at cross-purposes. This is the strongest sense in which rival theories can be said to be 'incommensurable': that they are mutually unintelligible.

This very radical thesis of incommensurability has the paradoxical consequence that rival theories do not contradict, but just talk past one another. If this were really so, then it is hard to see how they could be in conflict. Kuhn subsequently retreated into a less radical version of incommensurability, but still held that there were no objectively justifiable decision procedures for basic theory choice. This leaves the way open for a sociological approach to understanding such changes in science. In the absence of objectively rational, paradigm-neutral criteria for theory choice, scientific revolutions are accomplished by way of power struggles in the scientific community, in which editorial control over key journals, capture of particular university departments, the use of rhetoric and propaganda may all have a place. In fact, however, Kuhn himself remained committed to the view that science does progress through revolutions, and that the successful new paradigm does constitute an advance over its defeated rivals.

Kuhn's great achievement was to have brought to the centre of the debate the recognition of historical transformations in scientific beliefs (including transformations in concepts of what science itself was) and the role of social processes within the scientific community in bringing about such transformations. Although Kuhn himself was not a relativist, and believed that science does progress through paradigm shifts, many of his arguments pointed in a relativist direction. This sparked off a major debate in the philosophy of science, and made possible a revolution in the sociology of scientific knowledge.

The philosophical debate turned on whether it was possible to accept the social and historical processes of scientific change which Kuhn had drawn attention to, but still believe in the rationality of science as providing ever-more adequate knowledge of an independently existing reality. However, for other philosophers of science, Kuhn's earlier thesis of radical incommensurability between different paradigms, and the absence of theory-neutral tests to choose between them, led to more radically relativist conclusions. P. K. Feyerabend was the boldest and best known of these. He was a self-styled 'anarchist' (Feyerabend 1975) in the theory of knowledge, but, in case this implied that he took himself seriously, he was more inclined to call himself a 'Dadaist' (referring to the inter-war avant garde art movement), implying playful but subversive irreverence. Like Kuhn, Feyerabend took his philosophical views from his interpretation of episodes in the history of science. He argued that what came to be recognized as key advances in scientific thought were in fact achieved by deliberate *breaches* of accepted scientific method. If sciences progress by breaking the rules, then the appropriate motto should be 'Anything goes'. For Feyerabend, there are no methodological principles which distinguish science from non-science, and so no reason for thinking science is superior to other forms of understanding of the world. This position supports a tolerant pluralism within science, but also, more broadly, a dethroning of science itself from its privileged social position:

> And yet science has no greater authority than any other form of life. Its aims are certainly not more important than are the aims that guide the lives in a religious community or in a tribe that is united by a myth. At any rate they have no business restricting the lives, the thoughts, the education of the members of a free society where everyone should have a chance to make up his own mind and to live in accordance with the social beliefs he finds most acceptable. The separation between church and state must therefore be complemented by the separation between state and science. (Feyerabend 1978: 299)

However, others, most influentially Imre Lakatos, a follower of Karl Popper, attempted to use historical analysis to defend the rationality of science (Lakatos 1970). Lakatos's term 'research programme' is close to Kuhn's concept of 'paradigm'. Like the paradigm, a scientific research programme provides rules ('heuristics') and topics for empirical research – it is able to recruit and sustain the activities of researchers in the field concerned (what Kuhn called 'normal science'). Unlike Popper, Lakatos accepts that *early on* in the development of a research programme scientists may be justified in holding on to their basic propositions, or hypotheses (the 'core' of the programme) in the face of apparently adverse evidence. They may justifiably protect this core from falsification by surrounding it with a 'periphery' of *ad hoc* hypotheses. This is necessary to give the supporters of an embryonic research programme a chance to develop it to a point where its explanatory potential can really be shown. In the longer term, the programme can be shown to be succeeding to the extent that it generates unlikely predictions which turn out to be confirmed. Where research programmes fail to do this over a prolonged period of time, they are said to be 'degenerating', and a shift to a successful programme is 'progressive'. Since Lakatos's work, considerable ingenuity has been devoted by philosophers of science to the task of offering historically and sociologically sensitive defences of the rationality of science. Examples include Newton-Smith (1981), Hacking (1983), Brown (1994), Longino (1990) and others. The work of the critical realists (discussed at greater length in Chapter 8) can also be understood in this way.

So far as sociology of scientific knowledge was concerned, Kuhn's work was seen as liberating the discipline from the requirement to treat the content of natural scientific beliefs as a special case: as outside the scope of sociological explanation because determined exclusively by evidence and logic. Influential texts by Barry Barnes (1974) and David Bloor (1976, 1991) inaugurated what presented itself as a '*strong programme*' in the sociology of knowledge. In his classic statement of this approach, Bloor defined it in terms of four commitments: to seek causal explanations; to treat 'true' and 'false' beliefs impartially; to explain 'true' and 'false' beliefs, as far as possible, in the same sociological terms (the 'symmetry' principle); and to accept these commitments as also applying to the explanations provided by the sociology of knowledge itself (the principle of reflexivity).

This new approach to the sociology of science satisfied at least one of Lakatos's criteria for a progressive research programme: it inspired a large number of sophisticated and insightful empirical studies of science in the making, by MacKenzie (1990), Pickering (1984), Collins (1985), Shapin and Shaffer (1985), Pinch (1986) and many more.

These studies showed the extent to which social processes of negotiation and consensus-formation were involved in the construction and authorization of scientific knowledge-claims. Despite some disclaimers (for example, Bloor 1976, 1991: 7), the tendency was to give the impression that sociological explanation could account wholly for the content of science. So scientific knowledge-claims about nature were presented as 'constructs' of the social processes whose outcome they were. Further, given the symmetry principle, no special status could justifiably be assigned to scientific as against other sorts of belief. There was no direct access to nature-in-itself by which to compare alternative representations of it. The drift towards radical relativism about knowledge, and a social constructionist view of nature itself, seemed both necessary to sustaining the empirical enquiries, and a conclusion supported by the results of the studies themselves. This led to sharp divisions both within the sociology of science and between its more relativist wing and philosophers and natural scientists who were determined to defend the objectivity and rationality of scientific work; see, for example, the entertaining report on the confrontation between Wolpert and Collins at a British Association meeting by Irwin (1994) and the debate between Collins and Murphy in the UK journal *Sociology* (Murphy 1994; Collins 1996).

Gender and Science: The Feminist Vision

Once science had been shown, by the radical science movement and by sociologists of science, to be a thoroughly social process, the way was open to an exploration of a variety of *different aspects* of this sociality: science could be seen as following the dictates of instrumental reason in its 'modernist' mission to subdue nature, as expressing the world-view of a dominant class or culture, or, more narrowly, as the arena for the power play of scientists themselves. The emergence of a renewed and energetic feminist movement at the end of the 1960s ensured that yet another dimension of science's social character would be exposed: its relation to gender.

At first, feminist scholars emphasized the exclusion of women from science, analysing the mechanisms by which this exclusion took place (for accounts of this literature, see Harding 1991: part 1; Rose 1994: chs. 3, 5 and 6). They held not that women were absent from science, but that their presence was predominantly confined to ancillary and supporting roles, providing the practical support for research almost always defined by men. The aim of this 'liberal' feminist research was to bring the obstacles to female participation and advancement in science to public attention. That science itself would benefit from greater female participation followed from the obvious fact that a huge reservoir of talent was simply not being tapped.

But this assumed that women had the inherent capacity for science, and at the same time did not pose the possibility that women in science might make a *qualitative* difference to the way science was done. Studies of the work of that small minority of women who have been allowed to make their mark as scientific innovators (see Keller 1983; Rose 1994; also this volume, Chapter 9) revealed interesting answers to both questions. Despite immensely greater obstacles, some women clearly had made important contributions to science – this dispensed with the prejudice that women were somehow constitutionally incapable of major scientific achievement. But at least some of these women scientists (who did not necessarily identify themselves as feminists, or even attach significance to their gender in relation to their work as scientists – see Keller 1985: 173–4) could be shown to challenge the ruling self-image of science by their distinctive visions and ways of working.

At its most fundamental, this challenge could be seen as one which identified the whole project of an objective knowledge of nature as inseparable from a (white, Western) masculine aggressive desire to dominate nature, women and racial 'others'. In the face of this, the liberal feminist agenda of increased female participation in science was clearly far too narrow. But what were the alternatives? Here feminists remain divided, and we will consider some of the subsequent debates in Chapter 9. For the moment, however, we focus on an influential line of feminist analysis of the natural sciences which explores the relation between the prevailing ideology and practice of science, on the one hand, and gender and sexuality on the other. This approach does not abandon science altogether, but instead poses the possibility of a different practice of science on the basis of changed gender-relationships, and identifies trends in current science which point in that direction.

Influential work by the pioneering 'eco-feminist' (see Glossary) Carolyn Merchant (1980) and Brian Easlea (1980) established connections between witch-hunting and male challenges to previously female roles (in medicine and midwifery, especially), on the one hand, and the shift away from an organic, holistic and feminine vision of the world to the impersonal, mechanical philosophy of nature proposed by the New Science of the seventeenth-century, on the other.

Evelyn Fox Keller (1985) draws upon this work, but subtly shifts its emphasis. She detects ambiguities in the sexual and gendered metaphors by which the New Science justified itself. She describes the rivalry between two versions. One, the *hermetic* tradition, deriving from the ideas of the sixteenth-century physician Paracelsus, saw matter as infused with spirit, so that knowledge involved 'heart, hand and head', as opposed to the divorce between reason and emotion, mind and matter insisted upon in the mechanical world-view. Both philosophies thought of knowledge in terms strongly suffused with images of sexuality and gender, but the imagery of the hermetic tradition recognized different but complementary masculine and feminine aspects of nature, and emphasized a receptive relationship between science and nature. By contrast, the mechanical philosophy emphasized its masculine pursuit of truth and renunciation of the emotions:

> [W]here the *Will* or *Passion* hath the casting voyce, the case of *Truth* is *desparate*
> ... The *Woman* in us, still prosecutes a deceit, like that begun in the *Garden*; and our
> *Understandings* are wedded to an *Eve*, as fatal as the *Mother* of our *miseries*. (Joseph
> Glanvill, quoted in Keller 1985: 52–3)

What Keller interprets as the 'hermaphrodite' image of science in the hermetic tradition was attacked by the advocates of the mechanical philosophy as complicit with witchcraft, disorder and the radical sects. So, the establishment of the Royal Society after the English Civil War consolidated the victory of a self-consciously masculine and socially conservative view of science as committed to the rational 'penetration' of the secrets of nature. For the mechanical philosophy, nature was still represented as female, though no longer as 'mother', or as partner, but rather as the object of dispassionate exploration and rational control.

Keller's argument is that wider cultural and social changes in gender relations contributed to the formation of this new masculine ideology and practice of science, and also that the growing authority of science as associated with masculine virtues contributed to a consolidation of new gender divisions in the wider society. The link between femininity, emotion and subjectivity was opposed to masculine objectivity and rationality as the 'separation of spheres' came to characterize the division of labour between men and (middle-class) women in early industrial capitalism.

Keller, like other contributors to the discussion of gender and knowledge, draws on the 'object relations' school of psychoanalysis, and in particular on the feminist development of it associated with the work of Nancy Chodorow (see Chapter 9). That approach emphasizes the problems encountered by the developing infant in forming a stable sense of self-identity. These problems are different for boys and girls, and they may lead, especially in the case of boys, to the formation of defensive personalities which can maintain their autonomy only through a sharp boundary between self and other, and by aggressive, dominating relationships with threatening 'others'. The association of object-ivity, autonomy and masculinity with domination of nature as 'other' in the prevailing ideology and practice of science can be understood in terms of these underlying psychological dynamics. The division of mothering and fathering roles, the cultural definitions of masculinity and femininity and the gendered character of science are thus a mutually sustaining system.

However, for Keller this does not imply a feminist rejection of science as such. On the contrary, she holds out a radical vision of a quite different practice of science, linked to changed gender-relations:

> the aim of these essays . . . is the reclamation, from within science of science as a human instead of a masculine project, and the renunciation of the division of emotional and intellectual labour that maintains science as a male preserve. (Keller 1985: 178)

But as the phrase 'from within science' implies, this is not some utopian vision imposed from without. Keller reworks the object relations approach to develop a vision of a personality structure in which objectivity, power and love might be connected in ways denied by current formations of both masculinity and femininity. In this alternative, self-identity becomes sufficiently secure to soften the boundaries between self and other, and to recognize interdependence and relatedness. For such a personality, other humans and non-human beings in the outside world can be acknowledged in their independence and integrity, without the need to dominate or destroy. These emotional dynamics make possible a cognitive relationship to the world of objects which does not frame them in the perspective of our own desires and purposes. In this sense, what she calls 'dynamic autonomy' is the basis for a 'dynamic objectivity' – an objectivity which respects and loves its object. Keller draws on Ernest Schachtel's concept of 'world-openness' in characterizing this notion of objectivity:

> For Schachtel, allocentric perception is perception in the service of a love 'which wants to affirm others in their total and unique being.' It is an affirmation of objects

as 'part of the same world of which man is part'. In turn, and by contrast with perception that is dominated by need or self-interest (autocentric perception) it permits a fuller, more 'global' understanding of the object in its own right. (Keller 1985: 119)

Keller's optimism about the possibility of a different science is grounded in her perception that the victory of the mechanical philosophy was never complete. The practice of science has always been pluralistic, with rival and subversive visions persisting despite their marginalization by the dominant approaches. Moreover, nature itself, given the methodology of orthodox science, can be expected to be an ally in bringing about change:

But nature itself is an ally that can be relied upon to provide the impetus for real change: nature's responses recurrently invite re-examination of the terms in which our understanding of science is constructed. (Keller 1985: 175–6)

And once we acknowledge that nature itself is active in requiring scientific traditions to adopt new ways of thinking, and new methods of investigation, the hope for change from within looks more plausible. Keller argues that, in fact, current developments in the sciences, and most especially in the life sciences, are leading to a recognition of complexity and interaction in dynamic systems, as against the mechanical philosophy's pursuit of unified laws which nature 'obeys'.

Keller's biography of the geneticist and developmental biologist Barbara McClintock (Keller 1983) illustrates the persistence, at least in the work of this scientist, of a cognitive relation to her subject-matter very like that identified by Schachtel. In McClintock's vision, nature is infinitely complex and resourceful, so that there is no hope for science to encapsulate it or subdue it in simple formulae. Rather, the method of science should be one of attention to particularity and difference, and of humility in 'listening' attentively to what the object of study has to say. This attitude of reciprocity and affection between scientist and subject of study is not a sacrifice of objectivity, but a necessary condition for it. As Keller puts it:

The crucial point for us is that McClintock can risk the suspension of boundaries between subject and object without jeopardy to science precisely because, to her, science is not premised on that division. Indeed, the intimacy she experiences with the objects she studies – intimacy born of a lifetime of cultivated attentiveness – is a wellspring of her powers as a scientist. (Keller 1985: 164)

The themes of respect and love for nature, and the recognition of the integrity, complexity and particularity of the objects of scientific knowledge, are widely shared among feminist commentaries on science. They are acutely present when feminist concerns intersect with compassion for the suffering of animals as subjects of research, and anxiety about the wider ecological destructiveness of modern capitalism. Lynda Birke, herself a former researcher on animal behaviour, has explored the interconnections between a certain 'masculine' training in scientific method and the suppression of sensibility to the suffering of animals as subjects of laboratory research (Birke 1994).

But she goes further than this in analysing the complexities in the intersecting dualisms of nature–culture, feminine–masculine and animal–human. Freeing ourselves from the desire to conceptualize 'animals' as other and inferior to the human, and as appropriate subjects for objectifying and reductionist science, is essential to the struggle against maltreatment of (non-human) animals. But it is also necessary to the feminist opposition to biological determinisms which denigrate women: recognizing the individuality and subjectivity of non-human animals is a key to resisting attempts to represent *humans themselves* as biological 'automata'.

The complex and indefinable work of Donna J. Haraway has also addressed the woman–human–animal–science nexus, with a particular focus on the discourses of primatology – both in their 'scientific' forms, and in the popular cultural forms of TV documentary, cartoon, advertisements and so on (Haraway 1992). A recurrent theme in her work is the post-modern one of dispelling dualisms, transgressing boundaries and the proliferation of hybrid forms (symbolized with the image of the 'cyborg' – see Haraway 1991). This takes material forms in the replacement of human organs by mechanical parts, or by organs taken from transgenic animals, and discursive forms in the overcoming of sharp human–animal dichotomies. The way we represent our primate kin, especially the great apes, is clearly a very fertile field to explore this shift. Haraway's analysis remains ambiguously poised between several of the approaches we have discussed in this chapter, and which she calls 'temptations'. But Haraway's apparent abandonment of any clear cognitive or normative stance, as implied by this ambiguity, seems problematic. As Birke points out:

> We are already witnessing suggestions that pigs be bred to supply hearts for human patients; and transgenic animals sometimes become factories for human use. These kinds of boundary transgressions are not ones I would wish to celebrate. (Birke 1994: 147)

The Reflexive Turn: 'Constructing' Nature and Society

By the early 1980s the followers of the 'strong programme' in the sociology of science, and related approaches, were facing criticisms from a new direction. Previously enmeshed in debate with realists and rationalists over their relativism about scientific knowledge, they were now criticized for their (supposedly) unquestioning realist assumptions about society. There were, in fact, two distinct lines of criticism. According to one, the sociologists of science, in their focus on controversies, and talk of 'strategies', 'interests', 'sides' and so on, were committed to a 'decisionist' model of social life as constructed by the conscious 'rational choices' (see Chapter 5) of agents. Against this, the critics emphasized the importance of studying the embedded routines and cultural contexts of scientific practice.

However, a more fundamental line of criticism noted the inconsistency involved in the strong programme's systematic scepticism about the reality claims made by natural scientists, while accepting as 'real' and 'given' the sociological variables in terms of which scientific controversies were to be explained. Consistency could be restored only by 'reflexively' extending scepticism to the sociologist's own explanatory concepts and methods. Sociologists were now not only to see nature as a socio-cultural construct, but also to 'problematize' the individual and collective actors, their interests and power relations, alliances and so on which had so far been drawn upon as explanatory variables (see, for examples, Gilbert and Mulkay 1984; Woolgar 1988; Latour and Woolgar 1986; Latour 1987, 1993). Both social and natural worlds were now to be treated as 'constructs'. ('But of what and by whom?' one might ask.)

This reflexive turn in the sociology of science was connected to a wider debate in social theory between advocates of post-modernism (see Chapter 10) and others about how to characterize contemporary institutions and social processes. For some, the authority of scientific knowledge-claims, and of scientific rationality, was taken to be definitive of 'modernity', so that the sceptical and relativist tendencies of sociology of science chimed in with post-modernist themes.

The work of Ulrich Beck in Germany shared this sense of epochal change, but he understood it as a shift within 'modernity', from an earlier 'simple' modernity towards a 'reflexively' modern future. For Beck, 'reflexivity' referred to the way modern institutions, most especially science and technology, were, through their own development, putting themselves in jeopardy. Beck's *Risk Society* (not published in English until 1992) emphasized the significance of a new order of risks associated with new, large-scale technologies such as nuclear power, the chemical industry and genetic manipulation. These risks were literally incalculable, potentially universal in their scope, and exceeded the capacities of private and public sector to insure or guarantee security. In the face of these risks, the scepticism about particular knowledge-claims which had always been central to scientific method was now being generalized to science itself. A new 'sub-politics' was emerging, in which the authority of science was under question, with the hopeful prospect of wider democratic participation in scientific and technical decision-making (for evaluations of Beck's *Risk Society*, see Rustin 1994; Benton 1997).

However, for all Beck's use of the term 'reflexivity', his work remains realist about the ecological risks he describes. The work of other leading advocates of the reflexive turn has been strongly anti-realist (see, for example, Wynne 1996), or deeply ambiguous. The very influential work of the French philosopher-sociologist Bruno Latour and his associates comes into this latter category. This work, known as 'actor–network' theory, shares with the feminist approaches we discussed above an attempt to overcome rigid dichotomies between nature and human agency, and subject and object of knowledge. Latour pioneered what he thought of as an 'ethnographic' or 'anthropological' study of scientists and engineers at work (Latour and Woolgar 1979, 1986). The aim was to capture in detail the daily practices of science and technology in the making, as opposed to the abstract representations of the philosophers and the retrospective certainties of the historians. In this respect, Latour's work was continuous with earlier work in the tradition of the 'strong programme'. However, the key innovation of his 'anthropological' approach was to attempt a reconstruction of scientific activity as a seamless form of life, incorporating all its many aspects, just as the ethnographer of other cultures claims 'to be reconstituting the centre of those cultures: their belief-system, their technologies, their ethno-sciences, their power plays, their economies – in short, the totality of their existence' (Latour 1993: 100). One implication of this is that the instruments, buildings, reagents, microbes, particles and so on involved in laboratory practice all play their part in the story of the making of science. And, if we think more broadly, as Latour recommends, then the spread of the railways, of telegraphy, of practices such as vaccination, of information technology, of robotics and so on are at the core of transformations of modes of life. So central are these features of our existence that the practice of the social sciences, and the wider culture, in sharply separating society from nature is unsustainable: 'History is no longer simply the history of people, it becomes the history of natural things as well' (Latour 1993: 82).

At the heart of actor–network theory is this intention to break free of the dualism which separates off, or 'purifies', society from nature. The ethnographic study of laboratory life (see Latour and Woolgar 1979/86) is what enables this break, because it is here more than anywhere that we can observe the production, or generation, of ever more 'objects': chemical substances, micro-organisms, instruments, devices and so on. Under certain circumstances these generated 'objects' may escape from the lab to participate in the wider constitution of both nature and society. These 'objects' are, at first, Latour claims, no more than a set of readings or measurements, and they acquire established status as real 'things' only to the extent that the scientists in whose labs they are generated are successful in acting as their 'representatives' in the wider world of science, and so persuading, or 'enrolling', other scientists into an alliance. This process of enrolment is presented by Latour as a Machiavellian struggle to acquire, extend and maintain power through building and consolidating alliances. In his analysis of scientific literature, he emphasizes the role of rhetorical devices, the appeals to authority and the extensive deployment of citations to embed the current text in a network of already established knowledge. The visual displays provided by laboratory demonstrations add further authority, and this in turn is made possible only by virtue of the success of teams of scientists or engineers in enrolling into their alliance political and economic support from those who already command authority and resources in the wider society: the state, business, and, above all, the military; the following quotation is from his *Science in Action* (1987):

> Essentially, R. & D. is an industrial affair (three quarters is carried out inside firms) financed out of tax money (amounting to 47 per cent in the US). This is the first massive transfer of interest: scientists have succeeded only insofar as they have coupled their fate with industry, and/or that industry has coupled its fate to the state's . . . by and large, technoscience is part of a war machine and should be studied as such. (p. 170)

Latour's attempt to overcome the dualistic separation of nature and culture focuses on the way modern science and technology ('technoscience', as he calls it) is constantly proliferating new 'objects', as candidates for subsequent ratification, or 'stabilization', as accepted, taken-for-granted realities, pieces of equipment, measuring devices and so on. These objects typically involve fusion of human agency with natural substances or beings: frozen embryos, expert systems, digital machines, hybrid corn, databanks, whales outfitted with radar sounding devices, gene synthesizers, psychotropic drugs, the hole in the ozone layer and many other examples. This ever-proliferating multiplicity of produced objects is at the centre of our social life, yet its components cannot be allocated to either side of the great divide between nature and society: they are 'hybrids', 'quasi-objects' and 'quasi-subjects'.

Successful science and engineering consists in deploying the whole gamut of persuasive, rhetorical and material resources to extend and maintain alliances beyond the laboratory and the scientific journals. Crucially, these alliances are composed out of previously unconnected elements which cut across conventional divisions – they are heterogeneous 'networks of actants', which include human groups, animals, pieces of equipment, synthetic materials, measuring devices and so on. The term 'actant' is used to include the full range of elements which play a part in the establishment and consolidation of the network, irrespective of our subsequent wish to allocate them to one side or the other of the nature–society dichotomy.

It is only by virtue of a subsequent practice of what Latour calls 'purification' that nature and society are constructed as separate, unconnected domains. At this point, Latour is establishing a double distance between his approach and that of more orthodox sociology of science. On the one hand, he brings non-human beings and objects into the account of the processes of science and technology. To this extent (and with some ambiguities) his position is realist about the objects of scientific investigation: 'It is hard to reduce the entire cosmos to a grand narrative, the physics of subatomic particles to a text, subway systems to rhetorical devices, all social structures to discourse' (Latour 1993: 64).

But this leads to a second departure from more traditional sociologies of science. If our lives are lived through participation in collectives, which are, in turn, made up of heterogeneous networks of human and non-human elements, and if society and nature are merely secondary, 'purified' constructs, it follows that we can't use 'society' to explain science. What we have constructed as 'pure' society is a consequence of scientific and technical practices, and so cannot be used to explain them. This conclusion he calls, following Michel Callon, 'the principle of generalized symmetry' (Latour 1993: 94–6; Callon 1986. See also the exchanges between Collins and Yearley and Latour and Callon in Pickering 1992):

> Thus it [the strong programme – TB] is asymmetrical not because it separates ideology and science, as epistemologists do, but because it brackets off Nature and makes the 'Society' pole carry the full weight of explanation. Constructivist where Nature is concerned, it is realistic about society. (Latour 1993: 94)

Latour's proposal, then, is to treat both society and nature as constructs which stand in need of explanation, and to place the weight of explanation on the centre 'between' these poles – that is, on the networks of actants, and the processes by which they get put together, extended and stabilized. However, it is not at all clear that these concepts are up to such a demanding task. For one thing, Latour's key concepts for defining 'actants' are those of 'hybridity', 'quasi-object', 'quasi-subject' and so on. These terms get such meaning as they have only in terms of the *prior* understanding of what 'subjects', 'objects' and the 'pure' elements of the 'hybrid' are. Latour contravenes his own methodology in the very act of defining his most basic ideas.

Moreover, Latour's desire to find terms which link humans to non-humans into seamless networks leads to metaphorical excesses which carry little conviction. An example is his account of the way the windmill succeeded in forming a more powerful network than the pestle and mortar (Latour 1987: 129), binding together corn, machinery, bread and the wind. He writes of 'translation' of the 'interest' of the wind, and 'complicated negotiations' which have to be conducted with it to secure its alliance. Far from representing the windmill as something irreducible either to nature or society, Latour's language reduces the wind to a conscious quasi-human interlocutor, with its own interests and capacity for compromise. What is of value in the account is the recognition of the independent causal power of the wind, and its role in shaping the range of possible human responses to this, but this insight is put at risk by the resort to anthropomorphism.

Similarly, if we follow his argument about the extension and stabilization of 'networks' beyond the laboratory, we find Latour, as in the above quotation on R&D from *Science in Action*, explaining successful science in terms of the ability of scientists to establish alliances with states, businesses, the military and so on. As he puts it, scientists and engineers can succeed only in so far as they interest

> more powerful groups that have already solved the same problem on a larger scale. That is, groups that have learned how to interest everyone in some issues, to keep them in line, to discipline them, to make them obey; groups for which money is not a problem and that are constantly on the look-out for new unexpected allies that can make a difference in their own struggle. (Latour 1987: 169)

So, scientific success, which for him includes the power to define reality itself, depends on powerful groups, money, alliances, states, military institutions, businesses . . . This certainly *looks* very much like an explanation in terms of the forbidden 'society'!

So, despite his rhetoric, it seems that in practice Latour has not moved far from the sociologists of science whose approach he criticizes. Even what seems most distinctive – his inclusion of the activity of non-human 'things' in the processes of science – is compromised by ambiguity and contradiction. What exactly is the status of the 'objects' ('quasi-objects', 'hybrids', and so on) which science 'generates'? In his *Pasteurization of France* (1988) we read: 'Did the microbe exist before Pasteur? From the practical point of view – I say practical, not theoretical – it did not' (p. 80). In *Science in Action* (1987) he writes of the way laboratories 'generate' 'new' objects, but that at first these 'new objects' are no more than their responses to certain laboratory 'trials'. He goes on:

> This situation, however, does not last. New objects become *things*: 'somatostatin', 'polonium', 'anaerobic microbes', 'transfinite numbers', 'double helix', or '*Eagle* computers', things isolated from the laboratory conditions that shaped them, things with a name that now seem independent from the trials in which they proved their mettle. (pp. 90–1)

In some places he expresses scepticism about the realism of science when networks are consolidated, and controversy ended, but elsewhere he follows scientists themselves in shifting 'modality' from relativist non-realism in periods of controversy to conformist realism when controversy is settled. But can any coherent sense be made of a world in which 'objects' simply come into existence and depart again in a ballet perfectly choreographed with the power struggles of scientists? If success in defining reality is just a matter of superior strategic skills, owing nothing to either rational argument or what the world is actually like, why should we meekly accept the outcome? After all, a new power might be installed tomorrow!

Latour's account of technoscience presents it as a struggle to recruit powerful allies and material resources, as 'part of a war machine', and as an 'intolerable source of pathology':

[W]e find the myth of reason and science unacceptable, intolerable, even immoral. We are no longer, alas, at the end of the nineteenth century, that most beautiful of centuries, but at the end of the twentieth, and a major source of pathology and mortality is reason itself – its works, its pomps, and its armaments. (Latour 1988: 149)

Much of today's 'big science' conforms well to this description, but even as a description it is selective and one-sided. Not only have many courageous scientists sacrificed their careers out of a sense of social responsibility, but also there is a long tradition of scientific dissent, while much of what has come to be called 'environmental science' has been open to mobilization by oppositional social movements in their resistance to the destructive and exploitative impositions of the wealthy and powerful. Most seriously, however, the cynicism of Latour's demonic view of contemporary technoscience leads him to an outright rejection of reason itself. But if we abandon the means of criticizing power exercised in the name of science, or military force posing as reason, if we have no vision of an alternative practice of knowledge creation, what then does Latour's strong language amount to? 'Yes – it's terrible, but that's just the way things are'? The positive visions of an alternative science, respectful of its objects, democratically accountable to its wider citizenry, and open to full participation on the part of previously excluded or marginalized human groups, which are offered by the feminist and other radical critics of science, provide an alternative to this apparent defeatism.

Conclusion

This chapter has noted the shift, closely associated with the influence of the French tradition of historical epistemology, and the work of Thomas Kuhn, away from the prevailing empiricist orthodoxy in the philosophy of science. 'Post-empiricist' philosophers, historians and sociologists of science have emphasized the extent to which scientific knowledge-claims are shaped, even constituted by the moral values, prevailing interests or cultural contexts of their production. This has frequently given rise to scepticism about the special status generally claimed for scientific knowledge, and to various forms of relativism in the theory of knowledge. In the absence of any 'direct', or unmediated, access to reality, on the basis of which to compare rival accounts of it, one set of beliefs is as good or bad as any other.

But if we take as a methodological requirement that all scientific knowledge-claims are to be treated with equal scepticism, then what about the knowledge-claims made by the sociologists and historians of science themselves? This is the key question posed by Callon, Latour, Woolgar and the other advocates of the reflexive turn in science studies. But such radical scepticism is both self-contradictory and unwarranted. As our analysis of Latour's work showed, his attempt to dispense with the concepts of 'nature' and 'society' implicitly presupposed them, and his denunciation of reason itself employs reason (if, ultimately, less than *convincing* reasons!). Such radical scepticism is unwarranted since, though we may lack unmediated access to external reality, we *do* have mediated access to it. From our earliest attempts to survive and make sense of the world we encounter mismatches between our hopes, desires and expectations, on the one hand, and what reality (social and/or natural) actually does – the experiences of frustrated desire, disappointed expectation, failed ambition and so on repeatedly emphasize the difference between knowledge and wishful thinking. Our capacity to learn is testimony to the liability of our understanding to be questioned and revised in the face of the way the world is – social constructionists are right to emphasize that this questioning and revision take place within the sphere of human communication and discourse, but what provokes and necessitates them is our practical engagement with a world which is only partly made up of communication and discourse.

The feminist view of scientific objectivity advanced by Keller adds force to these notions, emphasizing the encounter with the 'otherness' of the objects of scientific knowledge as an indispensable dimension of scientific practice. The critical realist understanding of both social and natural science is also consonant with these considerations. We will return to a fuller discussion of recent arguments advanced by feminists and critical realists in Chapters 8 and 9, respectively.

Further Reading

There is no comprehensive work covering the field of social studies of science and technology. There are, however, several excellent journals which include not only empirically based articles but also reflective and controversial pieces on the rival approaches. The journals *Social Studies of Science*, *Science, Technology and Human Values*, and *Science as Culture* are particularly recommended. On questions posed by current public concern about environmental consequences of scientific and technical change, see A. Irwin (1995) *Citizen Science*.

Post-script

The broad approaches to the philosophy and social studies of science outlined in this and in the previous chapters have continued to have their advocates, but one approach, in particular, has attracted attention – from both advocates and critics. This is the 'reflexive' development of social studies of science and technology pioneered by Bruno Latour, Steve Woolgar, Michel Callon and others – and loosely known as 'actor network theory'. I say 'loosely', since advocates of this approach tend to resist the term 'theory'. Their work is marked by a strong commitment to detailed case-studies of specific episodes, with the implication that theoretical generalizations are always likely to abstract from this complexity in ways that are misleading.

Some of those influenced by this approach now readily concede that earlier formulations, such as those criticized in our first edition (pp. 69–74), can be dispensed with (see Law and Hassard 1999; Law 2004, 2007). Still, they argue, the central 'intuitions' of the approach retain their value. In defence of what he calls 'after-ANT', John Law characterizes it as 'a form of attentiveness and respect to the world' (Moog and Stones (ed.) 2009: 68. See also Law 2009). This means, among other things, that nothing is simply social – but is always at the same time 'material'. Perhaps, the main concept here is that of 'practice', with the emphasis on intertwined meanings and materiality – and the 'messiness' of such practices. Another feature of the approach as represented by Law is the importance of relations – complex and heterogeneous relations through which 'things', 'beings' and 'actors' get their identities, and are even 'generated'. Above all, there is a strong sense of the inadequacy of any discursive account of 'reality' to do full justice to its complexity – and there may be as many 'realities' as there are ways of 'constructing' reality in discourse.

The attempt to take seriously the complexity of the events and episodes that figure in the case-studies produced by this approach is commendable. Also of value is the inclusion, as with the earlier versions of the actor network approach, of the non-human elements in human social practices. However, some of the criticisms of the earlier version presented in our first edition seem still to apply. In particular, the resistance to developing general theoretical ideas in favour of rather unspecific 'intuitions' makes it difficult to see how the approach might be tested. A valuable argument for the compatibility of Marxian realist analysis and actor–network theory is Castree (2002).

5

Interpretive Approaches 1: Instrumental Rationality

We now turn to a very different approach to social science and a very different notion of science. This tradition of thinking is closer to the rationalist than the empiricist traditions in philosophy, and the starting-point is that whether or not positivism is an adequate philosophy of the natural sciences, whatever its advantages or drawbacks, the social sciences are qualitatively different from the natural sciences. The social sciences have objects of study that differ from those of the natural sciences, and they must develop their own specific methods to study these objects.

We find the difference between the objects of the two types of science expressed in different ways. Perhaps the most obvious distinction is that the objects of the social sciences – human beings and human groups – possess a property that we know as self-consciousness. They are able to reflect on themselves and their situations and their relationships. Human life is essentially a life of meaning, of language and reflective thought and communication. Sociologists often refer to this as 'reflexivity' (Giddens 1984), and there are a number of very different approaches that are based on this human capacity for self-consciousness and reflection – but they all involve ways of interpreting the meanings that people give to their actions, and most are concerned with the nature of rationality. They ask questions about what exactly it is that we do when we understand human action? How do we know whether our understanding is adequate, and indeed what do we mean by adequate? What is the relationship between understanding and explanation? Can we understand action at all if it takes place in the context of another culture? These are clearly different concerns from those of the natural scientist, but they can be seen as related to the concerns of the philosophers and historians of the natural sciences as discussed in Chapters 3 and 4.

In this chapter we are concerned with a cluster of approaches which, for reasons that will become apparent, can brought together because of their concern with an *instrumental* notion of rationality. The end of the nineteenth century and the early years of the twentieth saw a shift in philosophical attention towards the nature of language and language use. The principal subject of this chapter – Max Weber – was less explicitly concerned with language, but he was profoundly concerned with meaning. After discussing Weber we will go on to look at related interpretive approaches which fall into the same broad category: phenomenological sociology, which provides a deeper philosophical underpinning for Weber's categories, rational choice theory which takes us closer to late nineteenth-century economics with which Weber was familiar, and approaches developed from American pragmatism.

Weber's Discussion of the Objects of the Social Sciences

Weber, who lived from 1864 to 1920, comes from a tradition of philosophy originating in Kant whom we met in Chapter 3, as it was developed through the 'neo-Kantian' school of philosophy at Heidelberg. To summarize the work of the neo-Kantians very crudely, the 'forms of intuition' and 'categories of understanding' became a locus for the human or 'spiritual' sciences, and these were seen as based on mutual understanding and a shared culture (Dilthey 1961; Rickert 1962). We can find in Dilthey in particular many of the themes that reappear not only in Weber but in other interpretive philosophers and social theorists we will be examining in the following chapters: the importance of moving back and forth between the part and the whole of what we study, the intimate link between understanding and narrative, the importance of values and value choices, the movement between individual subjectivity and collective objectivity. We will see that these themes recur in Weber's work.

Weber seems to have been 'captured' by sociology, but he was a man of immense learning and could equally well be classed as an economist, a historian or a scholar of law. Like all really important thinkers, he overflows the disciplinary labels we might try to put on him. The one thing certain about him is that he conceived of the social sciences as primarily concerned with meaning, and in particular with individual meaning or the ways in which shared cultural meanings affected the actions of individuals. We might describe Weber as an 'ontological individualist': the world studied by the social sciences is made up of individuals interacting together. There are no collective social entities such as classes except in a limited sense that we will consider shortly, nor can we talk about social structures or overarching social phenomena which impose themselves on individuals. One might reasonably ask why, if there are only individuals interacting, we can make any sense of society at all. At the centre of Weber's answer to this is that we can make sense of social life because human beings act rationally. What he means by rationality emerges through a series of classifications in which he defines the proper object of the social sciences more and more closely. This hermeneutic or interpretive tradition is often seen as the main and radical alternative to positivism and the two are seen as mutually exclusive; overall, we will be arguing that both approaches have their place and that although we might argue about which philosophical presuppositions and consequent methods are appropriate in any particular case, we are not faced with an either – or choice between the two.

Weber's starting-point is that the social sciences study *meaningful action* as opposed to behaviour – movements which are the end result of a physical or biological causal chain (Weber 1947) As I write I blink, but I do not deliberately blink for some purpose of which I am conscious, and I do not attach a meaning to my blinking, even though in some circumstances others might do so. If, for example, I were talking to a psychoanalyst, he or she might take my blinking as indicating that I am being troubled by some unconscious and possibly rather embarrassing desire. There is an important point here: in Weber's various classifications, we are not dealing with absolute distinctions but with continua. We can think of the merging of behaviour into meaningful action without being able to draw a distinct line between them. The nasty cough which follows my cold might also be useful for drawing attention to my presence.

Meaningful action, as opposed to behaviour, still doesn't take us to the proper object of the social sciences. We have to go one step further to meaningful *social* action, action which is directed to another human being. The classic example here is that a cyclist might be engaging in meaningful action – riding her bike along country lanes for pleasure; her collision with another cyclist is not action at all, it is intended by neither; the argument that they have afterwards, however, is meaningful and social.

Weber goes on to distinguish four different types of meaningful social action. The first two are distinguished by the fact that they are carried out primarily for the satisfaction that they bring, not to achieve any other purpose in the world. The first is *traditional* (Weber 1922, 1947: 116) action, which we carry out because we have always carried it out: if somebody asks me why I am doing this I say because it has always been done. This is rare in contemporary society, although there are elements of it in everyday life – perhaps in some family routines which often have a long life and bring a sense of comfort.

Weber's second type of meaningful action is *affectual* action – that is, action based on emotion. Such action is on the borderline of the rational: if I am overwhelmed by my feelings then it is less rational or not rational at all, but if I guide my feelings into actions geared to achieve something, then it is closer to the rational. If I lose my temper and hit my friend, I am not acting rationally; if I am angry with my friend and decide to avoid him for a while, or discuss why I am angry, I am acting more rationally.

The third type of action is also on the borderline of properly rational action. It is for Weber a feature of human beings that we are valuing creatures and there is a class of actions which are oriented to ultimate values, values which we choose but cannot justify on any rational basis. Once we have chosen a value, however, we can make rational sense of actions we take in pursuit of it. Here for the first time an exterior purpose comes into play. If I am a Christian, I can, in Weber's terms, find no rational reason for my belief, but the actions as a result of my belief can be understood as rational. It is rational, for example, that if I am a Christian I should go to church and pray and adopt certain attitudes to my neighbours.

Finally there is action oriented towards achieving something in this world – *practical* action, the sort we take every day that is directed towards concrete, achievable ends. We calculate possible outcomes and make judgements. In contemporary society it is sometimes difficult to conceive of any other sort of action: the cultural emphasis on achievement, success, profit, practicality and so on leaves us feeling that an action which doesn't have an identifiable or even measurable objective is a form of self-indulgence or laziness. Perhaps the difference between these last two types of action-those closest to what Weber regarded as properly rational action-is best illustrated by attitudes to education, which is still to some degree a contested area. For some people education is a value in itself, something to be sought after because the more educated we are, the more civilized we become. Through education we become better people, more sensitive, able to appreciate the true and the beautiful, able to find sophisticated pleasures in the world; we become better citizens. Education is a value and people seek degrees because of their belief in that value.

More dominant is the practical–rational attitude to education: that it has some purpose outside itself. We must increase the proportion of children going to university in order to keep up with our competitors. We must increase student numbers in the natural sciences for the same purposes. From the individual point of view one pursues education not for enjoyment, the pleasures of learning or the discipline of learning for its own sake but in order to get a better job and earn more money.

The true object of sociology, and of the social sciences generally, is, then, meaningful, rational, social action, action to which the actor gives a meaning, directed to other people, intended to achieve practical purposes in the world. This is what we mean by *instrumental rationality*, since it is the use of rationality in order to bring about change in the world in the interest of the actor. This distinguishes this conception of rationality from other conceptions of rationality which can be found in the social sciences and which will be discussed in the following chapters.

This conception of rationality is intimately bound up with Weber's sociological histories of the world religions: Confucianism (Weber 1915, 1951), ancient Judaism (Weber 1921, 1952) and Hinduism and Buddhism in India (Weber 1921, 1958), culminating in his classic study of modern European Christianity, *The Protestant Ethic and the Spirit of Capitalism* (Weber 1904–5, 1930). His argument was that the difference between Western Europe and North America and the rest of the world, that enabled capitalism to develop first in these areas, was the presence of a specific religious ethic, ascetic Protestantism, which indirectly encouraged the development of capitalism, a system in which instrumental rationality dominates. The value-oriented rationality of particular Protestant groups contributed towards the development of instrumental rationality, the 'rational calculability' of modern capitalism.

Weber's Methodology: Understanding and Ideal Types

If the social sciences have their own specific object – meaningful social action – then they also have their own specific methodology. This Weber described as interpretive understanding – hence the use of 'interpretivist' to describe this approach. Weber used the German word '*verstehen*', sometimes translated as 'empathy', an emotional identification with the actors we are trying to understand. Weber himself makes it clear that this translation is not correct: *verstehen* involves an understanding of what is going on in the actor's head, and this in turn involves an understanding of the logical and symbolic systems – the culture – within which the actor lives. Leat (1972) makes this clear with a discussion of the way we understand statistical correlations. If, for example, there is a significant statistical correlation between the number of people living below an officially defined poverty level and an increase in theft, we are likely to think that the two are related. In a society where there are large and increasing differences in wealth, we might also find a statistical correlation between increasing numbers of poor and an increase in sales of more expensive consumer goods – say computers. A meaningful connection between these two would not strike one as likely.

Why do we react to the two correlations differently? The answer is that we have a common-sense and shared understanding of the meanings which situations have for people. In the case of theft, the one we take seriously, we reason that living in poverty is likely to leave the individual more open to the temptation to steal and that the more people who live in poverty the more likely we are to see an increase in theft. On the other hand we do not expect the poor to scrape together whatever money they can find and carefully save it so that they can surf the net. We need a little more thought to understand the second correlation in the same way as we do the first: if disposable income is rising for some groups, we can expect the temptation for people in these groups to buy computers will become more difficult to resist. More computers are sold not because there are more poor people, but because of an increasing number of comparatively wealthier people. We can, then understand what Weber calls the 'states of mind' of the actors concerned (Weber 1922, 1947: 87). More fundamentally we know the meaning of the symbols – we know what computers are, we know what poverty means, and so on, and we know the sorts of connections that people make between financial states and purchases – we know what we might call 'the logic' of their behaviour. The shared culture is essential to interpretive understanding.

Weber talks of two types of understanding: observational and explanatory. Observational understanding is simply a matter of recognizing what somebody is doing. I see somebody standing on the kerbside, peering up and down the road. This is simply a description of what the person is doing – it is what I see in front of me. An explanatory understanding is achieved when I understand the reason they are standing there – perhaps to check that the road is clear so that he or she can cross over; there is an even fuller explanation available if I can discover why this person wants to cross the road. There is a sense here in which an explanation is as full a description as one can achieve. This would be the case as long as the person whose actions I try to explain is behaving in a rational, instrumental way – each stage of the action leading on to the next in a chain which leads to the person's desired goal.

If interpretive understanding is the *method* by means of which the social scientist studies his or her object, then the *tool* that he or she uses is the 'ideal type' (Weber 1949). This is not ideal in the sense that it is desirable, something to be aimed at, but ideal in the sense that it is a construction in the social scientist's head, an idea. For Weber *the process of thinking rationally* produces knowledge, and the ideal type is a an account of what the object being studied would be like in its most rational form. Weber's ideal type of bureaucracy, therefore, is not a model of bureaucracy, nor is it something which can exist in the real world, nor is it an average type: it is a rational construction, a catalogue of purely rational procedures and organizational structures. We can then use the ideal type and compare it with bureaucracies that exit in the real world and so learn how real-world bureaucracies differ, and so better understand their functioning. Similarly, Weber, in his account of the connection between Protestantism and capitalism, constructed ideal types of both.

The next question is: 'How do we judge our explanation of social phenomena?' It should be evident that what Weber is suggesting is that we construct stories about the social world. We do not aim to discover universal laws of society – he suggests that even should we find such a law it would not be of much use to us because the task of the social scientist is to understand individual events and explain them through the meanings that that the individuals involved attach to their actions (Weber 1949). This also means that we cannot refer, as many social scientists do, to collective bodies such as social classes or the state. Strictly speaking such bodies cannot exist, but we can talk about them if the people we are studying think they exist and act as if they really exist. Weber modifies this position a little when he talks about class and status groups, but for him the general rule is that we can talk about such groups only when people think they exist or are conscious of belonging to them.

However, none of this takes us very far towards judging the explanations that we do construct – it just lays out the sort of ideas that we should not use in our explanations, or only use in limited circumstances. Weber suggests that there are two criteria. The first he calls 'meaning adequacy', or adequacy on the level of meaning. This seems to be a matter of telling a reasonable or believable story about those we are studying. The story has to be rational: it should be credible, for example, that the beliefs held by the members of some Protestant sects should encourage them to adopt a particular attitude towards work and towards reinvestment of profits, and that the attitude that they adopted to work should result in business success.

The second criterion is causal adequacy, but by 'cause' here Weber means something different from what natural scientists mean by the term. We cannot give any over-arching or general account of the rise of capitalism, but we can identify a number of contributing factors, so at different points in his work Weber discusses the legal and the economic preconditions for the rise of capitalism, and his argument in *The Protestant Ethic and the Spirit of Capitalism* is that Protestantism is the decisive factor. This is established on the level of cause by his other religious studies, which show that in certain situations the other preconditions for the rise of capitalism existed but the missing condition was an equivalent to the Protestant ethic. Establishing causal adequacy, then, involves a comparative examination of different but similar situations, trying to identify crucial features leading to different outcomes. This sort of comparative analysis is sometimes seen as the social scientist's equivalent to laboratory testing.

Weber on Objectivity and Value Freedom

Weber presents a sophisticated discussion of values in social science (Weber 1949). He certainly talks about the necessity for 'value freedom' and sociologists at least have often taken him to mean something equivalent to the more positivist notions of objectivity in the natural sciences. As we will see in the following chapter, at least one philosopher has read him in a similar way. But a more careful reading indicates that social science – or any sort of science – is bounded on every side by values and that values penetrate to the heart of the scientific enterprise.

To begin with science itself is a value choice, an ultimate value in the sense discussed earlier. There is no rational justification for a choice to make a career out of social science or natural science. Once that choice is made, the value can be pursued rationally and a level of value freedom can be achieved. However, this can be achieved only in a social and cultural context. First, there is the context of the scientific community, where value freedom is achieved through scholarship and studies are subjected to mutual criticism and argument (the context of justification in the language of Chapters 2 and 3). Second, there is the wider cultural context with its standards of rationality or reasonableness and its dominant concerns and values. All of these impinge on social science, and value freedom is relative to these contexts. This could be taken as a thoroughgoing relativism – in the social sciences, what is accepted as knowledge depends upon the norms and values of the scientific community and the wider culture, and of course these change over time: what is acceptable in one period will not necessarily be acceptable in another.

The alternative interpretation of Weber's position is more complex and interesting. The processes and events studied by the social sciences have many causes and there can be no final, overarching explanation. Within the process of cultural change, the values of social science change and social scientists concern themselves with different aspects of a complex reality. The Protestant ethic thesis concerns itself with one aspect of the rise of capitalism which is bound up with arguments against and about Marxism which were important in the late nineteenth and early twentieth centuries. Another historical period, the end of the twentieth century, for example, might not be concerned with these issues at all, or might be concerned with a different aspect of the process. This does not mean that the Protestant ethic thesis is wrong, but simply that it describes part of a reality which we no longer think of as being so important because of a change in cultural values. Reality is complex, and we concern ourselves with different parts of it at different times.

Phenomenology: A Philosophical Foundation for Instrumental Rationality

During the late 1960s and 1970s, the term 'phenomenology' or 'phenomeno-logical' was in common use among sociologists (Lassman 1974; Wolff 1978). A 'phenomenological approach' or a 'phenomenological method' was juxta-posed to what was taken to be a dominant 'positivist' method in social science. These phrases are in quotation marks because they were often used loosely – the latter to refer to any study that used statistics, the former to any that considered the actor's point of view. The terms are now less popular, but they are still sometimes used in this way in sociology and social psychology.

The ways in which philosophical approaches influence social research are never quite clear-cut. Weber was not a phenomenologist, yet he was concerned with the actor's point of view and some classic Weberian studies employ statistics (see, for example, Rex and Moore 1967). In psychologically oriented disciplines, phenomenology was perhaps more appropriately opposed to behaviourism, which denied that introversion could possibly be a source of knowledge; it might now be appropriately opposed to cognitive psychology since it is concerned with much more than the development of conceptual thought. Used in its proper sense it refers to a complex philosophical position which can be placed in the same wider Kantian framework in which we placed Weber – concerned with the way in which we impose meaning on the world.

The prime mover of phenomenological philosophy was Edmund Husserl (see, for example, Husserl 1930–39, 1965). His way of linking consciousness to the external world was to try to describe the way in which consciousness worked on and transformed our sense perceptions into recognizable objects.

'Sense perceptions' for the phenomenologist go beyond what we can see and measure, which is often all that matters for the strict positivist and empiricist. We can gain knowledge not only from sense perceptions other than sight but also from works of the imagination and the use of language (see, for example, Merleau-Ponty 1974).

A phenomenological investigation involves an exercise known as a 'reduction' or a 'phenomenological reduction', an attempt to set aside what we already know about something and describe how we come to know it; it is a matter of tracing the processes by means of which we give meaning to the world. It involves a suspension of our everyday, common-sense beliefs and an attempt to describe how we come by those beliefs. The translation of this philosophy of consciousness into a philosophy of social science comes primarily through the work of Alfred Schutz (1962–6, 1972), who studied under Husserl and who fled to Europe on the rise of Hitler, smuggling out some of Husserl's work. He spent the next decades dividing his energies between social philosophy and banking.

His relevance here is that he offers a phenomenological foundation of Weber's methodology which supplies us with a good example of the phenomenological reduction and adds to our awareness of the processes involved in understanding. If I set aside my common-sense knowledge of the world, if I try to stop seeing these things in front of me as a computer screen, a printer, a desk, a window, trees, grass and so on. I am left simply with a jumble of sense perceptions, colours, sounds and sensations. Schutz suggests that out of this stream of sensations we identify elements which are similar, perhaps because they share a colour, a shape, a certain texture or quality of movement. We identify what Schutz would call typical or recurrent elements from the stream of experience–a process of *typification*. If I look directly ahead I see a lot of green, some blue, some white, some brown and so on The green remains comparatively constant, but I begin to distinguish different shades at different heights in different places, whereas the blue and white stuff seems to be moving. These are the first stages of typification. As the process continues, my consciousness makes finer distinctions but also carries out syntheses which go beyond what is perceived. I can only see one surface of my desk when I look down, yet I grasp it as a three-dimensional solid object.

Eventually we end up with a description of what phenomenologists call the 'natural attitude', the everyday world of grass and trees and sky and clouds, desks, computers and so on. We build up typifications of typifications – I come to distinguish between different types of grass, clouds that threaten rain and those that do not and so on. All this is achieved through acts of differentiation and synthesis carried out by my consciousness.

The Phenomenology of the Social World concerned itself with the way we build up typifications of other people, classifying them into types with particular qualities from whom typical courses of action can be expected. This gives us our common-sense, taken-for-granted knowledge about the social world which guides us in our actions from day to day. We know things about human beings in general, what typically distinguishes them from cows and monkeys and trees; and we know things about particular types of human beings – men, women, blacks and whites – which enable us to distinguish them from each other. As we move beyond this type of group we build up typifications of family and friends and the closer the relationship the more specific our expectations. But however close our relationship, it is still based on a bedrock of typification.

For the phenomenologist, then, the social world is built up from a complex multitude of typifications which we organize into 'meaning contexts', a taken-for-granted stock of knowledge which we share with others. We choose which typifications we employ according to the ends, the projects we pursue at the time. The social scientist has his or her own specific project and here we move into Weber's methodology. The specific project of the social scientist is to build rational, ideal types of social action. Schutz calls these ideal types 'second-order typifications'. They are constructed out of the typifications of the actors we are studying, the everyday stocks of knowledge that they employ. He talks about constructing 'rational puppets', in a sort of rational puppet theatre. We can put our puppets in different situations, and if we know their goals we can predict their actions, were they to act rationally in pursuit of their goals.

In sociology Schutz's work was one of the starting-points for Harold Garfinkel's development of ethnomethodology, the study of the taken-for-granted rules which provide us with a sense of social relationships and social structures (Garfinkel 1967). Similar ideas are taken up by Anthony Giddens in his development of structuration theory (Giddens 1976, 1984). However, it does not tell us anything new about that reality. The meanings we subject to the phenomenological reduction, which we 'bracket' at the beginning of the investigation, are the same meanings we end up with after the investigation – we just have a better understanding of their construction. This emphasizes what is already implicit in Weber's work: that social sciences construct their theories and explanations out of our everyday knowledge of the world, or rather the knowledge of the social actors we are studying. Unlike the natural sciences, the social sciences do not produce a new conceptual language, rather they modify everyday language. It is often said that sociology especially, and to a lesser extent psychology, simply tell us what we already know, and these versions of the interpretive approach tend towards doing just that. The assumption of rationality in Schutz's work is still an instrumental one – it is the pursuit of practical ends.

There is however an important shift in Schutz's work. Whereas Weber was clearly concerned with flesh-and-blood people acting in the world, Schutz tends to move everything into consciousness. The first use of the term 'social construction' was in Berger and Luckman's book *The Social Construction of Reality* published in 1967, and they owed a heavy debt to Schutz. However, they were able to integrate phenomenological ideas with more structural and materialist explanations. Increasingly, the term has come to refer to processes within consciousness, to different interpretations of the world rather than actions upon an external world.

Instrumental Variations I: Rational Choice Theory

Schutz's work can also be seen as offering a foundation for rational choice theory, an approach developed out of the marginalist revolution in economics in the second half of the nineteenth century, a development with which Weber was intimately acquainted. We can find similar ideas in behaviourist psychology, nineteenth-century utilitarianism and exchange theory in American sociology.

The basic assumption is that people will act in a way which brings them benefits and will avoid acting in a way that does not bring them benefits. Exchange theory, for example, is based on the idea that people will exchange activities when seeking to maximize profits. If, for example, I decide that time to relax is more important to me than the satisfactions I gain from housework and from the income I would have to give up to pay somebody to do the housework, I will employ a cleaner. The cleaner I employ will have decided that the satisfactions of his or her free time is less important than the satisfactions to be gained from the wages I pay.

The whole of society can be seen in terms of a series of such decisions and exchanges. The assumptions of the economics of supply and demand are the same: I am an agent on a free market, and I have a disposable income and a set of needs and preferences which I order into a hierarchy – some are more important than others. I then decide how to dispose of my income to fulfil my most important needs or realize my most important preferences, whether they be for heroin or for books. The market, the 'perfect market' (perhaps the ideal-type market) consists of other equally free individuals pursuing their own interests and preferences in similar ways, and the end balance is the price of goods on the market; the price will settle at a point where the demand for the good equates with the willingness of suppliers to supply and the largest possible number of people are satisfied. As an individual I then have to decide whether the price of, for example, heroin is so high that I then have to take the risk of going out stealing in order to boost my funds.

Weber tended to think that all social orders were rather precarious and unstable, and he saw such market relationships as binding a society together; however, his conception of rational action is much wider than that of the rational choice theorists, according to whom the most distinctive feature of human beings seems to be that we are constantly calculating the benefits that come from our action. Weber recognized other types of action and most importantly that rational action could be undertaken in pursuit of values that did not bring any measurable benefit to the actor. Many of the arguments and developments of rational choice theory are attempts to integrate wider definitions of self-interest and other aspects of subjectivity into rational choice models, or to limit the scope of rational choice explanations (Abell 1991; Carling 1986; Sen 1977). Generally, however, rational choice theorists seem to want something much closer to the natural sciences in the ability not only to explain but also to predict. Whether this can be achieved is another matter.

There are important questions to be raised about rational choice theory in terms of its ability to understand the complexity of human motivations, limiting the role of values, and internal contradictions and conflicts in human psychological life. Weber was to some degree critical of the dominance of rationality in Western life, but rational choice theory can be seen as assuming an extension of that rationality to people's internal lives. It is much closer to positivism than Weber, adopting implicitly or explicitly, a positivist psychology – behaviourism – which attempts to explain human action through a process of conditioning involving rewards and punishments (Sen 1977). Whereas phenomenology is a philosophy of consciousness, rational choice theory is closer to a natural-science, cause–effect model.

Instrumental Variations II: Pragmatism and Symbolic Interactionism

We now turn to an interpretive approach which does not stress rationality in quite the same way, although a notion of instrumental rationality under-lies it. Pragmatism is a philosophy which developed in the USA during the second half of the nineteenth century, and is most often associated with names of C. S. Pierce (Pharies 1985), William James (1975) and John Dewey (1939).

There is a limited resemblance here to the instrumentalism espoused by positivists, who have problems with the status of 'theoretical' entities that cannot be seen or measured. Such concepts are seen as useful fictions which enable us to achieve our purpose and organize our perceptions and knowledge. Peirce defined our conception of an object as the total of the practical bearings that the object has on our actions. Our knowledge of objects arises in the prac-tical relationship we have to those objects, and it follows that as our practical relationship changes so our knowledge changes. This is not necessarily a theory of truth – in fact it tends towards a relativism, as we will see when we look at pragmatism in the social sciences, but it can easily be seen as involving the notion that what is true is what works. Clearly this is not a very helpful epistemological criterion – the theory that the earth is flat works perfectly well for me in my day-to-day actions.

We can already see the similarity between Weber's ontological individualism and pragmatic notions of truth – there is no such thing as a society, but if the people we are studying think there is and take it into account in their everyday actions, then we can take it as existing – it is real in its effects, and these effects are achieved through individual actions. Paul Rock, in his philosophical exploration of symbolic interactionism, states the same point emphatically: 'The character of society is so obscure that scientific attempts to discuss it are generally absurd' (Rock 1979: 227).

Rock traces the development of pragmatism through the American interpretation of Hegel, and although the details of this interpretation need not concern us here, the end point is very close to that of the neo-Kantians: that knowledge in social science is based on the shared culture of a community. However, this culture is not a structure of fixed components; it is an ongoing process. Interactionism concentrates on process. Knowledge of external objects is also a process: my knowledge of the computer I am working on at the moment grows and changes as I employ it for different and more complex purposes. My knowledge of the social world also changes as I do different things in relation to other people. The difference is that other people also have their own meaning contexts, their own knowledge of the social world and the development of that knowledge becomes a joint enterprise.

Pragmatism deploys a combination of evolutionary theory and Hegelian idealism, the view that reason, or rationality, creates the world to claim or assume that the division between knower and known has been bridged – not just in the human sciences but also in the natural sciences. Sociology and social psychology students will recognize here another source of the approach which now goes under the name of social constructionism. What happens in the course of our action, and our interaction, is that we *negotiate* (or construct) the meanings of the objects in our world. As we abstract from this negotiating process, our knowledge becomes, in Paul Rock's word, less 'authentic'. Notice that he uses the word 'authentic', not 'objective' or 'true'. For the interactionist there is no knowledge apart from that known by the people studied by the social scientist. And the work of the social scientist is again to elaborate and make intelligible the meanings negotiated and constructed by the people he or she is studying. Blumer's classic formulation sums it up well: people act on the basis of the meaning that objects have for them; these meanings are developed through social interaction, and modified through interpretive processes employed in further interaction (Blumer 1969).

Interactionist social psychology developed through Mead (1938) conceptualizes the self in pragmatic terms: the self is a *process*, not an entity – an internal conversation between what those around me tell me about myself and my interpretation of that information as I go about my practical purposes in the world; in the work of Goffman (see, for example, Goffman 1968) the instrumentalism of the approach becomes clearer: I use myself as a tool in my relationship with others, doing my best to manage the impressions I make on others in order to achieve my purposes. In both cases, however, the self arises in action, in doing rather than in being. Pragmatism draws neither explicitly on the common-sense notion of means–end rationality of Max Weber nor on the more rigorous conception of rational choice theory, but talks more about the different rationalities that exist in different situations. There are many different means–end chains, varying from situation to situation. The fundamental premiss, however, is the same as that for the other approaches: the job of the social sciences is to understand meaningful human action, and society – if it exists – consists of individual actions in relation to each other; the meanings and relations can be understood in the context of pursuing practical purposes in the world.

Reasons and Causes

So far we have taken for granted the relationship between what a person desires to achieve and the action they take to achieve it, and it is now time to look at it more closely. There is a debate among philosophers about whether the relationship is a causal one or not. One of the best discussions of these issues, which have become less central over recent years, is to be found in Keat and Urry (1975). They argue that the relationship is in fact a causal one, but 'cause' in this context must not be understood in the positivist sense of a contingent regularity.

If we hold to the positivist view then we tend to fall into an either – or conception of the relationship between the natural and social sciences. The natural sciences are concerned with contingent regularities between two phenomena out of which we construct universal laws of nature. The social sciences deal with people's ideas about the world, with logical relationships and with relationships between concepts. This view of rationality and action will be explored more fully in the next chapter. For the moment we will concentrate on Keat and Urry's suggestion that we can develop a non-positivist causal explanation of human action. They claim that

> it is part of our concept of rational agents that their beliefs and desires cause them to act in the appropriate manner. Systematic failure to act in this manner will lead us to withdraw the application of the concept of rationality to them. But this does not mean, that where the concept *is* applicable, the relations between beliefs, desires and actions is non-causal. (Keat and Urry 1975: 156)

The problem with this argument is that the simplicity of the terms employed to capture human action and the simplicity of the relationships posited between these terms. There is no doubt that human beings have beliefs and desires and that these are related to human actions. But it is possible, for example, for human beings to have and act on desires of which they are not necessarily conscious, or conscious only in distorted ways; people can have conflicting desires, or be unclear about what they want; they can be driven by desires which run counter to reasons for acting in a certain way; recognition of this can be found throughout Western literature and philosophy, although it is most systematically stated in various forms of psychoanalysis. Modern forms of sociology such as ethnomethodology and structuration theory emphasize the taken-for-granted and implicit nature of rules on which action is based. It is questionable whether interpretive approaches are compatible with anything but the broadest sense of causality – a sense which perhaps covers up rather than illuminates significant differences and complexities. And of course beliefs and desires are processes in themselves and parts of wider interpretive processes, not discrete entities which can be isolated for study (Giddens 1976).

One of these complexities is the nature of language. The linguistic turn in twentieth-century philosophy has generated several important theories of language and the way language works, and they all point to there being a hiatus between language and language use, and causal explanations. This does not mean that human beings are not subject to causal processes which operate through their physical and biological and psychological make-up as well as through the social structures in which they are placed, but the way in which they represent their own understanding of themselves and their situations and actions, and the way that identify and talk about their lives, will be processes which cannot be understood through notions of cause. The next chapter will outline one very forceful argument along these lines.

Individualism, Holism and Functional Explanation

One of the features that distinguishes Weber, and some other versions of interpretive sociology, is the explicit or implicit individualism that underlies attempts to explain the social world. There has been a much-drawn distinction between individualist and holistic approaches in the social sciences, and the opposition is dramatically illustrated by juxtaposing Durkheim's account of suicide which we discussed in Chapter 2 to Jack Douglas's *The Social Meanings of Suicide* (1967), where the author attempts to build up a sociological understanding of suicide through an analysis of the meanings that individual suicides, their families and friends and the authorities attach to their acts.

There is a question as to whether these approaches are as incompatible as it is sometimes claimed; one way of looking at them is that Durkheim's use of statistics and his positing of social facts (his positivism) and society as being over and above the individual (his holism) take us only part of the way – they tell us that we might expect more suicides in Protestant communities, but not all Protestants commit suicide. There is still an explanatory space to be filled by individualist and interpretive processes. This argument points to the fact that the social world might be comprised of different types of being, in this case social structures, social processes *and* individuals, and that they are different from each other. This possibility will recur through the coming chapters and will be explored more fully when we discuss critical realism.

There are certainly difficulties involved with sticking either to individualist arguments alone or to holistic arguments alone. An individualist approach has difficulties in explaining the social uniformities that Durkheim and others have been able to identify. A holistic approach has problems with explaining the mechanisms of social change and development. In Durkheim and later in Talcott Parsons's sociology there is a tendency to see society as equivalent to a biological organism, and both approaches employ a form of functional explanation. Each part of a society is seen as existing, functioning, to support the other parts, just as the heart and liver and other parts of the body function to support each other and the body as a whole. A functionalist explanation involves arguing that a society as a whole has certain 'needs' which must be met if that society is to survive (Parsons) or that some levels of society (the mode of production in Althusser's Marxism) have needs which are met by other levels of society (Althusser 1969).

The argument against functional explanation is quite simple: even if we can attribute 'needs' to a society or a social system or part of a social system, there is no way of showing that these needs *must* be met or that they must be met in a particular way. For example, the development of capitalism towards the end of the nineteenth century could be said to 'need' an education system, but the rate of development and type of system depended on all sorts of other factors; different capitalist societies developed different educational systems. A Weberian account would look at the historical process of the development of education systems on a comparative basis. One way of summing up this argument is that holistic explanations need to identify the *mechanisms* of change in social systems and structures, and one way of doing this might be through historical interpretive approaches. Rather than talk about 'needs', some thinkers talk about 'conditions of existence' – which do not *cause* something to appear but which create the space for its appearance and which interact with a multiplicity of other processes to produce whatever the outcome turns out to be.

Conclusion

This chapter has introduced the idea that the social sciences proceed in a way very different from that taken by the natural sciences, as a result of the differences between the objects studied by the social and natural sciences. The crucial difference is that the objects of the social sciences, like the social scientists who study them, are conscious, reflexive beings who endow their actions with meaning. We have looked at four different philosophical approaches that we have grouped together under the label 'instrumental rationality'. They have in common an assumption that the object of social science is the action of individual human beings aiming to achieve this worldly goals.

Beyond this, there are significant differences between them. Rational choice theory, influential in economics and sociology, presents the simplest and most rigid view of rational action – a choice of what brings the greatest benefit to the actor. Weber, who has been appropriated mainly by sociologists, offers a much wider conception much closer to our common-sense notion of everyday rational action, and his conception of rationality is surrounded by the irrationality or partial irrationality of the other three types of social action: those based on tradition, on emotion and on the irrational choice of ultimate values.

Whereas rational choice theory and Weberian sociology tend to take meanings for granted, the phenomenological development of Weber and sociological and social psychological developments of pragmatism are more interested in the development or construction of meaning. For Schutz this development occurs through a process of typification from the stream of consciousness, and this leads neatly to Weber's ideal-type methodology. For Mead and symbolic interactionism, on the other hand, the focus is on the collective negotiation of meaning in everyday contexts. If we can talk about rationality at all it is a context-bound rationality, specific only to particular situations.

How are we to make sense of the overall argument and the variations? It would be a strange social science which at no point took account of what human beings thought of themselves and how they thought about what they were doing. It does not follow, as many seem to suppose, that this is all that social scientists have to look at; positivist methods can perhaps help us understand some aspects of human social life, and we might also be able to talk about the effect of social structures of which social actors are not completely away or are unaware.

It is arguable as well that there is no need to choose between the different approaches discussed here – they can each be seen as appropriate to some level of analysis or particular object of meaningful social action. Weber's ideas are perhaps the most generally applicable in setting out the task of understanding and the criteria it must meet; Schutz offers us a way of studying the processes of consciousness and the taken-for-granted world; interactionism gives us a way of looking at the social generation of meaning; and rational choice theory is perhaps most appropriate to looking at certain economic decisions. It might be however that none of them can make sense of what I do when I fall in love.

And, of course, these are not the only ways of making sense of what we think and of our actions.

Further Reading

The best original source for Weber's philosophy of social science are the opening sections of *The Theory of Economic and Social Organization* (Weber 1922, 1947) and the discussion of ideal types and value freedom in *The Methodology of the Social Sciences* (Weber 1949); Diana Leat (1972) offers an excellent discussion of the meaning of *verstehen;* for an alternative, more traditional view, see W. G. Runciman's *A Critique of Max Weber's Philosophy of Social Science* (Runciman 1972).

Schutz's *The Phenomenology of the Social World* (Schutz 1972) is a thorough account of phenomenological sociology, and Peter Berger and Thomas Luckman's *The Social Construction of Reality* (Berger and Luckman 1967) is an example of the phenomenological influence at its best.

Peter Abell (ed.) in *Rational Choice Theory* offers a useful collection of studies employing this approach (Abell 1991). For pragmatism and symbolic interactionism, Paul Rock's *The Making of Symbolic Interactionism* (Rock 1979) is an excellent account of the philosophical background. For a general discussion of pragmatism and social science, see Lewis, J. D. and Richard L. Smith: *American Sociology and Pragmatism* (Smith and Lewis 1980) and for a vigorous and impressive contemporary defence of pragmatism see Richard Rorty's *Consequences of Pragmatism* (Rorty 1982).

Post-script

Rational choice theory continues to hold powerful sway over several social science disciplines, most notably economics and political science. The emphasis that has been central to much sociology and anthropology on the role of normative rules, values and cultural traditions has tended to limit the appeal of rational choice theory in those disciplines. The work of Lawson (2003a) in economics has provided an important critique of the basic assumptions of mainstream approaches in that discipline. Archer and Tritter (eds) (2000) provide an excellent and wide-ranging set of critical evaluations of rational choice theory in relation to central problems of social theory. On the centrality of norms in social life, see Sayer (2009). On the relationship between markets and rational choice, see O'Neill (2007).

The contested issue of the role of causal explanation in the social sciences is addressed in the wide-ranging collection edited by Ruth Groff (2008).

6

Interpretive Approaches 2: Rationality as Rule-Following: Cultures, Traditions and Hermeneutics

Introduction

We move on now to a very different notion of rationality and a different conception of what is involved in understanding human action, a conception which gives more prominence than does Weber to the culture in which the social actor is situated and to the nature of language itself.

The starting-point here is the discussion in the previous chapter about whether reasons can be understood as causes. It was suggested there that these arguments employ concepts that are too simple and static to enable us to understand the complexities of human action. We begin to move into the complexity when we look at the other side of the argument: that reasons are not and cannot be causes of action. This argument has been important in Anglo-Saxon philosophy, which has been dominated by the originally Austrian Ludwig Wittgenstein (Wittgenstein 1958, 1997), a leading figure in the linguistic turn. The conventional interpretation of Wittgenstein's work turned into what was referred to earlier as the 'under-labourer' conception of the relationship between philosophy and science: science, as it were, delivers the goods and the philosopher is only important if the scientist runs into difficulties. The difficulties are linguistic and the job of the philosopher is to unravel the knots in the conceptual wool so the scientist can go on knitting.

This view was contested in a radical manner in the late 1950s in a book called *The Idea of a Social Science* by Peter Winch (Winch 1958). We will see that Winch uses Wittgenstein's ideas to raise a number of questions not only about the possibility of a social science but also about the possibility of understanding cultures other than our own and the issue of relativism. We will concentrate on Winch's work and its implications in the first part of this chapter; we will then turn to the more recent work of Alisdair MacIntyre (1981)

94

and then to a major figure in continental European philosophy, Hans-Georg Gadamer (1989). Although they do not explicitly develop each other's work, their ideas can be situated in the same broad family.

Peter Winch: Philosophy and Social Science

On the flyleaf of his book, Winch quotes the German philosopher Lessing:

> It may indeed be true that moral actions are always the same in themselves, however different may be the time and however different the societies in which they occur; but still, the same actions do not always have the same names, and it is unjust to give any action a different name from that which it used to bear in its own times and amongst its own people. (Winch 1958)

Winch's argument can be seen as a meditation on this quotation. He coined the term 'underlabourer' to describe the conception of philosophy he was criticizing. His own position can perhaps best be summed up with a point he makes about the relationship between philosophy and science. When philosophers ask questions about the existence of the outside world, they are not asking for a reply that can be 'proved' in some scientific sense, but rather are asking what it is we mean by the notion of externality: How do we, in our particular culture, decide what is external? As we will see, different cultures have different outside worlds. The philosopher is concerned not with particular linguistic confusions but with the nature of language itself and its relationship to reality. We cannot have access to any external reality without language, and Winch goes one step further: 'The concepts we have settle for us the form of the experience we have of the world' (Winch 1958: 15).

Thus different languages define different realities. We might say that different cultures *are* different realities. We can gain an intuitive sense of what Winch means when we think what happens when we adopt a new set of beliefs about the world. If for example, I become converted to Christianity, I do not see the world as I saw it before: whereas before I might have seen people who were miserable, I now see people who refuse to allow Jesus to touch them; whereas I would once have avoided such people I now believe it is my duty to bring the Word to them. Again, if I am trained as a psychoanalyst the world changes: whereas once I would have seen footballers congratulating each other after a goal, I now see a permissible expression of latent homosexuality.

Each language, each way of looking at the world, is a different way of trying to make the world *intelligible*, and the work of the philosopher is to explore the way in which different languages – religious, scientific, social scientific, literary and so on – try to do this. In the case of social science, however, something remarkable happens; philosophy and social science merge:

> A man's social relations with his fellows are permeated with his ideas about reality. Indeed 'permeated' is hardy a strong enough word: social relations are expressions of ideas about reality. (Winch 1958: 23)

The statement may suggest the reason why Winch's book was for many years ignored by social scientists – it would put them out of business! However, his ideas are worth taking seriously. What he is saying is in effect very similar to the approaches discussed in the previous chapter: that the task of the social sciences is to understand the meanings that people give to their social world. But for Winch this is also the job of philosophy.

Language, Games and Rules

Winch thinks of himself as making an epistemological argument, but it is important to remember that, at least when we consider the objects of the social sciences, he is not talking about what '*really*' exists but how we decide, through our use of language, what we think really exists. Crucial to his understanding of this is Wittgenstein's conception of rules, rule-following and 'language games'. Understanding is a matter of how we use words and how we recognize that we use them in the 'right' way.

One of the intriguing things about our use of language, shown up for example in Garfinkel's ethnomethodological studies (Garfinkel 1967), is that we are constantly involved in interpretative processes when we talk, but we can never arrive at some final, definite interpretation. If you keep asking somebody what they mean by a particular word or phrase, you get a lot of anger and frustration but no conclusive answer. The word 'course' presents us with a good example. There is no final, dictionary-type definition of the word. Most of the people who read this book will be taking an academic course in a particular subject; while you read it, the chances are that somewhere in the world horses will be racing around courses; journalists will be reporting on the course of events in many different places; dogs will be engaging in hare coursing; radars will be tracking the course of many thousands of aircraft; a doctor and a patient will be speculating on the course that a cancer is likely to take and whether a course of chemotherapy or radiotherapy is the best way to treat it; and millions of people will use the phrase 'of course' in many different contexts. And, of course, in the course of preparing this manuscript I might come across a new idea that knocks me completely off course. I might comfort myself by going out for a three-course meal . . .

All these can be considered 'correct' ways of using the word; we can also identify incorrect ways of using it: it would not make sense to talk about a 'football course' rather than a football pitch, or to talk about the course followed by my house, or of the university offering a course in walking around corridors, although we might plot various courses of action as we walk around them.

The point of all this – before we get carried away completely – is that there is no single, clear definition of the word. We have already come across this idea in the last chapter, and Winch's interpretation of Wittgenstein has also played a part in the development of ethnomethodology. Winch argues that we know whether 'course' is being used in the right or the wrong way because we know – implicitly at least – the rules that govern the use of the term. The rules enable us to understand what the word means. But from here we go in a very different direction from that taken by ethnomethodology. Being a philosopher, Winch is concerned with the concept of a rule and what it is to follow a rule, and we return to the issue of reasons and causal explanations.

The first point is that if we can identify the right way of following a rule, then we can also identify a wrong way, we can make mistakes. Winch argues that:

> . . . the notion of following a rule is logically in seperable from the notion of *making a mistake*. If it is possible to say of someone that he is following a rule that means that one can ask whether he is doing what he does correctly or not. (Winch 1958: 32)

So far I have developed the argument using language as an example, but we can think of the whole of our social life as language use – we give meaning to what we do, and therefore our life, our language and our social world can be seen as rule-following. If we can follow a rule in at least two ways, a wrong way and a right way, it means that we cannot offer causal explanations in the social sciences, and that our understanding of reasons is always *evaluative*: we ask whether a rule is being applied in a right way or a wrong way. Causal explanations are not evaluations but statements of (putative) fact. Therefore social sciences cannot predict, for there is no guarantee that a rule will always be followed in the same way.

A second implication of rule-following is that all action is social, for if action is meaningful, or rule-following, there must be somebody to evaluate how the rule has been followed – otherwise I could do what I like with no check. As Winch develops his argument, so he criticizes Weber – particularly the latter's notion of causal adequacy and the idea that there can be meaningful action which is not social – and develops his argument against others who argue for the possibility of a social science that is not concerned with explicating the rules of social action.

The social scientist (who is not a scientist but a philosopher) is concerned with explicating the rules of social life, what Wittgenstein called 'forms of life' or 'language games' – the social rules that are implicit in meaningful behaviour. This implies a relativism: different societies, different cultures have their own forms of life and there is no overarching form of life or language which is neutral and into which other languages can be translated. The distinction from positivism here is that, as we saw, the latter implies a neutral observation language, a 'scientific' language.

Winch then takes us beyond even the moderate notions of cause, objectivity and value freedom that we find in Weber's work. What exists in the social world and people's ideas of what exists are one and the same thing; there is no privileged access to an external reality. We understand cultures, and presumably subcultures, by elaborating on the rules that people use in their understanding of their relationships. For the sociologist there are certain questions that spring to mind immediately, such as 'Who makes the rules?' and 'How do we look at different relationships to the rules?' (see, for example, MacIntyre 1974), but these objections seem to assume that rules are 'external', out there between people. Winch is not talking about an object that we study, but about the way in which we create our sense of there being an object to study; not about whether there are differential relationships to rules but what rules are applied in the recognition of differential relationships.

Understanding Other Societies

We can take our discussion further by looking at what Winch has to say about witchcraft in a classic paper on the Azande (Winch 1974). It also enables us to develop some criticisms of his position. He begins with a critique of the British anthropologist E. E. Evans Pritchard who published a study of the Azande as long ago as 1937. The Azande believe in witches, and witches play a central role in their lives. If I were to develop a fever I would consult my doctor; if I were an Azande (at least at the time when Evans Pritchard studied them), I would consult a witch-doctor to discover who had cursed me. He might consult the poison oracle; this would involve ritual preparation of a mixture known as *benge* which we would regard as a poison, although the Azande have no equivalent concept of our 'poison'. The *benge* would then be fed to a chicken, again with the proper rituals and a question – perhaps 'Has my neighbour put a curse on me?' – would be asked. It would be agreed beforehand whether the death of the chicken would mean 'Yes' or 'No', and the answer would be confirmed by putting the question the other way round as the poison was administered to another chicken.

For Winch, Evans Pritchard is not sufficiently critical of the view that Western science is (at least in limited ways) better at dealing with these things than the Azande. Winch argues that, as a matter of principal, we cannot show that science is superior because to do so would require drawing on a language into which all other languages could be translated and compared, a language which had a privileged access to reality, a language which today might be called a 'meta-narrative'.

Winch draws again on Wittgenstein, who had

> come to reject the whole idea that there must be a general form of propositions. He emphasised the indefinite number of different uses that language may have and tried to show that these different uses neither need, nor in fact do, all have something in common . . . He also tried to show the what counts as 'agreement or disagreement with reality' takes as many forms as there are different uses of language, and cannot, therefore, be taken as given *prior* to the detailed investigation of the use that is in question. (Winch 1974: 90)

Each language has its own criteria, its own rules about what is right and what is wrong, about what exists and what does not exist.

The only things we have access to, says Winch, are forms of life – the languages spoken by different cultures, the rules that enable the attachment of meaning to the world. There is no super-language with access to a 'real' reality: all realities are real in the context of the language that defines them as such. The Azande have witchcraft, the British (and others) have science; each society has its own forms of rationality which are likely to be unintelligible to members of the other society. If, for example, a Zande native were to knock on my door and tell me that the hens I keep in my backyard were not the right sort of fowl for the oracle, then he or she might very well be right, but the statement would puzzle me and it would have no meaning except as a strange story. If I, as a British native, were to point out to the Zande native that his or her beliefs were logically contradictory, I would be right but my statement would be as irrelevant to my visitor as his or hers was to me.

Two consequences seem to follow from this position. The first is that we are unable to take moral positions on other forms of life, on what goes on in other cultures. This is an issue that will recur in various ways, and all that we need say about it at the moment is that there is an attraction to Winch's position in the context of contemporary debates about multi-culturalism and the general distaste with which traditional and imperialist attitudes are regarded, particularly in the academic world. Winch gives us no basis for converting the heathen, either to Christianity or to science, but nor does he give us any basis for criticizing what we might regard as the unacceptable features of other societies – female circumcision, for example, or authoritarian dictatorships. If there is no meta-language into which forms of life can be translated and compared in terms of their relationship to an external reality (the epistemological question) or any meta-logic which enables us judge forms of life in terms of their rationality, there is also no meta-ethic which enables us to makes moral judgements about different forms of life.

This type of debate is not unrelated to the questions that arise around Thomas Kuhn's concept of the paradigm in the philosophy of the natural sciences. Can we judge between paradigms? This is related to the question of whether we can translate from one paradigm to another. Here is the second consequence of Winch's argument: it raises the question of whether we can actually understand another culture at all, whether we can translate from one form of life to another in a meaningful way.

Winch's answer to this is a subtle one which can be seen as a plea for making the effort to understand other forms of life and a criticism of the Western society from whose form of life he speaks. He refers to another linguistic philosopher, Rush Rees (1960), who points out that, within our own culture, we tend to participate in numerous language games (or components of wider forms of life) as we go about the diverse activities of our lives, and the meaning of a statement in one language game will depend not only on the particular game in which the actor is engaging at that particular moment but also upon its relationship to all the other games in which the actor is involved. There is an overlap between the language games in which I am situated – the language of the sociologist, of the family member, of the British citizen, the cricket lover and so on. For the individual:

> Whether a man sees a point in what he is doing will then depend on whether he is able to see any unity in his multifarious interests, activities and other men; what sort of sense he sees in his life will depend on the nature of this unity. The ability to see this sort of sense in life depends not merely on the individual, though this is not to say that it does not depend on him at all; it depends also on the possibilities of making such sense which the culture in which he lives does, or does not, provide. (Winch 1970: 106)

One assumes that Winch might include women in this as well. He goes on, in a discussion of an argument, put forward by Alisdair MacIntyre, that Azande witchcraft is a way of trying to increase production, to argue that MacIntyre misses the interconnectedness of Azande practices:

> ...a Zande's crops are not just potential objects of consumption: the life he lives, his relations with his fellows, his chances for acting decently or doing evil, all spring from his relation to his crops. (Winch 1970: 106)

And he seems to see the tendency to miss these connections as representing a lack in Western culture – the blinkers which come from our instrumental way of looking at the world. The reason we should study other cultures is that it extends our own awareness of life and its possibilities.

This still does not answer my second question of how we gain access to other cultures, of how we can begin to translate or move from one form of life to a very different one. Winch's answer is that all cultures face certain problems that are in one way or another at the centre of being human – they all have to handle birth, sexual relations and death; these notions are implicit in the idea of life itself. There are many different ways in which new members of a culture are raised and socialized, many different ways in which sexual relations are organized and many different ways in which the dying and the dead are handled. But all societies have to do these things, and they provide the possibility of mutual understanding – of recognizing the other in ourselves and vice versa.

What Can We Do with Winch?

Winch takes us to the heart of some central problems in social science. Whether we are sociologists, anthropologists, historians or psychologists, our work must involve understanding the meaning that our subjects give to the world. It is difficult to imagine a social science that did not make some sort of assumption about meaning. Perhaps the nearest we get to a social science that does not do this is behaviourist psychology, and most, if not all, behaviourists would regard themselves as natural scientists.

As we have pointed out before, however, to say that the social sciences *have* to be interpretive does not mean that they are *only* interpretive. For Winch and for others we will encounter later, there is a basic ontological and epistemological commitment to idealism – the things that exist in the social world are defined by our culture, our language. There is, if you like, an essential transparency to social life: if we can understand the language games of those we study then we can understand their social life. Associated with this there is what Taylor (1985) calls the 'incorrigibility thesis', namely that we cannot criticize other cultures from the point of view of our own, that there is no neutral language.

There are two points to be made here: first, that Winch's account only gives us part of the task of social science, and second, following the work of Taylor, we can recognize the force of the incorrigibility thesis without, as it were, swallowing it whole.

The first point is that our social life is not that transparent; all sorts of things happen to us which we struggle to understand, and for which our ideas often seem inadequate. If the social sciences were only a matter of interpreting meaning, then, one can't help feeling, life would be much easier. This can be coupled with an interesting absence in Winch's list of 'life problems' with which all cultures have to find some way of dealing. Not only do we all have to deal with birth, sexual relations and death, we also have to eat, and there are not many societies where our food falls from the sky and we have to do nothing with it. In other words, all societies have to deal with the production of goods. This gives us a further link to the Azande – both our society and theirs, for example, grow crops.

One route into understanding other cultures, then, is though grasping the social systems within which they produce goods. This takes us towards Marxism, but we do not necessarily have to go all the way, nor do we have to give Western science – instrumental reason – priority. This is where Taylor's argument comes in (Taylor 1985). He argues that for Winch we are faced with an either – or choice: either we see the Azande culture from the point of view of our own culture, as working with a primitive or inadequate scientific method or we understand them from their own point of view as achieving an integration of meaning in tribal and individual life. Taylor suggests that it is possible to develop a language of 'perspicuous contrast'. The dictionary definition of 'perspicuous' is 'having mental penetration', and such a language would be one in which we could formulate both their way and ours as alternative possibilities in relation to some human constants at work in both. It would be a language in which the possible human variations would be so formulated that both our form of life and theirs could be perspicuously described as alternative such variations. Such a language of contrast might show their language of understanding to be distorted or inadequate in some respects or it might show ours to be so (in which case we might find that understanding them leads to an alteration of our self-understanding and hence our form of life . . .) or it might show both to be so. (Taylor 1985: 125–6)

In other words, the Azande might be good at providing coherent meaning to their lives, while we might be better at producing knowledge of nature.

This seems an eminently sensible position and one that is perfectly compatible with Winch's argument, at least when he is talking about the connections between cultures which might enable understanding. These points of contact enable Winch to avoid a strong relativism as far as understanding is concerned, although it might be more difficult to move to moral arguments about other cultures.

We can, then, maintain the value of Winch's arguments for the social sciences but also engage in other types of social analysis. It is also clear from more recent work by other philosophers that this cultural/linguistic level of analysis can be deepened beyond the comprehension of the rules that people follow.

Alisdair MacIntyre: Narratives and Communities

Winch's work raises a wealth of epistemological, ontological, political and moral issues relevant to the philosophy of the social sciences and they can be developed in different ways. Alisdair MacIntyre, another English philosopher, has, in the course of his career, engaged in the debate around these issues from different positions. In his earlier work he was close to Marxism and his criticisms of Winch that I mentioned earlier come from that time. In the latter part of his career, however he has moved towards the work of Thomas Aquinas, a thirteenth-century Benedictine monk and follower of Aristotle. There is not sufficient space here to elaborate on what that means, but the contrast with Marxism should be apparent. Whereas Winch was able to criticize the younger MacIntyre for only being able to see Azande practices in relation to the production of consumer goods, the later MacIntyre is highly critical of such an emphasis and highly critical of the instrumentality of modern cultures, and of modernity as a whole.

MacIntyre's central concern is moral philosophy. He argues that it is only in the context of a *tradition* that any sort of morality can be meaningful, and that we can talk about a tradition only in the context of two other concepts: practice and narrative. By 'practice' he seems to mean a coherent social practice which enables a moral life to be pursued, and this enables human beings to tell coherent stories about themselves. He argues that human beings are by nature story-telling animals, and the stories we tell about ourselves are rooted in ancient myths where everybody is given a clear role. It is this sort of coherence of meaning in individual life that Winch suggests could be the advantage of Azande society.

MacIntyre's criticism of modern society is developed though a distinction between external and internal goods – 'goods' here meaning what is valued and desired, 'goods' as opposed to 'evils'. External goods are objects and involve ownership; internal goods are moral or ethical goods – this is an over-simplification, but is sufficient for our purposes here. MacIntyre's example is of teaching a child to play chess: the child might not be very interested but might be persuaded into learning by the offer of sweets if he or she does well. The sweets are, for the child, external goods. (And they do *not* become internal goods when they are eaten!) The hope is that the child will learn to enjoy and value the skill of playing the game for its own sake. The ability to play well and the satisfaction of winning become internal goods and they are goods which benefit the community – a good chess player (like any good games player) can give pleasure to others.

For MacIntyre, there is a contradictory or dialectical relationship between practices and institutions. Practices, the pursuit of internal goods, are dependent upon institutions, but the latter are also concerned with the pursuit of external goods so there is always a danger of corruption. What is important in all of this is that MacIntyre is putting forward an argument which is epistemologically similar to Winch. We can understand human action only within its context, within the language game or within the form of life within which it takes place – which MacIntyre seems to deal with as practices and institutions. The epistemology carries with it implications for moral philosophy: in his discussion of the Azande, Winch plays with the idea that the advantage of Zande culture over Western culture is that it offers a more coherent meaning to the individual life than does the modern world – it is therefore wrong to see Zande witchcraft through one or another set of scientific spectacles. MacIntyre turns this into a full-scale critique of modernity, arguing that we have entered a new dark age in which the pursuit of external goods has eaten away at the pursuit of internal goods and the coherence of social life which is both a condition for and a source of coherent individual and social narratives. He provides a philosophical basis for an emphasis on communities and traditions.

More important, MacIntyre provides a philosophical foundation for the contemporary emphasis on narrative in sociology, social psychology and sociology and perhaps to a lesser extent in social history. The emphasis has developed in different ways in each discipline. Dan P. MacAdams (1993), for example, influenced by the work of the psychoanalyst Carl Jung, talks about the importance of building up personal myths for a sense of identity and meaning in life; Jerome Bruner (1987), the cognitive psychologist, in a seminal paper suggests that there is only narrative in people's lives, that there is no difference between the life as lived and the life as told. The culture supplies the narrative structures around which we organize our personal lives, and in this organization we are bound into our culture. In sociology the idea of narrative has been particularly important in looking at the way in which people deal with illness or life crises such as divorce (Andrews *et al.* 2000) In all cases it is suggested that a coherent narrative is a source of personal identity and connection to the wider social group.

We can, then, think of narrative as providing another basis for the interpretive approach to the social sciences. The emphasis on narrative presents an alternative to instrumental rationality and extends the notion of rationality as rule-following to take into account the way we give significance to our lives within a form of life.

Hermeneutics: Hans-Georg Gadamar

In the last chapter we looked at different forms of the interpretive approach to the social sciences sharing in common a concern with instrumental rationality. In this chapter we have looked at different forms of rationality, concerned less with doing than with being: how do we find meaning in our life, how do we endow it with meaning? The answers have all involved reference to communities, forms of life, traditions, the collective; to rules and lastly to narratives. They have taken us from questions of epistemology through a first encounter with the problem of relativism to questions of moral philosophy and the relationship of morality and the social world. They have also taken us from the individual emphasis of instrumental rationality through to the collective emphasis of culture and tradition.

'Hermeneutics' was a term given originally to interpreting the spiritual truth of the bible, but it was imported into the human sciences by Dilthey to refer to the investigation of intentional human behaviour and human institutions, and by thinkers after Dilthey to refer to processes of understanding within and between traditions and cultures. In its widest sense everybody we have looked at in this chapter and the previous one can be listed under this heading, but there are important distinctions. Max Weber can be seen as closer to the scientific spirit of the Enlightenment as well as tracing its triumph, whereas Peter Winch and Alisdair MacIntyre have recourse to different traditions – Wittgenstein and Thomism. Conventionally now hermeneutics refers to the ideas of a number of continental European philosophers one of the most central of whom is Hans-Georg Gadamer (Gadamer 1989). What marks this particular group is their hostility to what they see as the instrumental and manipulative spirit of the natural sciences.

Gadamer is a critic of all conventional notions of objectivity, insisting that knowledge is not a product of coming to understand the action of the individual (*à la* Weber) but of achieving an understanding of the movement of history, and history is the development of a common aim; we can only under-stand a text when we make ourselves part of that common aim out of which it emerged. The same can be said for understanding an argument with somebody from a different tradition – what is necessary is a gradual merging of horizons as each comes to understand the other, and this happens through the attempt to understand, independently of our will. If you have struggled to understand a difficult text with which you don't agree and you discover at some later point that your view of the world has somewhat changed, you should be able to understand what Gadamer is getting at.

Understanding is inevitably historical; the nature of a human being is itself historical and open to historical change. The process of understanding is paradoxical, involving the 'hermeneutic circle': we cannot know the part without understanding the whole of which it is a part, and at the same time we cannot understand the whole without understanding the parts that make it up. We cannot understand the meaning of, say, a Shakespeare play without under-standing the meaning of the individual scenes and acts within it; at the same time we cannot understand the meaning of the individual scenes and acts unless we understand how they relate to the whole play. Understanding involves a constant movement from the part to the whole and back again, and for Gadamer this is a description of our very existence as thinking beings. This is what we do when we think.

The individual is secondary for Gadamer; history (the culture, the tradition) is primary. We first come to understand ourselves through and as part of the social units in which we live, long before we understand ourselves as indi-viduals – individual self-awareness is merely 'a flickering in the closed circuits of historical life'. We understand, primarily through our prejudices, the prejudge-ments of the historical moment of which we are a part. The introduction of a word such as 'prejudice' in a favourable light, as what roots us in history and our life, indicates how far Gadamer is from conventional notions of science. Alan How describes well the way this works. We are understanding and inter-preting beings, caught up in the circular process of moving from part to whole and back again:

> It is something we undergo, something that cannot be finally controlled by us because our prejudgements are not our possessions. They are not things that, as it were, we could get round the front of us in full view. They are what we are before we know it, and in being so are also the positive pre-requisites for all our actual understandings and inter-pretations. We don't really know our own prejudgements till we bring them into view in the process of furthering our tradition. (How 1995: 47)

We cannot, then, know anything at all without prejudices, but they may change as we become aware of them in the ongoing historical project. The historical is a source of authority as well as necessary prejudice, and the process of understanding involves the recognition of the authority of tradition.

For the purposes of this book, these are the most important ideas we can take from Gadamer. Perhaps it might be useful to look briefly at some current debates in sociology to show the import of his ideas. It is not uncommon now to hear arguments that we no longer need the classical texts of the founders of sociological thought – Marx, Durkheim, Weber and Simmel. There are different versions of this: either modern sociology is a sophisticated empirical discipline, or modern thinkers have shown the restrictive or repressive character of 'grand narratives', or modern theorists are more relevant to the beginning of the twenty-first century than those who wrote in the late nineteenth.

Gadamer's position would be that the conditions of the possibility of sociological thinking are provided by the classic texts; they, if you like, provide the prejudices of sociology, and it is arguable that if we don't read them then we have no discipline – no authority for what we say about the world. It would be as if every generation had to build the discipline anew, from scratch. As How points out, new theories and apparently radical critiques of the classics appear, but over time they become absorbed into the tradition. And of course if we leave the classics behind, we end up reinventing the wheel (How 1998).

At the same time, there are problems with Gadamer's notions of tradition and authority. As we will see in the following chapter, there is a strong argument that if he is right then we cannot undertake the systematic investigation of our mistaken ideas about the world, the critique of ideologies. The arguments about relativism are relevant here as well – if the tradition from which I came is systematically racist (as it almost certainly is) and it frames my perceptions of the world and of other people, then how is it possible for me to learn, or if I do learn, to show others, that racism might be wrong. Of course, reality is more complicated than that, and a tradition is made of all sorts of contradictory streams of thought in a continuous process of argument and merging, but there is a perhaps unnecessary conservatism to Gadamer's hermeneutics, an overemphasis on the authority of tradition. Yet his picture of human beings as beings who by nature understand and interpret through a circular process that defines their being adds to Winch's view of humans as rule-following and MacIntyre's view of humans as story-telling animals.

Conclusion

This chapter has taken us a long way from the comparatively simple notions of human action discussed in the previous one. The basic assumption is the same: the social sciences are concerned with understanding meaningful human action, but the approaches discussed in this chapter all emphasize the significance of the wider culture, whether we call it a language game, a form of life, a tradition or a community. The individual and the meaning of individual action is framed by the wider culture in the same way perhaps as the sentences that I speak as an individual are framed by the rules of the language in which I speak. But they all leave us with an interesting question: To what extent are we prisoners of our own tradition, our culture? And can we see outside it or beyond it? How can we question it?

Further Reading

For the debates around Winch, see *The Idea of a Social Science* (Winch 1958), the essays by Winch, MacIntyre and Lukes in Wilson (1970) and the essay by Taylor (1985). For a good introduction to MacIntyre, see McMylor (1994), but it is also worth reading MacIntyre's own *After Virtue* (1981). For an excellent introduction to Gadamer and his debate with Habermas, see How (1995). Those who want to plunge into the deep end with Gadamer should have a look at *Truth and Method* (Gadamer 1989). For a straightforward and powerful advocacy of the notion of narrative see Bruner's paper 'Life as Narrative' (Bruner 1987).

Post-script

The death of Peter Winch in 1997 gave rise to renewed attention to his work, including an excellent intellectual biography (Lyas 1999). In Commentary on Recent Developments, I offer an extended critical discussion of a recent work (Hutchinson *et al.* 2008) that passionately defends Winch's view that there could be no such thing as a science of society. In the course of this discussion, I take up some arguments in relation to Winch and hermeneutics that open up differences between Ian's treatment in the first edition and my own thoughts.

7

Interpretive Approaches 3: Critical Rationality

Introduction: Hegel, Marx and the Dialectic

This last chapter on the interpretive tradition moves in yet another direction, taking up the political implications of the Enlightenment and bringing them forward into the contemporary world. In the introduction we pointed out that both strands of philosophy that developed in this period challenged the existing hierarchical social order, since both suggested that knowledge was available to the ordinary person, either because we can all experience the world directly or because we all, by virtue of being human, possess the faculty of reason. The former still lives on in appeals to the facts as against prejudice or dogma. An interesting contemporary illustration of this lies in Gordon Marshall's use of empirical evidence to dispute the 'prejudices' of some postmodernists about the decreasing importance of class in contemporary society (Marshall 1997). The latter lives on in the work of what became known as the Frankfurt School – 'critical theory'. Here, rationality not only becomes the means by which we can understand individual behaviour, cultures and forms of life but also offers the means by which we can judge different forms of life. To put it as crudely as possible, if all human beings possess reason then any society which excludes people, on the grounds of a human characteristic such as race or sex, from the rights and duties of citizenship, from exercising their reason as part of the collective life, is an irrational society.

The home of critical theory was Frankfurt, where the Institute for Social Research was founded in 1923. It developed a non-communist Hegelian Marxism, and the major figures that concern us here are the philosophers Theodor Adorno, Max Horkheimer and Herbert Marcuse and the-second generation, contemporary philosopher Jurgen Habermas. With the rise of Hitler the main figures emigrated to the US, and Marcuse stayed there, Adorno and Horkheimer moving back to Frankfurt in the late 1940s.

Clearly, critical theory presents a very different way of thinking about rationality, and is not as firmly rooted in the Kantian tradition as Weber or even

Gadamer. The direct line of descent is from Hegel through Marx, but with rather more emphasis on Hegel than Marx. Critical rationality is a form of dialectical thinking exploited to the full by Hegel, who saw both the history of ideas and the history of the world as a dialectical process. The two were directly related: the history of the world was a product of the history of ideas. In a famous formulation, Marx 'stood Hegel on his feet'. His 'materialist conception of history' saw ideas, from philosophical systems to common sense, as the product of social and economic relations rather than the other way around. The simplest but by no means the most accurate way of describing the dialectic, whether of ideas or of reality, is as involving a process of *thesis*, a proposition or a social system, an *antithesis*, the opposite to which it gives rise, and the synthesis of two. We start with capitalism, which generates the working class, its own antithesis, and the contradiction produces the socialist revolution. Nobody would accept such a simple formula now, and the attempt of Marx's collaborator, Engels (Engels 1949), to formulate 'laws of the dialectic' as 'laws of nature' is now generally rejected.

If we stick with the dialectic in its original form as a way of thinking which is thus implicated in human action and relationships, then we are on firmer ground. It has several important features. First, it is not linear in the way that instrumental thinking is linear. As with hermeneutics, the imagery is circular, and dialectical thinking involves a similar continual movement from the whole to the parts and back again. If we think of a developmental process as a dialectical development, it means it does not go forward in a straight line, but moves more in a spiral, perhaps coming back to the same point but at a different level. One can, for example, think of the development of modern capitalism from the middle of the nineteenth century as a movement from attempts to control the market system to attempts to free it. At each turn levels of technology and social organization are different, and at each stage arguments are different from but related to the ones that went before.

Whereas formal logic and much everyday thinking are based on notions of identity, dialectical thinking is built on opposites – that in any system of concepts, the meaning of one concept can be understood only in relation to those around it, and in particular to its opposite. As a simple example, we can only understand the meaning of 'up' in relation to the meaning of 'down' – the two go together. On a broader scale, we can never be satisfied with a simple 'positive' statement. It must be remembered that dialectical thinking only comes into play when we talk about ideas and about human actions and relations. If we take a statement about the world of nature – all swans are white, for example – we cannot say that the dialectic tells us there should be black swans as well. There are some classic mistakes in the history of dialectical thinking that come from using it this way. Hegel famously predicted that a star would be found where no star exists and more tragically harvests were lost in Soviet Russia in the 1930s through attempts to implement a 'dialectical' biology in agriculture (see our discussion in Chapter 4).

If we work with ideas and actions, however, we have a different result. We can, for example, suggest that one of the dominant themes of contemporary society and culture is fragmentation – put crudely, things seem to be falling apart. The dialectical thinker would also want to bring into play the opposite process – that of globalization and the increasingly highly organized nature of modern capitalism – and he or she would want to look at the way in which these contradictory processes effect each other. This introduces another vital element of dialectical thought – contradiction – and leads on to what at first glance might seem to be a defect rather than a part of the value of this way of thinking – negativity.

The idea of the negative or negativity features throughout the history of critical theory. In his *Phenomenology of Spirit*, Hegel (1807, 1977) talks about the 'labour of the negative', by which he means the careful and systematic criticism of philosophical concepts, and the idea is taken up in Herbert Marcuse's *Reason and Revolution* (Marcuse 1960), where negative philosophy is juxtaposed directly to Comte's positive philosophy (see Chapter 2). Comte is characterized, largely rightly, as attempting to impose the methods of the natural sciences onto the social sciences in the interests of establishing natural laws of society: if society, like nature, is governed by universal laws, we can do little to change them. However, we know what we can do, and we can stop speculating about what we might do, and this, Comte thought, would be a cure for the social disorder of his time. Negativity, the labour of the negative, on the other hand, is concerned with radical social change, a process of liberation. One of Marcuse's later books was entitled *Negations* (Marcuse 1968), and finally one of Adorno's most famous books is *Negative Dialectics* (Adorno 1973).

Dialectical thinking, then, involves a movement between parts and whole similar to that of hermeneutics, but it involves as well the notion that reason – thought – proceeds by contradiction and that human existence is contradictory in various ways; as a consequence, human relations and human thought are constant processes, not static entities. According to Horkheimer, traditional (positivist) social science is concerned with solving particular social problems. He is referring here to the sort of social engineering envisaged by Comte and later advocated by Popper (1957). He goes on:

> We must . . . add that there is a human activity which has society itself for its object. The aim of this activity is not simply to eliminate one or other abuse, for it regards such abuses as necessarily connected with the way in which the social structure is organized. Although it itself emerges from the social structure, its purpose is not, either in its conscious intention, or in its subjective significance, the better functioning of any element in the structure. On the contrary it is suspicious of the very categories of better, useful, appropriate, productive and valuable, as these are understood in the present order. (Horkheimer 1972: 206)

The Dialectic of the Enlightenment

> In the most general sense of progressive thought, the Enlightenment has always aimed at liberating men from fear and establishing their sovereignty. Yet the fully enlightened earth radiates disaster triumphant. (Adorno and Horkheimer 1969: 3)

This is a typical Frankfurt school statement, a vast generalization which, if it has any effect at all on the careful empirical social scientist or even the careful linguistic philosopher, would appal them. They might at the most grant it the status of bad poetry. The book which provides the heading for this section was originally titled *Philosophical Fragments* and that is precisely what it is, not a systematic philosophy because the idea of systematic philosophy – totalizing philosophy – was already (in 1944) becoming associated in the minds of the authors with totalitarianism.

A philosophical social science (they were primarily concerned with sociology) must always go beyond science if it is not to become meaningless measurement, and the style of argument is one of the ways in which it does this. This book gives as good a sense as any of the overall philosophical project of critical theory, which is full of paradox and manipulates concepts in a way distinctly foreign to Anglo-Saxon ears and minds. The book is about the play of rationality and irrationality, the attempts of human beings to liberate themselves and the nature of domination – which is best understood as that which occurs when a person's goals, and means of achieving them, are prescribed for him or her (Marcuse 1970: 12). The 'story' is about the way myth and enlightenment can turn into each other. Myths can be seen as early attempts to understand and control nature; although they were dismissed by Enlightenment thinkers as forms of superstition, they already contained elements of enlightenment in the broadest sense of the attempt to understand reality. In a world dominated by myth, however, human beings are still dominated by the nature they struggle to understand.

The Enlightenment splits humans from nature and puts them into the dominant place: we adopt an instrumental attitude to nature, seeing our task as classifying, measuring, explaining and using it for our own purposes. In this context knowledge is a tool of power – an insight at the centre of Nietzsche's philosophy and taken up by some contemporary post-modernists and post-structuralists (see Chapter 10). For Adorno and Horkheimer too, the domination of nature produces a technology which dominates human beings. The moral impulse of the Enlightenment – the emancipation of humanity from domination – is lost, and the Enlightenment sciences become another form of domination – a myth. One might say that the notion of God is replaced by the equally irrational notion of a triumphant science.

If the social sciences align themselves with the methods of the natural sciences, as many do, then they distort and misunderstand the reality they study. They isolate objects of study from the dynamics of history, and they remain ignorant and uncritical of their own thought processes.

Ideology

It is here that we meet for the first time in this book a theory of ideology, a notion which seems to have all but disappeared from contemporary social science with its emphasis on language and discourse and the assertion or implication that the way in which people see the world *is* the world. This idea is present in the varieties of instrumental rationality that we studied in Chapter 5 and the conception of rationality as rule-following and hermeneutics we looked at in Chapter 6. All these approaches recognize that people can be wrong in their perceptions and conceptions of the social world but not that they can be systematically mistaken or misled by the type of society in which they live.

Although 'ideology' was originally used to refer to a possible 'science of ideas', it was taken over by Marx and Marxists and used in various ways. At its simplest, it is used to mean a set of ideas which serve the interests of a particular social class. In the Hegelian tradition, developed through the work of Georg Lukács (Lukács 1971), the notion of totality and a 'second nature' is central. In the first volume of his *Capital* (Marx 1970), Marx argues that the market system works to disguise relationships between human beings as relationships between things, commodities, and that human beings themselves come to be seen, and see themselves, as commodities, governed by the workings of the market. The attempt to use the methods of the natural sciences in the social sciences reproduces this, also treating people and relationships as things. These things are isolated for analysis and seen as static and one-dimensional. They are separated from the dynamic totality of historical development. The separation of the social sciences from each other is part of this: rather as the chemist might break down and analyse a compound substance into its various parts, so the social sciences break down human beings and human relationships into supposed component parts and study those parts in isolation from each other – sociology, psychology, economics, history all develop along their separate paths, searching for their own laws, or at least their own forms of knowledge. In this way society itself takes on the status of an object as unchangeable as nature – it becomes a 'second nature' (Lukács 1971).

This process of analytic study might very well be important for the social sciences, but it remains ideological as long as we do not situate our study in the wider context. For example, to study male psychology or female psychology as if it were fixed and unchanging and unconnected with changes at all levels in the wider society is 'ideological', blind to a wider reality which thus remains beyond understanding and criticism. Similarly, when sociologists study the emotions simply in terms of the social rules about showing emotion, their work is ideological since it excludes understanding that comes through biology, different types of psychology and history.

But this is only one dimension of ideology; Adorno developed a radical critique of what he called the culture industry (Adorno 1967), and after the Second World War Marcuse developed a theory of one-dimensionality (Marcuse 1964). The ideal underlying these critiques is of an autonomous individual able to make more or less rational decisions of his or her own, able to analyse and criticize the different ideological discourses imposed upon him or her and able also to stand out against the group or the crowd, thinking for him- or herself and arguing with others. The implication is that such a figure can provide the basis for a real and open democratic system. The possibility of developing such abilities was undermined not just by systems of ideas but also by the cultural forms of modern capitalism. Art and music had become ways of lulling the senses and producing a feeling of ease rather than challenging people to think. Mozart was played to Jews as they were marched to the gas chambers, and Beethoven is played to cows to increase their milk yield.

Adorno, himself a major musical scholar as well as a philosopher and social theorist, was a champion of Schoenberg and twelve-tone music: it is impossible to listen to this with a sense of ease. The development of commercial radio stations playing brief extracts of beautiful music but never a whole symphony or concerto would have been the logical culmination of this process as far as he was concerned.

For Marcuse it was the development of consumer-based capitalism that produced 'one dimensionality' (Marcuse 1964), producing a false contentment and directing peoples' energies and ambitions into objects rather than relationships, binding them into the system by manipulating their desires. Frankfurt writers were among the first to try to hitch social theory to psychoanalysis in order to understand the ideological workings of society, particularly the way in which the working classes came to support Hitler in Nazi Germany (Adorno *et al.* 1950) and the way in which people could be enslaved to consumer goods in late capitalism (Marcuse 1966). The details of their social theory are less important for our present purposes than the way in which they develop the notion of rationality as part of an ongoing, and in fact never-ending, dialectical process. Too great an emphasis on one side of the thinking process, for example, the analytic method of the natural sciences, produces the myth of science and the very real result of fragmented knowledge. On the other hand, too much emphasis on the totalizing process of dialectical thought aligns thinking with the totalitarian dynamics of modern and late capitalism. In *Minima Moralia* (Adorno 1974) Adorno suggests that now the whole is the source of untruth, and that truth can only be found in individual suffering.

Rationality becomes in this view more than anywhere else a form of oppositional thinking, a constant process of criticism which produces a scepticism similar to that inherent in modern scientific practice – so that everything must be questioned – but in which that questioning is a process which must go beyond the immediate sense data with which the sciences are concerned. Thinking must criticize the process of thinking itself; the ability of a society to allow this sort of constant self-reflection, and to enable as many people as possible to achieve it, is one criterion by which we can judge that society. Rationality is thus at the centre of concerns about individual autonomy and political theory.

Towards the end of their lives, Adorno and Horkheimer became increasingly pessimistic about the possibilities of political change and the establishment of a full democracy. They opposed the radical student movement of 1968 on the grounds that the activism espoused by the students made critical and reflective thinking even more difficult. It was partly as a reaction to this pessimism that Habermas, a student of Adorno, developed his ideas.

Habermas: The Possibility of an Emancipatory Science

The work of Adorno and Horkheimer tended towards sweeping generalizations, a matter of thinking about thinking at its grandest level, and they tended to think themselves into a pervasive pessimism. There are moments in Adorno's work where he seems to believe that all thinking leads us into the totalizing system of modern capitalism yet to reject thinking achieves the same result, and there is no consolation to be found in beauty – after Auschwitz, even the blossom of the cherry tree must be regarded with suspicion; we cannot allow ourselves to enjoy it.

In comparison, Habermas is a sober and very careful, if often obtuse, thinker about the nature of society, science, social science and philosophy. There are two ideas of his which are particularly useful contributions to the debates considered in this book. The first is to be found in *Knowledge and Human Interests* (Habermas 1972) where he suggests a way of looking at the human sciences which brings together all the approaches we have considered so far. He does this not at the level of methodology, with which the positivists are primarily concerned, nor by distinguishing between the different objects of the social sciences – the concern, as we will see later, of contemporary realists. Rather, he organizes them according to their relationship to what he calls 'human interests'. He suggests a sophisticated pragmatism.

These ideas come from the earlier part of Habermas's work and have been modified, particularly as he has moved away from the Hegelian background of critical theory. Nonetheless, they are worth holding onto simply because they do bring together very different ideas of science and relate them to an overall human project of gaining understanding and knowledge in order to improve human life. He suggests that our scientific enterprises are rooted in and guided by different cognitive interests which we possess by virtue of being human. A defining feature of individual human beings, and of societies, is that they learn from their activities. They learn on different levels at different rates, and he develops a complex model of social evolution based on ideas taken from developmental psychology.

Habermas's critique of Marxism develops that of the earlier Frankfurt theorists – that Marxism concerns itself only with the economic, the instrumental aspects of human existence. Human beings are of course producers, and we have a *technical* interest in controlling and manipulating the objects around us. This gives rise to the natural sciences and the technologies that grow out of them and to those aspects of the social sciences that are most like the natural sciences; it also provides a place for at least some of the ideas of positivism.

There is also a *practical* interest, says Habermas, in being able to communicate with others – this enables cooperation to the mutual benefit of everybody and this gives rise to the hermeneutic sciences, the sciences of understanding. And there is a third interest, a reflexive interest that we have in understanding ourselves and our ways of thinking about the world which provides us with the possibility of autonomy as well as the possibility of reflexively understanding the existence of these interests. This is the *emancipatory* interest and takes us back to critical theory. To achieve autonomy we need to know about the objects in our world, we need to be able to understand the people around us, and we need to be able to understand what we ourselves are doing.

Habermas's example of an emancipatory science is psychoanalysis, which works on all three levels. First, it gathers information about our bodies and the way our bodies, through our sexuality for example, limit the things we are capable of. This is working at the level of the technical interest. Second, it is concerned with the meaning we give to the world and the way we communicate with others – it is a hermeneutics. And finally, it attempts to free us from distorted communication, our failure to understand and communicate that stems from our own hangups, our neuroses.

The above is of course an oversimplification of what Habermas is saying, but it should be sufficient to get across the general idea. It is important for two reasons. First, it takes us to two central arguments in this book: that there are different types and levels of scientific activity beyond the straightforward distinction between the human and the natural sciences, and that these can coexist with each other. Second, it is our first explicit encounter with a philosophical anthropology – a theory of human nature. Although philosophers still argue about these things, social scientists do not show a lot of concern about the issues when perhaps they should. Any social scientist carrying out research actually presupposes something about human nature, however limited and scientifically 'objective' the study. Rational choice theory seems to assume that human beings are rational actors, pragmatism that people have purposes, while Weber and hermeneutics assume that people are meaning-creating animals. These assumptions may not be very sophisticated but they are always there whatever we do, and for Habermas part of the work of critical theory is to elaborate and refine such assumptions.

In this sense Habermas can be seen as developing and criticizing the philosophical anthropology of Marx for whom human beings were primarily collective producers, forever transforming their environment and therefore transforming themselves. We can also find the communicative and emancipatory interests in Marx's work, but they are implicit, not developed as concepts. All critical theorists would argue that it is the centrality of instrumental reason in the development of Marxism which encouraged the development of Stalinist tyranny.

Critical Theory and the Linguistic Turn

Whereas perhaps Adorno abandoned his Marxist origins, Habermas tries to revise Marxism to rule out the possibility of it being dominated by the technical interest, by instrumental reason. He too moves to the philosophy of language, but not in the way that Winch and others do, to assert a relativism and an idealism, and argue that reality is created in and by language. As stated earlier, Habermas sees social reality as multi-layered and complex, evolving on a number of different levels, and he certainly sees it as having a real existence outside language. Rather he takes language as the basis for critical theory; it becomes a model for democracy. He talks of an 'ideal speech situation'. We are all speaking animals, and if we are to use that capacity to its full, we must all participate equally in public debates about political and social life. To do so we must have equal access to relevant information and we must have equal access to the debate and equal rights to be heard. It is again possible to develop an ideal standard against which to measure existing forms of society. This idea was already in embryonic form in *Knowledge and Human Interests* (1978) but was developed systematically in the two-volume *Theory of Communicative Action* (Habermas 1984, 1987).

Habermas's work in this area is very complex, and all that we can hope to do here is outline the main positions which he develops and changes throughout his as-yet-unfinished career. There are four points which are important in this context.

The first point is that with the exception of Gadamer all the philosophers we have discussed under the heading of 'interpretive' have concentrated on the meaning that individuals give to their actions, an approach Habermas calls the 'philosophy of consciousness'. Such a view point sees meaning and action in terms of a relationship between a subject acting on an object and this, Habermas argues, means that we are inevitably caught up in instrumental action and instrumental reason. In this context, critical theory is doomed to the sort of pessimism which claimed Adorno. His turn to linguistics is meant to avoid this.

Drawing on linguistic philosophy, Habermas adopts a distinction between 'performative speech acts' and 'communicative speech acts'. The former involve instrumental, purposive or strategic action. The latter involve an attempt to communicate with and understand the other, or to make oneself understood, and they are by definition open to revision: they are based on reasons and can be assented to or argued against by reference to other reasons, and the very possibility of argument implies that consensus may be reached. We move from the individual trying to achieve his or her ends through language (instrumental reason) to individuals participating in the play of reasons – or perhaps better, the play of reason in which the speaking subjects are, as they are for Gadamer, comparatively inessential in the overall development of knowledge.

This takes us on to the second point, Habermas's 'universal pragmatics'. The pragmatism discussed in Chapter 5 took the (instrumental) position that what works is right. Habermas's pragmatism asserts that what can be agreed upon is right. All areas of human endeavour, whether we are talking about science or ethics or aesthetics or anything else, is mediated through communicative rationality; all arguments can in principle achieve consensus. We have in this a consensus theory of ethics – we can argue about what is good until we agree; and a consensus theory of knowledge of the outside world – we can argue about what exists until we agree. This offers a way out of relativism, based on the nature of language and thinking itself.

This takes us to the third point, and a debate between Habermas and Gadamer, and (by implication) Winch and Weber. For all these three latter thinkers, the culture, the form of life, the tradition, or whatever we like to call it, defines what is true, and what exists, and different traditions define different realities. Habermas argues that the process of thinking itself challenges this. It holds open the possibility of an understanding that includes everybody. Different forms of life can, therefore, be mistaken or corrected through argument, a position very similar to that of Charles Taylor, discussed in Chapter 6. The other side of this coin is the possibility of 'systematically distorted communication' – either on the personal level, where psychoanalysis shows that our neuroses can lead us to be systematically mistaken about the world, or on a social level, where differences in power can lead to the same result. There are therefore limits to the straightforward hermeneutic approach. We need a 'hermeneutics of suspicion' – a critical hermeneutics.

Fourth and finally, Habermas develops a different analysis of instrumental rationality as opposed to communicative rationality. The latter belongs to the life-world – a notion we met first in the discussion of phenomenology but which Habermas uses more in the sense of a level of open communication between people. The former becomes functional rationality, the rationality of the system, the rationality which enables it to keep functioning and which constantly threatens the life world, imposing itself upon us through the demands of our social roles or positions. One near-to-home example of this conflict is to be found in the modern British university system. The communicative rationality developing from the research interests and concerns of academics might lead in one direction (for example towards long-term, carefully thought out and argued projects with no immediate relevance), but the requirements of government-imposed surveillance in the form of research assessments and competitive ratings (the functional rationality of the system) push towards short-term, easily written-up research.

Conclusion

To try to summarize this chapter: we have discussed the notion of the rational as a critical standard, as a form of permanent criticism, of permanent dialogue, and as a way to developing a consensus on truth and morality. Once again these views are not an alternative to those discussed in the previous chapters, but they work on a different level and approach different questions – or perhaps more accurately approach the same questions but from a different angle, highlighting in particular questions of domination, ideology and communication in our judgements about the world. Such judgements were in the background in the discussions in Chapter 5, and were put into question in Chapter 6 and received complex answers in this chapter. The process of rational thinking is seen as part and parcel of freeing ourselves from all sorts of domination, but we also run the risk of rational thinking itself dominating. Hence Adorno's movement towards a permanent insistence on the importance of the negative.

For Habermas, the negative is not so important, and he has been accused of wanting the world to be like a seminar. One response is that a seminar is preferable to a concentration camp, but in his social theory and in his interpretation of psychoanalysis Habermas can be criticized for an over-rational view of humans and society. He loses the insight present in the work of the earlier Frankfurt thinkers that irrationality – the mythical – can also be a form of liberation, and underestimates Freud's insistence on the power of the irrational.

Overall in these three chapters we have moved from a focus on the rational as a way of understanding individual actions in the world to a way of understanding and analysing different cultures, and then on to a way of making critical judgements about the nature of the social and comparing ethical systems in the world. People working at one end of this movement – say, the cognitive psychologist, the social psychologist, the Weberian sociologist or the marginalist economist – would be likely to be bemused by Adorno or Habermas, yet the philosophical assumptions of the practising social scientist lead back to the wider issues of hermeneutics and critical theory.

We find in Habermas's work the integration of a hermeneutic and a structuralist approach, although in the end he seems to come down on the former side of the divide. In the following chapter we will be looking at an approach which tries to combine both. But what we would want to keep from Habermas is the importance of argument, even if agreement always remains on the horizon. In the context of this book, the important arguments are between and within the different conceptions of science and their philosophical foundations.

Further Reading

The best introduction to dialectical thought (although it might be difficult to find) is Henri Lefebvre's *Dialectical Materialism* (Lefebvre 1968), and perhaps all students should attempt to read Hegel's preface to the *Phenomenology of the Spirit* (Hegel 1807, 1977). There is no easy reading on critical theory, but the best overall account is David Held's *Introduction to Critical Theory* (1980); of the original texts we would suggest Adorno's *Prisms and Minima Moralia* (Adorno 1967 and 1974 respectively) and Horkheimer's *Critical Theory* (Horkheimer 1972); it is worth attempting Habermas's *Knowledge and Human Interests* (1986). William Outhwaite's *Habermas: A Critical Introduction* provides an excellent entry to his work.

Post-script

Central to the tradition of critical theory has been a concept of universally valid rational principles for making and justifying knowledge-claims as well as for organizing human social life. Jürgen Habermas is acknowledged as the most significant thinker in this tradition today. For a more extended discussion of his ideas than was possible in our book, see, for example, White (1988).

Recent intellectual fashion has turned against the prospect of universally valid rational principles that might provide a basis for criticism and even transformation of social life. However, one major thinker who has risen to the challenge of re-working the heritage of critical theory as a resource for emancipatory knowledge and practice in the twenty-first century is Axel Honneth. His vision is one of emancipation as cooperative self-realisation through mutual recognition. This possibility for human society, and the way the estrangements, instrumental rationality and relations of domination of capitalist society obstruct its realization, still provides an appropriate framework for theoretical and empirical work in sociology and psychoanalysis (see especially Honneth 1996, 2009).

The work of Honneth, Habermas and others influenced by critical theory is included and commented upon in a number of collections, including White (1995); Freundlieb *et al.* (2004) and Rundell *et al.* (2005).

8

Critical Realism and the Social Sciences

Introduction

Most debate in the philosophy of social science still works on the assumption that there are two basic options: positivism or some form of interpretivism. However, as we have seen (Chapter 4), there are alternative, non-empiricist views of the natural sciences, and there are also significant limitations to even a critical form of interpretivism, such as that offered by Habermas. In this chapter we will be exploring some of the ways of thinking about the social sciences made possible by an account of the natural sciences which is anti-positivist, but still 'realist'.

Although the implications of this 'critical realist' approach for the conduct of the human sciences remain controversial, it has proved very fruitful in stimulating new research agenda in a number of human sciences and interdisciplinary fields. The approach was pioneered by a number of writers in the UK during the 1970s. Rom Harré's realist philosophy of the natural sciences was influential (Harré 1970, 1972, 1986; Harré and Madden 1975), as was the work of Mary Hesse on models and metaphors in scientific thinking (Hesse 1966). Roy Bhaskar's *Realist Theory of Science* first appeared in 1975, while attempts to develop new ways of understanding the social sciences in realist terms included Russell Keat (1971), Keat and John Urry (1975), Ted Benton (1977) and Roy Bhaskar (1979, 1998). The work of Roy Bhaskar has provided the most systematically developed and influential version of the approach, especially in its account of the natural sciences. The implications of this for the social sciences are subject to more disagreement among critical realists, and we will attempt to convey something of the issues which remain unresolved. However, Bhaskar's more recent development of an ambitious 'dialectical' philosophy and engagement with eastern philosophies take us beyond the scope of this introductory book.

So, what is 'realism', and what is 'critical' about this version of it? In non-technical contexts of everyday life people often claim to be 'realistic', commonly meaning that they don't have very high expectations of themselves, or of some activity they are about to engage in. The word often expresses a resigned and world-weary acceptance that the way things are can't be expected to live up to our hopes and desires. (Something of this was evident in the shift to an approach called 'New Realism' in the UK trade union movement. This followed massive defeats in the 1980s, and signalled a new attitude of collaboration and compromise with the employers.) However, the term also comes into play in some art-forms – the novel, painting, sculpture, and drama especially. Here, realism often signals a contrast with fantasy, escapism, imagination, or generally non-representational forms of expression. In these contexts, adopting a 'realist' mode of expression may be motivated by quite the opposite of resigned acceptance. The school of British Victorian painters known as the 'Social Realists', for example, used detailed representational forms to bring home to the middle classes the suffering associated with poverty, unemployment, and ill-health among the working classes of the period.

Critical realism takes something from both these uses of the term 'realism', but it also differs from them in important ways. It takes from the 'resigned acceptance' usage the latter's clear recognition of the existence of an external world, independent of, and often defying, our desires of it and attempts to understand and change it. However, as the adjective 'critical' might suggest, critical realists tend to share the social realists' commitment to *changing* unsatisfactory or oppressive realities. In this respect, at least, they inherit the Enlightenment's optimistic view of the role of knowledge in human self-emancipation.

So, realists in the theory of knowledge are committed to the existence of a real world, which exists and acts independently of our knowledge or beliefs about it. However, they hold that this external world is in principle knowable, and to some (discoverable) extent open to being changed on the basis of such knowledge as we are able to achieve. Sometimes this view is caricatured by its opponents as claiming an absolutely certain, one-to-one correspondence between existing belief and the supposed reality of which it is the knowledge. It seems unlikely that there are, in fact, any 'realists' of whom this is true, but it certainly does *not* apply to critical realists.

There are four features of critical realism which distinguish it from this caricature. First, critical realism holds that we can make sense of cognitive practices such as the sciences only on the assumption that they are *about* something which exists independently. It does not pronounce on whether the truth claims of any *particular* science at any *particular* time are true – only the science concerned can make and evaluate such claims. Second, critical realism shares with most contemporary philosophy a *reflexivity* about the conditions of possibility for thought, or language, to represent something outside itself: as we will see, critical realism differs from empiricism in theorizing knowledge as a social process which involves variable 'means of representation'. Third, critical realism differs from some other forms of realism in regarding the surface appearance of things as potentially misleading as to their true character. This is why knowledge has to be a process and an 'achievement': work has to be done to get beyond or behind misleading appearances. This is why it is sometimes called a 'depth' realism, as distinct from the 'empirical' realism of the empiricists. Finally, and most importantly, critical realist insistence on the independent reality of the objects of our knowledge, and the necessity of work to overcome misleading appearances, implies that current beliefs will always be open to correction in the light of further cognitive work (observations, experimental evidence, interpretations, theoretical reasoning, dialogue and so on). Critical realism is thus 'fallibilist', in contrast to idealist and relativist theories of knowledge which insulate themselves from the possibility of being proved wrong by doing away with the idea of a knowable independent reality.

We will begin by giving an account of the critical realist view of natural science, focusing in particular on the version pioneered by Roy Bhaskar. Then we will consider to what extent that view of natural science might provide a model for a 'scientific' but non-positivist approach to the social sciences.

Realism and Natural Science

Observable Phenomena, Metaphors and Mechanisms

In Chapters 2 and 3 we noticed the problem faced by empiricism in accounting for the apparently important role played in scientific theory by reference to whole classes of entities and processes of which we would otherwise be completely unaware: atoms, molecules, subatomic particles, fields of force, viruses, genes, quasars, black holes and so on. Modern science not only tells us of the existence of this unsuspected 'deep' structure in the world, but it also uses this to explain those aspects of the world which we do experience and acknowledge – such as the changes in the properties of foods when we cook them, the symptoms of illnesses we have, the similarities between parents and children and so on.

Strict versions of empiricism have difficulty in accepting this as the core of scientific knowledge, since so many of these theoretical entities are not accessible to direct observation. However, realists argue that the great intellectual achievement of science is to have discovered that the world is so much more complex in its structure than common-sense understanding could have imagined. The task of philosophy of science is to try to understand the forms of investigation and reasoning that enabled scientists to do this. Philosophers such as Rom Harré and Mary Hesse emphasized the role of analogy and metaphor in scientific theory-building. The synthesis of proteins by the molecules of DNA is likened to the interpretation of a sign system, when biologists speak of the genetic code. The concept of an electric current contains an analogy with the flow of a liquid, and Darwin's concept of natural selection contains an analogy with the selective breeding of domesticated animals and plants.

We can think of theory-building through the use of metaphors as a three-stage process. First, there is the collection of evidence about patterns of observable phenomena. Second, the question is asked, 'What underlying structure or mechanism would, if it existed, explain this pattern?' It is here that the creative use of metaphorical thinking comes in. 'If nature worked on wild animals and plants as domestic breeders do, then the observed patterns of organic diversity would follow.' 'If electrons flowed along a conductor in the way water flows along a river, then the observed patterns of electrical charge, resistance, magnetic attraction, and so on would follow.' And so on. The logic of this phase is sometimes, following N. R. Hanson, referred to as 'retroduction'. The third phase in the process is to conduct further experiments and observations on the hypothetical assumption that the mechanism attributed on the basis of the metaphor really does exist.

This does not, of course, settle the issue of when scientists are justified in moving from the tentative use of a metaphor to the claim that the hypothesized mechanism really does exist. It is important at this stage, however, to recognize that there is a difference between (a) being able to prove the existence of some particular class of entities or mechanisms claimed by science and (b) being able to justify the realist account of science as an attempt to discover and study such mechanisms. Realist theories of science are attempts to do (b) not (a). However, the historical evidence of the simultaneous discovery of mechanisms by independent groups of scientists (for example, the independent invention of the concept of natural selection to explain the formation of new species by Charles Darwin and Alfred Russel Wallace), and the various ways in which different sciences converge around common beliefs about underlying mechanisms (for example, the theory that matter is made up of atoms, and that these combine in various ways to form molecules, is the basic ontology of physics, chemistry and modern biology) are hard to explain unless we assume that there really are independently existing things and processes which are more or less adequately grasped through the theories which scientists invent. However, critical realism offers apparently much stronger philosophical arguments for this view of the nature of science. These are called 'transcendental arguments' (see pp. 57–8), and their use is central to the view of science proposed by Roy Bhaskar.

Transcendental Arguments

These arguments begin with what is taken to be an uncontroversial description of some phenomenon, p. The question is then asked, 'What must be the case for p to be possible?' Let us suppose that some condition, or state of affairs, c, can be identified as a necessary condition for p. Since we have already accepted that p is *actual*, then it must be possible, and so the conditions which make it possible must be satisfied. So, c must be the case. An example from social life might be: 'Jane is a student.' For anyone to be a student there must be teachers, bodies of knowledge to be taught and learned, educational institutions to define the roles of teacher and student and so on. Since Jane is a student, the necessary conditions of possibility for someone to be a student must be satisfied, and so, for example, we can conclude that educational institutions exist. Another well-used example is: 'Jay cashed a cheque.' For anyone to be able to cash a cheque there must be a banking system, a money economy and so on. So, we can conclude that there is a money economy. In these rather obvious cases, the transcendental argument has conclusions which are not very surprising or interesting. However, in Roy Bhaskar's realist theory of natural science, arguments of this type have led to some very interesting and important conclusions.

Science: Transitive and Intransitive Dimensions

Bhaskar constructs transcendental arguments on the basis of (presumably) uncontroversial descriptions of scientific practices such as experimentation, scientific disputes and the application of scientific knowledge in technology. If we ask the question, 'What must be the case for (for example) scientific experiments to be possible?', the answers fall into two groups. These will be, on the one hand, statements about what the world must be like for experiments to be possible, and, on the other, statements about what scientific investigators must be like for them to be able to conduct experiments. Bhaskar uses the term 'intransitive dimension' to characterize the referents of the first set of statements, and the term 'transitive dimension' for the second. For the moment, we will focus on the intransitive dimension – what must *the world* be like in order for distinctively scientific practices such as experiments to be possible? (Note: it is arguable that the same form of reasoning could be applied to any other human social practice, with comparable results.)

Experiments, Laws and Mechanisms

The empiricist view of scientific laws as general statements about regular patterns of observable events has already (in Chapter 3) been shown to be open to a number of serious criticisms. The starting-point for the critical realist argument is to note that such regular series of observable events are rather rare in nature. One of the very few such regular sequences is the movements of the planets in the solar system. This gives us the regular patterns of night and day, the seasons and so on. However, if we consider, for example, the weather, then on a day-to-day basis, prediction is notoriously difficult and unreliable, even when meteorology is a well-resourced and established science. This is because the actual sequence of climatic conditions in any particular place is the outcome of the interplay of many different factors (pressure gradients, air movements, electrical potentials, temperatures at different altitudes, humidity levels and so on).

In Bhaskar's account, scientific experiment is a practical intervention which seeks to isolate just one mechanism, so that its operation can be studied without the interference of its interactions with other mechanisms. To go back to our earlier example of the simultaneous emergence of dragonflies (see pp. 19ff.) one might want to know whether it was caused by day length, by temperature, or by some form of communication across the population. This could be tested experimentally by taking some dragonfly larvae into a labora-tory where they could be isolated from one another but subjected to exactly the same conditions of temperature and light/dark sequences. Each of the other conditions could then be artificially controlled in turn, and the effects on emergence studied. Bhaskar's argument is that when a single mechanism is isolated in this way, regular event sequences can be 'triggered'. But since these have been produced by the scientific investigators, and it would be absurd to say that the laws of nature are produced by the actions of the experimenters, it follows that the laws of nature must be something else, something independ-ent of the event sequences which are artificially produced in the experiment.

In Bhaskar's account, the laws discovered by experiments are 'tendencies' of the underlying mechanisms, which may or may not issue in regular and observ-able event sequences when the mechanism is interacting with other mech-anisms outside the artificial experimental situation. So, for example, further research might show that the underlying mechanism in the dragonfly case is the secretion of a particular hormone in response to a given temperature threshold. However, the action of this hormone might be affected by other physiological mechanisms linked to maturational stage, light-exposure, contact with other individuals of the same or other species and so on, such that in nature the temperature threshold often may not trigger emergence.

This account of laws as tendencies of mechanisms, as disclosed by scientific experiments, is the key 'realist' conclusion from the analysis of experimen-tation. Experimentation as a practice would be unintelligible if the mechanisms and their tendencies under investigation did not exist independently of the activities and beliefs of the experimenters.

Reality as Stratified

But Bhaskar argues that we can conclude more than this. Something about the basic structure of the intransitive dimension can be inferred from the analysis of the conditions of possibility of experiment. This analysis implies three levels of reality:

a. the 'real' world of mechanisms, powers, tendencies and so on, which science seeks to discover;

b. the 'actual' level of flows, or sequences of events, which may be produced under experimental conditions, or occur in more complex and less predictable 'conjunctures' outside the laboratory;

c. the 'empirical' level of observed events, which must necessarily be only a small subset of b.

A strict empiricism can recognize only level-c phenomena as real. A more relaxed empiricism may recognize the existence of unexperienced, but still *experienceable*, events (level b) as real. Bhaskar calls such a position 'actualism'. But the distinctive feature of transcendental – 'critical' – realism is its claim to demonstrate the independent reality of the third, 'real' level of mechanisms, their powers and tendencies (level a). This third level can be inferred from the intelligibility of experimental practice as such, and it is also, of course, what makes experiments necessary. Were there nothing but the flow of experienceable events, there would be nothing for experiments to discover, and knowledge would be merely a matter of observing and summarizing. Remember, however, that the analysis of experimentation shows only that there *must be* underlying causal mechanisms and powers. It does not tell us anything about what they are. That is a matter for substantive research in each scientific discipline.

So, the claim made by critical realism is that there is a reality independent of our scientific investigation of it, but also that this reality is stratified, or layered. The key levels identified in Bhaskar's philosophical ontology are, as we saw, the real, the actual and the empirical. Of course, Bhaskar accepts that each of these levels is real, so there is some terminological confusion, with the word 'real' also being used to denote one level of reality. The metaphor of levels implies that critical realism is a form of 'depth' realism, such that scientific investigation attempts to penetrate behind or below the surface appearances of things to uncover their generative causes.

Stratification, Emergence and Reduction

The idea of reality as layered, or stratified, can be taken further. Once a science has discovered mechanisms which constitute the level, or aspect of reality, which it has as its subject-matter, it is then possible to ask what deeper-level mechanisms are responsible for those, and so on. So, for example, physiological mechanisms explain many of the characteristic activities of animals and plants – metabolism, reproduction, respiration and so on. But these physiological mechanisms can themselves be explained in terms of the chemistry of the complex organic molecules of which living organisms are composed. There is no obvious stopping-point to this process of probing evermore deeply into the microstructure of the natural world. To the extent that the different scientific disciplines are each concerned with a particular level of reality, they, too, can be ordered into a hierarchy of levels. So, we might put the sciences into an ordering something like this:

social sciences
psychology
physiology/anatomy
organic chemistry/biological chemistry
physical chemistry
physics

This way of ordering the sciences could be justified in terms of the way the mechanisms characteristic of each level are explicable in terms of those of the next one below it. This corresponds to a view of science as explaining wholes in terms of the parts of which they are composed. It will be noticed that several sciences don't seem to fit into this hierarchy at all. These include ecology, geography, meteorology, oceanography, palaeontology and so on, and we will consider them in the next section.

Although the general idea of sciences uncovering layers of a stratified reality is quite widely shared, there remain many issues which divide critical realists among themselves, and also divide them from other realist approaches. There is space here to deal with only two of these issues. One has to do with the way we think about the relationship between levels. If the mechanisms of one level are held to explain those at a higher level, then it might seem that as soon as the lower-level science has been established it can replace the higher-level one: that physiology becomes redundant when biochemistry is developed, for example. This, in some versions, leads to the view that ultimately all sciences will be reduced to the basic laws of physics (see the sections on theoretical entities and the hypothetico-deductive account of theories in Chapter 3). Much more influential versions are concerned with the explanation of human mental and social life in terms of physiology, genetics or natural selection.

Such 'reductionist' interpretations of the layering of reality are opposed by critical realism. There are three main reasons why reductionism does not work. First, the lower-level science explains (at best) only the constitution of the *mechanisms* at the higher level. It does not explain when or with what effects the powers established with those mechanisms will be *excercised*. So, for example, having the right anatomy and physiology (hearing, vocal organs, appropriately constructed cerebral cortex and so on) may explain why humans have the power of speech (which, for example, closely related primates do not), but it does not explain when and how any particular human will learn to speak, which language she will learn, or what she will say.

Second, once higher-level mechanisms are formed, their activities have effects on lower-level ones. For example, an emotional trauma can have effects on the interactions of the central nervous and endocrine systems, so altering the rate of the chemical reactions involved in respiration, the rate of blood supply to muscles, and triggering anaerobic chemical reactions at the level of cells and tissues. So, causality can flow down the hierarchy as well as up it. It follows (on the critical realist equation of 'being real' with 'having effects') that the mechanisms constituted at each level have their own specific reality. It also follows that the sciences of the lower-level mechanisms can *contribute* to explaining, but never *completely* explain, the behaviour of the higher-level mechanisms.

Finally, the association between levels and particular sciences is in part explained by the way entities at higher levels have properties and powers not predictable in advance on the basis of properties of lower-level entities. The macromolecules we call genes play a part in explaining the characteristics of the living organisms in whose cells they reside, but unless we had first encountered living organisms (including ourselves) we would have no idea what properties of living things were explicable in terms of them. Again, it is reasonable to believe that human consciousness depends on a certain level of complexity in the organization and functioning of the brain and central nervous system, but 'consciousness' could not have been predicted from even the most sophisticated neurophysiology unless we first knew what it was to be conscious. Indeed, since all knowledge depends on the activities of conscious beings, this higher level has to be presupposed in the discovery of the lower and more fundamental levels. As we saw in Chapter 3, the formation of qualitatively new properties or powers at each level of organization is termed 'emergence', and critical realists are often committed to some form of 'emergent powers materialism'.

The second area of controversy among realists concerning the relationships between different levels focuses on the higher levels. In particular, it concerns the relationship between the human biological, the psychological and the social, and so we will return to it in a later section of this chapter. For now, it should be noted that the hierarchy of sciences listed above puts the social at the top, the psychological below it and the biological below them. This reflects the common-sense view that bodily organization and functioning is the basis of psychological mechanisms, and that society is formed by the conscious actions of individual people.

However, it can be argued against this that at least some psychological mechanisms (for example, whatever mechanisms enable us to form sentences according to the grammatical rules of our own language) can only be explained in terms of social processes (in this case, the learning of our own language). This is the sort of argument that a follower of Durkheim or Saussure might advance. On that basis, psychology should be above sociology in the hierarchy of the sciences, since we explain psychological processes in terms of social ones. Society is not created by the conscious decisions of individual people, but pre-exists them and moulds their mental life.

Equally, however, it seems clear that unless human beings had certain innate psychological capacities and dispositions (for example, to learn *some* language) it would not be possible for society to shape them in the way it does. Considerations like this point to a branching hierarchy, in which psychology and the social sciences would figure at the same level, with mutual interdependence of the mechanisms described by each. This would be consistent with contemporary views of human evolution, according to which modern humans and their distinctive patterns of sociability evolved together (for contrasting views on this issue, see New 1994, 1996: ch. 2; Collier 1994: ch. 4).

However, a view of human social life as involving only human individuals, and involving them only in virtue of their mental activities, would be drastically impoverished. Central features of human societies, the way they organize production of food, clothing and shelter, the relationships through which they regulate sexuality, reproduction and child-rearing, and so on, are all unintelligible unless we understand humans as embodied beings, with organic-functional needs and vulnerabilities. So, we are essentially social beings through our embodiment, not just our mental lives. But in noting this we are also committed to an understanding of the relationships which constitute society as binding embodied humans to other living and non-living beings: to physical spaces, raw materials, tools and machines, domesticated and wild animals and plants, agricultural and semi-natural ecosystems, buildings, highways and so on. All of these things and relationships are produced, reproduced or transformed as elements in the overall metabolism of society. It follows that society cannot reasonably be represented as a single level in the hierarchy. Rather, it is a heterogeneous complex of mechanisms and processes constituted by the combination of mechanisms drawn from several of the other levels: psychological, physiological/anatomical, ecological, chemical and so on. We will return to this view of the nature of social life later in this chapter.

Reality as Differentiated: Closed and Open Systems

For the moment, we have to consider yet another feature of the world which is disclosed by the possibility (and necessity) of scientific experiment, and also the application of science in technology. If it is necessary to design experimental conditions under which mechanisms can be isolated in order to study their powers, tendencies and so on, then this is because most mechanisms most of the time do not exist under such conditions. The constantly shifting patterns of (especially British!) weather are the outcome of complex interactions between many different mechanisms. It is similar with historical processes such as the origin of a new species, or the formation of modern capitalism. These cannot plausibly be explained as the outcome of a single underlying causal mechanism. In these cases it is hard to see how the various interacting causal mechanisms could be isolated experimentally, and this poses serious problems for the scientific status of the disciplines (such as meteorology, geography, evolutionary biology and most of the human sciences) which take them as their subject-matter. We will return to this question later in the chapter.

However, in other cases, such as the extraction of pure samples of chemical elements from the mixtures and compounds in which they generally exist in nature, or the rearing of organisms under artificially controlled conditions, experiment is a practical possibility. Where mechanisms coexist and interact with one another in contingent ways, Bhaskar speaks of 'open' systems. Where mechanisms naturally exist in isolation (or there is a balance of interfering mechanisms), or where there is artificial isolation (or control of interfering mechanisms), Bhaskar speaks of 'closed' systems. Experiments would not be either possible or necessary if all mechanisms naturally occurred in closed systems: the world would be as the empiricist ontology takes it to be. Equally, experiments would not be possible if the artificial creation of closed systems could not be achieved.

When experimental work under controlled conditions discloses the properties and powers of particular materials – for example, that certain plastics are good electrical insulators, or that electric currents generate magnetic fields – then this knowledge can be applied to make instruments like electrical safety devices, electric bells, locks and so on. But this application makes sense only on condition that the causal powers attributed to the materials concerned on the basis of study in closed systems continue to be their properties in open systems. So, both scientific experiment and the application of science presuppose that causal mechanisms can exist and act in either open or closed systems, and that the laws of nature (but not necessarily regular event sequences) apply 'trans-factually' (that is, in both open and closed systems). Bhaskar calls this feature of the 'intransitive dimension', as disclosed by the analysis of experiment and scientific application, its 'differentiation'. The world thus exists *independently* of our beliefs about it, is *differentiated*, and is *stratified*. These are the key claims made by critical realists about what the world must be like if it is to be a possible object of scientific investigation.

The Transitive Dimension

We can now turn to the second set of answers to the question, 'What must be the case for science to be possible?' These concern what the human scientific investigators, their modes of communication and society must be like for science to be possible, and together they constitute what Bhaskar calls the '*transitive*' conditions or dimension of science. Here, critical realism is close to Kuhn, Feyerabend and the sociologists of science, in recognizing (against the empiricist tradition) the social and historical character of science. Science as a social practice presupposes the institutions of scientific communication and criticism, and the role of metaphor in scientific reasoning implies the existence of a culture which can be drawn on for the conceptual 'raw materials' for the production of scientific knowledge. But there is in critical realism also an emphasis on experimental practice. This presupposes humans as embodied agents capable of deliberately intervening in the world, monitoring the consequences of their interventions, as well as entering into critical dialogue about how to interpret those consequences.

The distinctive features of critical realism as a theory of science, then, are:

(i)   it recognizes science as a social practice, and scientific knowledge as a social product;

(ii) it recognizes the independent existence of the objects of scientific knowledge;

(iii) it has an account of scientific experiment and discovery as simultaneously material and social practices in virtue of which both (i) and (ii) are sustained.

By contrast, Kuhn, Feyerabend and constructionist accounts of science fully recognize the social character of science, but have great difficulty in maintaining a coherent account of the independent reality of the objects of scientific knowledge. On the other hand, empiricist accounts of science have little or no room for the social dimension of scientific practice, though neither can they fully sustain the independent reality of the objects of scientific knowledge. At best, they are restricted to a view of reality as a flow of 'surface' events, and science as a summary record of them.

Realism and Social Science

But does this realist account of science have any bearing on the social sciences? Is it any more acceptable as a model for the social sciences than the positivist programme? Here, there is quite a lot of disagreement among realists. Rom Harré (one of the most influential advocates of a realist approach to natural science) is strongly committed to methodological individualism in the social sciences, and denies the reality of social structures. The prominent critical realist Andrew Collier has argued that because experimental closure is impossible in the social sciences, and the use of measurement and quantification is ruled out (Collier 1994: 162), they cannot be sciences in the full sense of the word. Collier coins the term 'epistemoids' to characterize the less-than-scientific social science disciplines (see Collier 1989: ch. 4). By contrast, Benton has argued (1981) that so long as we recognize the diversity among the different natural sciences there is no reason to draw a strong dividing line between natural and social science.

Roy Bhaskar advocates yet another position, which he terms 'critical naturalism' (Bhaskar 1998). This approach accepts the main burden of the interpretivist, or hermeneutic critique of the positivist version of 'naturalism' (that is, in this context, the proposal to study society on the model of the natural sciences). However, he argues that despite, and even *because of*, the fundamental differences between natural and social objects of knowledge, it is still possible to have a science of society in the same *sense* as the sciences of nature, but not necessarily of the same form as them and not employing the same methods.

The sort of knowledge that can be achieved, and the methods for achieving it, will vary according to the subject-matter of a discipline. An implication of realism, then, is that the answer to the question 'Can there be a science of society?' will turn on what sort of thing 'society' is. But how can we answer this without first having a social science to tell us? Benton (1977) dealt with this problem by analysing the explanatory theorizing of representative figures in three rival traditions of social science. In each case he discovered key realist assumptions. All three (Marx, Weber and Durkheim) were committed to the existence of social realities independent of the beliefs held about them by individuals, to the difference between social structures and their forms of appearance and hence to social scientific enquiry as a fallible process of explaining appearances in terms of the social realities which produce them. However, the theories of knowledge in terms of which they reflected upon and justified their explanatory work often obscured or explicitly ruled out some or all of these realist commitments. This was particularly true of Weber, whose self-proclaimed methodological individualism was systematically overridden in his actual explanatory work in sociology. It was argued that each of these research traditions had suffered distortions and contradictions as a result of the influence of inappropriate epistemological precepts (methodological individualist, empiricist, subjective idealist and so on). Realist philosophy could play a useful underlabouring role in offering an epistemology more appropriate to, and capable of defending the legitimacy of, realist moves already made at the level of substantive research practice.

Bhaskar's (1979, 1998) starting-point was one of scepticism about existing strategies in the social sciences. For him, indeed, what has to be established was, precisely, whether a scientific study of society was *possible*. To begin with, existing explanatory work in social science would beg the question at issue (in a way that using this strategy in relation to the natural sciences would not). Bhaskar's approach to the question 'Is society the sort of thing that can be studied scientifically?' is, as before, to rely on transcendental arguments. This time, however, the premises of these arguments are familiar social actions and practices. He begins with what are taken to be uncontroversial descriptions of them and asks what human society and social agency must be like for them to be possible. In turn, the answers to these questions 'give' him a social ontology, on the basis of which he can consider whether a science of such things is possible. As we will see, this takes us onto the familiar and hotly contested terrain of the 'structure/agency' problem in social theory.

Social Ontology: Structure and Agency

The examples we used earlier, of someone cashing a cheque or being a student, will do as a starting-point. Both actions, as described, are possible only on condition that the agent is situated in a set of institutional relations, which exist prior to and independently of their actions. For someone to cash a cheque there has to be a money economy, a banking system and so on, but also they have to be located in that system as an account holder (not to mention having money in their account or an overdraft facility!). This is the sort of point that a structuralist might make. However, it is also true that without individual people and their activities there could be no such things as accounts, cheques, banks and economies. Institutions do not exist independently of the activities of people, but, on the contrary, are nothing but regularities in the aggregate patterning of those activities. This is the sort of point a methodological individualist might make. A third possibility might be a synthesis of the two rival views. Bhaskar refers to the dialectical view of Peter Berger and his associates (see especially Berger and Luckman 1967). On this account, society is an outcome of individual agency, which then reacts back upon individuals. But Bhaskar rejects this account, too, since it does not sustain the persistence of social structures as both conditions and outcomes of human agency, or of people as both products of and conditions of possibility of social structures. On Bhaskar's own account, society and persons are distinct 'levels' – both real, but interdependent and interacting with one another.

This solution to the structure/agency problem, then, involves a commitment to the reality of social structures, conceived as relations between social agents in virtue of their occupancy of social positions. Structures are causally efficacious, in that they both enable actions which would otherwise not be possible (cashing cheques, getting degrees and so on), and constrain actions (bouncing cheques, imposing structural adjustment policies on Third World governments, enforcing essay deadlines and so on). To complement this account of social structure, Bhaskar develops what he calls his 'transformational model of social action'. On this account, it is only through the activities of social agents that social structures are kept in being (reproduced), but individual or collective agency may also modify or transform social structures. The outcome of social action in either reproducing or transforming social structures may be *unintended*, as when employees go to work in order to earn a living, but in doing so also help reproduce capitalist relations of production without (usually) particularly wanting to do so. Or it may be *intended*, as in the case of successful social movement or political mobilization. It is central to this account of the relation between social structures and human agents that they are ontologically distinct from each other. This distinguishes Bhaskar's account (and that of most critical realists) from what Margaret Archer calls 'elisionist' approaches (such as Anthony Giddens's 'structuration') which collapse structure and agency together (see M. Archer 1995; M. Archer *et al.* 1998, ch. 14;

A. Giddens in G. A. Bryant and D. Jarry 1997; see also R. Stones 1996: ch. 4; I. Craib 1992).

These arguments and the concepts they give rise to are very effective against both methodological individualist and empiricist tendencies to dismiss the reality of (unobservable) social structures. However, Bhaskar's (1979, 1998) treatment of society as a continuous transaction between intentionally acting human agents and the social structures they reproduce or transform seems to neglect both human embodiment, and the significance of non-human materials, processes, living beings and so on as participants in human social life. To do this explicitly would be to commit himself to a rather different social ontology, and so to a very different view of the relation between the natural and social sciences. Such a shift is discernable in some of his subsequent work.

Naturalism and Its Limits

In this context the term 'naturalism' generally means the view that there can be a scientific study of social life, in the same sense of science as in the natural sciences. Bhaskar is, as we have seen, committed to naturalism, but his account of social structure and agency implies some radical ontological and other differences between nature and society, with implications for the possibility of our knowledge of them. It is for this reason that his position is termed 'critical naturalism'. So, first, what are the relevant differences, and how is it still possible to assert the possibility of a social science?

Bhaskar lists three ontological, one relational and one epistemological limit to naturalism. The ontological limits have to do with supposed differences between social and natural structures. Social structures are maintained in existence only through the activities of agents (*activity-dependence*), whereas this is not true of structures in nature. Social structures are *concept-dependent*, in the sense that they are reproduced by actors in virtue of the beliefs actors have about what they are doing (but, as we saw above, the reproduction of the structures may not, and usually will not, form part of the pattern of beliefs which are the actor's reasons for acting). Finally, social structures are only relatively enduring (are '*space–time-dependent*'), unlike structures in nature. The relational limit to naturalism derives from the fact that social science is itself a social practice, and so is part of its own subject-matter. This seems to make unsustainable the distinction between the intransitive dimension (the independently existing objects of knowledge) and the transitive dimension (the social process of production of knowledge) in the case of the would-be social sciences. The epistemological limit to naturalism is the impossibility of experimental closure in the social sciences. This is what Collier takes to be a decisive obstacle to a scientific study of society (Collier 1994: 162).

Though the terminology is different, most of these limits to naturalism are fairly familiar items in the anti-naturalistic arguments of the hermeneutic tradition (already encountered in Chapters 5 to 7). Both Collier and Benton (Collier 1994: ch. 8; Benton 1981) have argued that Bhaskar makes too strong a contrast between natural and social reality. Benton has argued, for example, that Bhaskar's commitment to the activity-dependence of social structures comes close to undermining his own ontological distinction between structure and agency. Social scientific explanation often makes use of the notion of un-exercised powers. Modern nation-states, for example, have at their disposal an immense capacity for the use of violence to maintain order. This power is, however, rarely used – in part, at least, because dissident subjects know it is available. Benton also argues that space–time dependency of social structures is not peculiar to them. There are historical natural sciences such as geology and evolutionary biology, as well as developmental sciences which deal with often quite ephemeral but naturally occurring structures. The thesis of concept dependence, too, can be misleading. Much of social life is habitual and routine, involving bodily activity rather than conscious thought or symbolic meaning. Some important sociological knowledge – such as the well-established links between social class and occupation, on the one hand, and likelihood of premature death and chronic illness, on the other – points to causal mechanisms in society which operate independently of the conscious awareness of human agents.

Benton's view was that Bhaskar's strong contrast between social and natural ontology was based in part on his taking 'basic' sciences such as physics and chemistry as the paradigms of natural science. Natural sciences such as meteorology, evolutionary biology and developmental biology share many features with the social sciences, and the social sciences themselves have very diverse subject-matters. It seems clear that a strongly anti-naturalistic social ontology will be a serious obstacle to the development of research programmes to address such questions as the relation between socio-economic processes and ecological change, where collaboration across the social/natural divide is essential (see Benton 1991).

However, for Bhaskar, his largely anti-naturalistic social ontology and related arguments can still be harnessed to a naturalistic defence of a scientific approach to social life. In some respects, this is because there are substitutes or compensations for the absence in the social world of features which enable the scientific study of nature. In some respects, he argues that social science is possible just *because* of the differences between the social and the natural.

The concept and activity dependence of social structures *enable* social scientific work, rather than limit it. This is because the beliefs actors have about their social life are available as a resource for social scientific thinking. This hermeneutic dimension of social life is, for Bhaskar, the necessary starting-point for social science. However, the common-sense ideas of social actors are not treated as the final authority. Theoretical argument (including, notably, the use of transcendental arguments) and empirical evidence can lead to accounts of the social structures which differ from, or even contradict, those of the lay actors. The fact that social structures are only relatively enduring does not prevent their being real, and nor does it prevent their being objects of scientific investigation either during the time period, or within the spatial limits of their occurrence. That social science can take itself as its own object of study does not obliterate the transitive–intransitive dimension. Social science is only a part, and not the whole, of the subject-matter of the social sciences, and when it is being studied it is still possible to distinguish what is being studied from the process of studying it. It could even be argued that the self-referential character of sociology encourages a beneficial methodological reflexivity which is less evident in the natural sciences (this has been emphasized most strongly in feminist approaches to social scientific knowledge – see Chapter 9).

The epistemological limit, deriving from the necessary occurrence of social phenomena in open systems, and the consequent impossibility of experimental closure is a more tricky issue. As we saw, not all critical realists think it can be overcome. Bhaskar's response is to look for analogues or substitutes in social science for the role of experiments in the natural sciences. One analogue is the occurrence of crises in the social order, during which structures which are concealed in normal times become transparent. An example might be the 1984 miners' strike in the UK. The widespread acceptance of the police as a neutral force for maintaining public order was called into question by the use of extensive physical force by the police against the miners' pickets. However, while this was certainly manifest to the miners, who were at the receiving end of police action, and their supporters, it was by no means a consensus. In general, social and political crises tend to polarize opposed interpretations of the social world, rather than settle differences of opinion.

Another alternative to experiment is the use of transcendental arguments. Everyday social practices under agreed descriptions can be analysed in terms of their conditions of possibility, and accounts of the underlying social structures built up in that way. Bhaskar considers it a plausible interpretation of Marx's *Capital* that it consists largely of such arguments from the experiences and understandings of those involved in economic activity to an account of the underlying structures and dynamics of capitalism (Bhaskar 1979, 1998: 65). However, this would seem to imply a very limited role for empirical research in the social sciences. Similarly, Collier's pessimism about the possibility of genuinely scientific social science is based on his view that measurement and statistical analysis are not a substitute for the impossibility of experiment. However, it is not clear why he believes this, and a good case can be made for non-positivist and critical realist uses of statistical analysis in the social sciences (see, for example, Levitas and Guy 1996).

Critical Realism and Human Emancipation

Critical realism was developed during the 1970s at a time when Marxism (in one version or another) was strongly represented among social scientists.

Marxism was one of the few approaches to social science whose explicit philo-sophical commitments coincided with the main outlines of critical realism. It remains open to question how far the continuing association with Marxist ideas is implicit in critical realism, and how far it is a merely contingent phenomenon. However, at least in Roy Bhaskar's version, there is a necessary connection between critical realist philosophy and emancipatory politics. In this respect (though not necessarily in others), Bhaskar's version of realism is like Habermas's social theory (see ch. 7). Both see a close connection between knowledge of self and society and human emancipation, or freedom from domination. Indeed, the link between knowledge and emancipation is made on a very closely related basis by the two thinkers (see Outhwaite 1987 for a fuller discussion of the relationships between critical realism, critical theory, and hermeneutic approaches to social theory).

In Bhaskar's argument (see Bhaskar 1979, 1998: 69–91 and Collier 1994: Chapter 6), the key concept is that of an 'explanatory critique'. The paradigm case of this is Marx's critique of the wage form (in Volume 1, Chapter 19 of *Capital*). Marx takes the common-sense understanding of the wage contract as an exchange of a given amount of labour for a sum of money. Since employee and employer are free agents, there is no reason to doubt the normal assumption that this is generally an exchange of equivalents, and so that expressions such as 'a fair day's work for a fair day's pay' are at least sometimes apt descriptions. However, the condition and consequence of this relation of employer and employee under capitalism is that the product of the employee's work is sold by the employer for a profit, whereas the wage supplies only the subsistence needs of the employee. The capitalist gets rich, while the worker remains poor.

Marx's analysis of this is that what is exchanged is not labour but *labour-power* (the capacity to work). The employer's use of this capacity involves the extrac-tion of more value than was paid for in the wage, and this relation of exploit-ation is achieved through the coercive relations of power and domination which characterize the process of production. What appears, as an *exchange* relation, to be a transaction between free and equal agents, is, as a *production* relation, coercive and exploitative. Marx argues that the ideas through which capitalism is legitimated, such as freedom and equality, only get their plausibility from representations of market exchange relations in abstraction from the unfree and unequal relations of production upon which market exchanges depend. The wage form, then, is misleading: it entails false beliefs about people's real relationships. But, more importantly, these false beliefs are actually engendered by the relations themselves and, as ideological legitimations, they play a part in maintaining the coercive relations they disguise.

So, this is a case in which (if Marx's theory is true) a structure of social relations causes agents to have false beliefs. Since it is better, other things being equal, that people have true beliefs than that they have false ones, it would be better, other things being equal, that this structure of relations be abolished or transformed than allowed to continue. In short, Marx's explanation allows us to draw a negative value judgement about the causes of the phenomenon he explains. This argument, like Habermas's notion of an ideal speech situation (Chapter 7), attempts to give an objective grounding to certain critical value judgements, and so to justify an emancipatory project of social change.

In the case of Bhaskar's notion of an explanatory critique, a crucial step in the argument is the claim that it is better, other things being equal, to have true rather than false beliefs. It is accepted that there will be occasions when it is better for someone not to know the truth, but these occur because of some exceptional circumstance which outweighs the normal presumption in favour of having true beliefs. That this presumption in favour of truth is not merely arbitrary or subjective can be confirmed by thinking about the conditions of possibility for practices of linguistic communication itself. Were there no normative presumption in favour of truth-telling, such practices could not be sustained (this is also something which Habermas includes in his account of the 'pragmatics' of speech). So, there is a logical incoherence in the behaviour of someone who continues to participate in language use, but denies the norm of truth-telling.

Of course, one might well argue that causing false beliefs is not the only or the main problem with capitalism. Alternatively, one might take up the invitation of the 'other things being equal' clause and argue that the benefits of capitalism outweigh its unfortunate side-effect in causing a few false beliefs.

One way of dealing with objections such as these is to expand the scope of the idea of explanatory critique to expose other deleterious consequences of (for example) capitalism. This is the path taken by Bhaskar (1986) and by Collier (1994: ch. 6). They argue that while having false beliefs is (other things being equal) a bad thing, acquiring true beliefs about one's oppression (exploitation and so on) by no means necessarily entails emancipation. Sometimes, indeed, one can be oppressed simply by living with false beliefs – for example, that one was abandoned, unloved, by one's parent at an early age when in fact one was abducted. In this sort of case, merely finding out the truth may be in itself emancipatory. More generally, however, as in the case drawn from Marx, false beliefs are only one aspect of the system of power. But this suggests the possibility that explanatory critiques might be used to generate arguments in favour of social transformations for reasons other than their propensity to spread false beliefs.

Both Collier and Bhaskar take this line of thinking in the direction of a distinctively realist account of ethics and practical reason in general. It would take us beyond the scope of this book to discuss these ideas in depth, but some indications can be given. The most direct extension of the notion of explanatory critique would be to show that a prevailing system of social relations causes the frustration of certain human needs:

The extension of emancipatory critique from cognitive error to unsatisfied needs makes it clear that false belief is not the only chain that binds us, and it is massively outweighed by others in terms of urgent human problems. Peasants who grow food they cannot afford to eat, unemployed workers, homeless families, bullied wives, tortured prisoners, may all know exactly what would make them free, but lack the power to get it. (Collier 1994: 191)

The argument is that if it can be shown to be factually true that frustration of need is caused by a certain social structure, then, other things being equal, it should be changed or abolished. As with the explanatory critique of social structures which cause false beliefs, there is a value premiss in the argument, namely, that if something is a need, then it is wrong to frustrate it if that can be avoided (other things being equal). Collier concedes that it is not actually self-contradictory to say that something is a need, but it is right for it not to be met, but he thinks that it 'doesn't make sense' (unless, of course, there is some other overriding priority).

This realist approach to values takes Collier towards a form of moral realism, according to which moral disagreement turns out to be (mainly?) about facts, and moral conclusions can be drawn directly from social scientific knowledge. One virtue of this approach is that it avoids the sort of moral relativism which makes dialogue between different moral standpoints seem impossible or point-less. It makes moral disagreement amenable to rational argument, a preferable alternative to coercion and violence.

However, it is arguable that it makes such rational settlement of moral disagreement look *too* straightforward. First, while many (but not all) might agree that human needs should be met (other things being equal), this may be because we count something as a human need only if we first think that it should be met. That is, the valuing is already there in the acceptance of the 'fact' that something is a need. Second, even if this problem can be solved, in open systems other things *never are* equal! Often removing obstacles to meeting one human need will create frustrations elsewhere. There may be no cost-free process of emancipatory social change. Ending poverty or protecting the environment may involve curtailing individual liberties in some respects, and so on. Questions of priorities in the satisfaction of needs and desires arise, and different moral traditions may view such questions of priority differently, in ways which can't be settled just by appealing to the facts.

Nevertheless, even if, against moral realism, we accept that there may well be irresolvable and permanent differences in moral perspective, it is still important to recognize the extent to which moral disagreement is always bound up with (though never fully determined by) differences of view about factual matters. This is enough to make reasoned moral dialogue both possible and worth-while. There are, for example, people who think that free markets facilitate expansion of the total social wealth, so that the poor are better off than they would otherwise be because of 'trickle down' effects. At least some of these people genuinely believe that poverty is a bad thing. However, if the social scientific evidence is that, in the absence of redistributive government policies, free markets make the poor even poorer, then the advocate of free markets has to find other grounds for the belief, or abandon it.

The issue of priorities and trade-offs in any proposed emancipatory project raises a further problem with reliance on explanatory critiques. As Andrew Sayer (2000: chs. 7, 8) has argued, this form of argument is primarily negative: it gives reasons why some existing social structure should be changed or abolished. However, implicit in such arguments is the assumption that some possible form of society could be created in which needs were not frustrated, false beliefs were not essential to social reproduction and so on. This assumption needs to be made explicit and justified. In other words, to make out a satisfactory argument for an emancipatory transformation of society it would be necessary to show that an alternative, and preferable (more transparent, more fulfilling and so on), form of social life can be achieved. A considerable amount of work within the critical realist tradition can be understood as attempting to meet this challenge. Kate Soper's 'alternative hedonism' (see Soper 1990, 1998) and work by Mary Mellor (1992), Peter Dickens (1992, 1996), John O'Neill (1993), Ted Benton (1993) and numerous others have been using critical realist ideas to think about possible futures – often attempting to link together feminist, green and socialist visions (see also Red–Green Study Group 1995).

Further Reading

Edited by M. Archer, R. Bhaskar, A. Collier, T. Lawson, A. Norrie, *Critical Realism: Essential Readings* (1998) is an excellent and comprehensive (if rather weighty!) collection of work covering the main issues covered in this chapter, and more. A. Collier's *Critical Realism* (1994) is the best introduction to this tradition – clear, witty and very accessible. R. Bhaskar's *Possibility of Naturalism* (1998) is the classic statement on the application of critical realism to the social sciences, while W. Outhwaite's *New Philosophies of Social Science* (1987) explores relations between critical realism and other philosophical approaches. A. Sayer's *Method in Social Science* (1992) is an excellent work on the methodological implications of critical realism, and his more recent *Realism in Social Science* (2000) is particularly valuable for its sustained encounter with post-modern currents in social science, and for its further development of important ethical issues in critical and emancipatory social science.

Post-script

Since we wrote the first edition of this book, critical realism has become much better known, and there has been a flood of new literature. Much of this provides clear and introductory accounts of realist philosophy and its application to the social sciences, while other works engage in substantive research in specific disciplines (or across disciplinary perspectives). There are now significant differences of approach within the broadly defined 'school' of critical realism. These have been provoked most especially by the attempts by some of the originators of the approach to extend it to a philosophical defence of religious or spiritual beliefs. This has been resisted by others as undermining the more modest role of the approach as 'underlabourer' for secular scientific work. Developments in the wider social and political context of social theorizing have also had their consequences for the directions taken by critical realism. There has been a growing concern with the approach as a basis for understanding the relationship between socioeconomic processes and the natural environment, and, along with the decline in explicit commitment to Marxian analysis among the social scientific academy, there has been continuing discussion about the relationship between critical realism and Marxism, as well as other 'critical' theories. In Chapter 12 of this edition, 'Commentary on Recent Developments', I provide a more detailed literature review of at least some of these issues.

9
Feminism, Knowledge and Society

Introduction: Objectivity and Cultural Diversity

Since the origins of modern social theory in the Enlightenment, there has been a tension between, on the one hand, the received model of objective (scientific) knowledge and, on the other, the recognition of the historical and cultural variability of patterns of belief. The paradigm of mechanical science, associated with Galileo and Newton, dealing with objectively measurable phenomena, and disclosing a world governed by mathematically specifiable laws, was widely adopted as the model for 'scientific' morality, law and government. Although the advocates of rival epistemologies – empiricists, rationalists and Kantians – differed from each other on many issues they still shared important thematic commitments, most especially their belief in the objectivity and universality of scientific knowledge and method. This belief can be summed up in the form of the following four statements:

(a) The concepts of science should be universally applicable, across time and space.

(b) The work of science should be objective, in the sense that it should aim at knowledge of the world as it is, and not as the investigators might like it to be.

(c) The personal characteristics of the investigator should therefore be irrelevant to the evaluation of the knowledge-claims they make, and the institutions of science should be designed to ensure this (for example, anonymous refereeing of journal articles and research applications).

(d) The standards, or criteria, in terms of which rival knowledge-claims are evaluated should be universalistic, and so neutral with respect to the rival positions being evaluated. Reason, observation and experimental testing are the standards most generally appealed to.

However, thinkers as diverse as Ferguson, Herder, Montesquieu, Rousseau, Vico and Voltaire were also well aware of the deep differences between the understandings and values which prevailed in different cultures. They not infrequently used the standpoint of a cultural outsider as a device for exposing the irrationalities and injustices of their own societies (see, for example, Montesquieu's *Persian Letters*). By the early nineteenth century it was also recognized that, within the same society, differences of social position and social experiences shaped different ways of thinking. Feuerbach, Marx and Engels developed this insight further into a systematic sociology of knowledge.

For those who took cultural diversity seriously, it posed a challenge to the project of objective and universal knowledge of the social world. But, since other cultures also had different ways of understanding nature, the recognition of cultural diversity could also call into question the special status of Western natural scientific knowledge. How could one escape the conclusion that scientific standards of objectivity and universality were themselves the product and property of a particular, historically and geographically localized civilization (modern Western society)? What justification could there be for imposing these forms of thought on radically different cultures? This is, of course, the recurring theme of our book!

The use of the word 'imposing' in the penultimate sentence of the last paragraph is one indication why this has become such an important question. What at first sight seems like a matter of which set of beliefs we adopt – those of Western science, or those of some other culture – turns out to imply far more than this. Modern science is not just a set of authoritative beliefs and methodological principles, but is part of a complex apparatus of power, one which spans 'cultures', and incorporates Third-World farmers, indigenous peoples, tropical rain forests, the upper atmosphere, pregnant women, the sick, industrial workers, consumers of processed food and hi-tech gadgets, ethnic minorities and sexual deviants – that is, all of us humans, and large parts of the non-human world, too. This immensely complex and heterogeneous web of power both produces and coexists in tension with a correspondingly complex and diverse array of 'subaltern' positions. These positions, in turn, sustain relationships and activities on the part of the people who occupy them which may provide alternatives to the dominant forms of knowledge and understanding. The struggles of such subaltern groups on behalf of their own autonomy, emancipation, or even mere survival necessarily involve struggles to redefine themselves and their relations to the world around them against the dominant world-view, including its 'scientific' legitimations.

The benign and comforting ethic of welcoming cultural diversity, commonly claimed by relativistic approaches to knowledge and rationality, is inadequate when it is applied to such complexes of knowledge and power. For subaltern groups, resistance to domination has to include challenging the forms of knowledge which are invariably complicit in such regimes. These forms of knowledge, so far as the modern West is concerned, have generally harnessed the authority of science. So, for example, the eminent German biologist Ernst Haeckel was able to say in 1865:

> That immense superiority which the white race has won over the other races in the struggle for existence is due to Natural Selection, the key to all advance in culture, to all so-called history, as it is the key to the origin of species in the kingdoms of the living. That superiority will, without doubt become more and more marked in the future, so that still fewer races of man will be able, as time advances, to contend with the white in the struggle for existence. (Haeckel, 1883: 85)

Haeckel's use of Darwinian ideas to justify the genocidal implications of Western imperialisms was in no sense exceptional. Indeed, the text was composed at a time when Haeckel's views were relatively liberal and progressive, and similar views were being expressed in Britain and the other Western powers. Such evidence clearly calls into question the objectivity and value-neutrality of scientific expertise, long before the emergence of modern military-commercial technoscience. From the standpoint of those on the receiving end of this knowledge, a tolerant, relativist acceptance of it as just one of an indefinite plurality of incommensurable discourses seems insufficient.

So, what would constitute an appropriate challenge? If we agree that the relativist response will not do, then there are three broad alternatives to it. One is to accept, in some version, the account of 'good science' bequeathed by the Enlightenment, and to use it against the *specific* knowledge-claims which are considered objectionable. So, for example, it could be argued against Haeckel that his extended use of the concept of natural selection to include genocide is not licensed by scientific canons of enquiry, or that his assumption of 'progress' as an outcome of selection involves an illegitimate importation of values into his 'science'. So, this sort of criticism accepts a certain normative concept of science, but uses it to criticize 'bad science', or 'misuses' of science.

The second sort of challenge would be to accept that all knowledge-claims, including scientific ones, are grounded in the interests or values of some social group. Since we have no 'Archimedean' point, neutral between such rival claims from which to assess their relative closeness to the truth, we can turn only to the values and projects which inspire them. Beliefs should be supported or rejected on the basis of their conduciveness to a just and good society. But this only poses further questions about the status and meaning of these appeals to values. Are they universally valid? What is to count as 'justice'?

The third sort of challenge to the authority and power-relations of Western science gives a central place to the metaphor of 'perspective', or 'point of view'. Patterns of belief are associated with social positions in a way analogous to the relationship between a view of a landscape and the physical location from which it is surveyed. However, there are different ways of taking this metaphor, and they result in rather different positions in epistemology. In the case of views of a landscape, the different perspectives obtained from different standpoints can easily be understood as partial but mutually compatible with some synthetic concept of the real shape of the landforms. This concept can then be used to predict how the view will look from different viewpoints. Alternatively, and more commonly, the notions of 'perspective' and 'standpoint' are used to indicate different and potentially conflicting views from different positions in society, in the absence of any direct, perspective-free, access to the real landscape. This, too, can be taken to support a relativism of incommensurable views or perspectives. But it can also support claims that some standpoints give better views than others. This is the use of the 'standpoint' metaphor with which we will be most concerned in this chapter.

The dilemmas involved in these various attempts to find a reliable basis for challenges to the dominant apparatus of knowledge and power have been explored in very sophisticated ways in a range of modern social movements – the gay and lesbian movement, the labour movement, the women's movement, the struggles against disablement, anti-colonial and anti-racist struggles, and in rather different ways in ecological and animal rights and welfare movements. An influential approach to the study of social movements (see Eyerman and Jamison 1991) gives a central place to their cognitive practice, not only in defining movements and the identities of their participants, but also in transforming the wider culture: 'For us, social movements are bearers of new ideas, and have often been the sources of scientific theories and of whole scientific fields, as well as new political and social identities' (Eyerman and Jamison 1991: 3).

Our focus in the rest of this chapter will be on how the issues of relativism and the status of rival knowledge-claims have been posed and understood in the contemporary feminist movement, but it should be kept in mind that there are both substantive connections and parallels which span these different sorts of social and political struggle.

Feminist Politics and Social Knowledge

All large-scale emancipatory struggles involve challenges to established beliefs. Consider the example of the long struggle for women's voting rights in Britain through the latter part of the nineteenth century and into the early twentieth. Suffrage campaigners had to challenge male power in the home, in the church, in the courts and prisons and on the streets. Women suffragists and their male supporters had to face outright violence and abuse, as well as more subtle forms of coercion, but an aspect of struggle in all these domains was the need to challenge patriarchal beliefs about women's nature and proper place in society.

The ideology of 'separate but complementary spheres', ordained by God and nature, demanded that women confine themselves to the domestic sphere, to housework, child bearing and rearing, combined, for women of higher status, with charitable works. Though this did not prevent working-class women from performing arduous and badly paid work in agriculture, industry, domestic service and as paid homeworkers, it did prevent them from entering higher education, or participating in elections. As Harrison (1978) points out, 'scientific' medicine was directly implicated in providing the theoretical backing to the anti-suffrage cause. Women were held to be in the grip of emotion rather than reason, to be physically weaker than men, to be too engaged by their reproductive functions to be distracted by political concerns. Even women's activism in favour of the vote was taken to be a pathological symptom:

> Physiologists wrote learned but strange letters to *The Times* in December 1908 ascribing suffragette conduct at public meetings to an outburst of 'Tarantism' akin to the dancing mania of the Middle Ages. T. Claye Shaw added, for good measure, that the phenomenon was akin to 'the explosive fury of epileptics'. (Harrison 1978: 67)

Similar medical expertise warned against the folly of allowing women into higher education. Lynda Birke tells of one Dr E. H. Clarke, a Harvard professor, whose view was that menstruation took such a toll of the female physiology that the extra strain of study would be damaging to health (Birke 1986: 27).

More recent, 'second-wave' feminism continues to be engaged in challenging patriarchal beliefs little or no more sophisticated than these. The renewal of social Darwinism which emerged in the 1970s under the name 'sociobiology' used the differences between male and female 'investment' in reproduction to declare male domination, patriarchy and the sexual double standard as both natural and inevitable (see Caplan 1978; Goldberg 1974; Rose *et al.* 1984: ch. 6; Rose and Rose 2000). A television series (*Anatomy of Desire*) shown on UK Channel 4 in November and December 1998 confidently pronounced that 'science' in the shape of parental investment theory explained the supposed fact that men have more extra-marital affairs than do women – to do so is programmed by their genes! Later it was acknowledged that there might be a statistical anomaly in the 'fact' to be explained. Just *who* were the promiscuous men having their affairs with, if it is in women's nature to be faithful? As Hilary Rose succinctly put the challenge posed by the new biological determinism:

> at the height of the struggle of the feminist movement to bring women out of nature into culture, a host of greater or lesser sociobiologists, their media supporters and New Right politicians joined eagerly in the cultural and political effort to return them whence they came. (Rose 1994: 19)

However, science is not *wholly* a masculine enterprise (see Chapter 4 of this book and associated references). Recent feminist scholarship has given more recognition to the significant role women have played in the natural sciences when they have been able to break down the barriers to those professions (see Harding 1991: ch. 2; and Rose 1994: chs 5–8). In the behavioural and social sciences women have also made important contributions, not necessarily as self-consciously feminist researchers, in such fields as primate ethology, cultural anthropology (MacCormack and Strathern 1980), sociology and history. (H. Rose 1994: ch. 3 offers a valuable account of the unevenness in the impact of feminism across different countries, and in different fields of research.)

But the transformative power of specifically feminist research in the social sciences has been witnessed most dramatically in sociology since the late 1960s. The link between 'second-wave' feminism and the wholesale restructuring of the sociological research agenda since then has been remarkable (though, of course, it remains unfinished). The ongoing debate between Marxists and neo-Weberians over the theorizing and explaining social class and stratification was thrown into disarray by feminist argument and evidence. Both traditions linked class to work and the division of labour, but in their different ways both had failed to recognize the gendered character of that division of labour, both in the wider economy and in the domestic sphere. Feminists in cultural studies have explored the production and reproduction of gendered identities in cultural and media representations, while new research agendas around intimate relationships and the social construction and regulation of emotions have been pioneered by feminist and gay writers. Feminists have also been at the forefront of questioning established methods of data-gathering in sociology and other social sciences. They have insisted on the dialogic relationship between researchers and the researched, and have pursued reflexivity about the power relations involved in research practice and the ethical implications which flow from them (see, for some examples, Gelsthorpe 1992; Hammersley 1992, 1994; Ramazonoglu 1992 and Morgan and Stanley 1993). In the process, disciplinary boundaries, too, have been broken down or transformed, as in the formation of the distinct cross-disciplinary field of women's studies.

So it is already clear that feminist work in some scientific disciplines has gone much further than simply gathering new factual information. Central theoretical paradigms and research agendas have been challenged and transformed, and alternatives tabled. Further still, this transformation of the discipline has posed questions of method, of the relation of knowledge to its subject-matter – questions about the nature of the discipline itself. For some feminist writers this has posed the *philosophical* question: may knowledge itself be a matter of gender? Can there be a distinctively female, or feminist, understanding of what knowledge is – a feminist epistemology?

Feminism and Epistemology

It has become conventional (following Sandra Harding's influential *The Science Question in Feminism* (1986)) to distinguish three approaches to this issue: what she calls 'feminist empiricism', 'feminist standpoint epistemology' and

feminist post-modernism. On Harding's account, *feminist empiricism* is characteristically the position of those feminists who have managed to gain entry
to scientific research (social or natural). These feminists acknowledge the way
science has misrepresented and mistreated women, but hold that this is not
essential to science. Rather, it is a consequence of the failure of male-domin-
ated science to live up to the norms of scientific research: the problem is not
science as such, but 'bad science'. Feminists should struggle to enter science
and correct the partiality and bias which stems from their current lack of representation there. We will consider this approach again later in this chapter,
but already we might question whether the term 'feminist empiricism' really
captures the depth of the challenge to mainstream approaches which has been
mounted by feminists working within such disciplines as sociology, history
and cultural anthropology.

Feminist Standpoint Epistemologies

The second sort of approach to the question of feminism and knowledge is
'feminist standpoint epistemology'. This approach emerged from debates in
the late 1970s among feminists concerned with the 'masculinism' of the natural
sciences, and especially with biology, the science most intimately connected
with defining women as a 'natural' category. The pioneering work of Jane
Flax, Sandra Harding, Nancy Hartsock, Hilary Rose and others drew upon the
campaigning activities and new forms of understanding generated by the
women's movement, in particular the revaluation of women's experience as
a resource for critically addressing orthodox biomedical knowledge. But the
new standpoint epistemology also synthesized this source of new understandings with other traditions of theoretical work, most especially a feminist development of psychoanalytic object relations theory, and the humanist
materialism of the early Marx, as developed by the Hungarian Marxist Georg
Lukács, and Alfred Sohn-Rethel.

Nancy Hartsock's Feminist Materialism

Perhaps the most comprehensive melding of these influences was to be found
in the work of Nancy Hartsock (1983a, b). She takes from the humanist Marxian
tradition a materialist understanding of the relationship between forms of
knowledge, on the one hand, and social relations and practices, on the other.
In the Marxian tradition from which she draws, social divisions are the basis for
different and opposed ontologies and epistemologies (not simply different or
conflicting factual beliefs). Sohn-Rethel had argued that the division between
mental and manual labour, intensified under modern capitalism, was the basis
for the abstract thought of modern science, and also the abstraction of the

dominant social and political ideologies of capitalism. Lukács had developed the Marxian notion of the relationship between ideas and social divisions into a historical 'grand narrative'. According to this, the working class's experience of being rendered a 'thing-like' commodity was in fundamental conflict with its potential for subjectivity and historical agency, and would eventually lead to an explosive transformation of consciousness and socialist revolution. Lukács's conviction that the liberation of the working class represented and in some sense contained the liberation of all oppressed and exploited groups led him to see it as a 'universal' class, whose revolutionary role was the culmination of human history. Since working-class revolutionary consciousness was in this sense the most all-inclusive, and its vantage-point one which encompassed all of history, it followed that the knowledge contained in it was superior to rival 'bourgeois' beliefs.

This version of standpoint epistemology is critically endorsed by Hartsock. She accepts the Marxian critique of the dominant, capitalist ideology, and the academic theories which refine and develop it. For these theories, the key concepts are abstract categories of exchange, and they are rooted in experience of market relations. However, the experience of male wage-workers under capitalism provides a basis for a different and rival understanding of reality, both social and natural. This derives from workers' direct participation in the more fundamental level of social activity – the *production* of the commodities exchanged in the market. This productive activity avoids the abstraction of mental labour, uniting mental and manual aspects of practice, engaging with the natural world and being alive to qualitative differences (as against the capitalists' merely quantitative concern with money and profit).

However, like Lukács, Hartsock recognizes that the workers' experience and consciousness is subordinated to the power of capital, so that this alternative consciousness, or form of understanding, exists only in a contradictory and partial state. It is, rather, a *potential* form of understanding, just as Lukács's representation of the revolutionary consciousness of the workers was an idealization, 'imputed' to them on the basis of Lukács's own version of history. But in Hartsock's view, the workers' alternative knowledge is limited and partial for another reason: the Marxian tradition does not carry its insight into the relation between social divisions and knowledge to its logical conclusion. The division between capital and labour, between manual and mental labour are primarily divisions of *male* labour. In the gender-blind categories of this tradition, women's contribution to the social division of labour disappears from view. Just as Marxism exposed the limited and distorted character of knowledge based on market exchange from the standpoint of workers engaged in production, what was now needed was an exposure of the limitations and distortions in Marxian theory from the standpoint of women's distinctive role in 'reproduction'.

There are three distinct stages in Hartsock's argument here. One is to show that women do, in fact, occupy a distinctive position in the overall division of labour in society. The second is to show why and how that can form the basis for a distinctively female, or feminist, way of knowing and experiencing the world. The third is to show that this is more than just different, but also superior, better grounded, or more reliable as knowledge. Only if this third claim can be made good can the approach count as an epistemology.

On the sexual division of labour, Hartsock notes the dual presence of women both in wage labour and in work in the household. As wage-workers they share the experiences of male workers of productive labour processes, but they also work in the home, outside the wage labour system, under male domination. Here they perform work which is concerned with necessities of survival, bodily and psychological renewal and the reproductive activities of childbearing and upbringing. Although Hartsock claims that the sexual division of labour is central to the general organization of human social labour, she tends to confine her analysis to Western class societies. She accepts that, even here, there are many differences in the life experiences of individual women. She is also sensitive to the specificity of the experiences of lesbians and women of colour. However, her concern is to identify commonalities in the lives of women that cut across these differences, and to focus on institutional-ized practices which might ground a distinctively female or feminist outlook.

One reason why Hartsock thinks the sexual division of labour is such a central feature of social organization is that, for her, it is not wholly socially constructed. Although not all women give birth, (at least so far) no men do. This fact depends on bodily differences between the sexes, and Hartsock speaks of the 'sexual', not 'gender', division of labour so as to emphasize the importance of embodiment and its consequences for the gendering of the social division of labour, and also of other dimensions of life experience. But this does not amount to an acceptance that 'biology is destiny': bodily functions and sex differences are partly 'given', but also are subjects of transformation and amplification in different ways by social relations and practices.

This already takes us to the second stage of the argument: the different 'way of knowing' associated with women's place in the division of social labour. This interweaving of the social and the bodily aspects of experience tells against any absolute duality of biology and society, and so suggests a more integrated and holistic form of understanding. Women's work in the domestic sphere involves the development of skills which acknowledge concreteness, qualitative difference and the basic materialities and necessities of life, often demeaned in the wider cultural value-system, and shunned by men. Women's bodily experi-ences of menstruation, lactation, coitus and childbirth give them a less strong sense of their bodily boundaries than is the case for men, and so make possible a greater sense of continuity with the world around them. Finally, in childbear-ing and upbringing women's reproductive activity is quite different from the male engagement with material production. Reproduction involves a transition from a foetus experienced as part of one's own body to the formation of an independent being. The process is one which engages many different and unique layers of experience and relatedness.

Hilary Rose: Hand, Brain and Heart

Hilary Rose's version of standpoint epistemology (1983, 1994) has much in common with Hartsock's emphasis on the division of labour. Rose also criticizes the Marxian approach for limiting its interest in the division of labour to the mental/manual divide only, and ignoring emotional work – the labours of caring and nurturing which are mainly allocated to women (hence the title of her pioneering article: 'Hand, Brain and Heart'). Rose argues that caring work potentially engages thinking and feeling, bodily and cultural dimensions, autonomy and relatedness in ways which undermine fixed oppositions between nature and culture, reason and emotion and self and other. It is, potentially, the basis in women's lives for an alternative rationality to the polarizing, abstract and destructive rationality of the patriarchal world. Rose's particular interest in the sciences leads her to make connections between these thoughts about women's caring work and distinctive approaches in anthropology, psychology and biology associated with feminist researchers (Carson 1962; Merchant 1980; Keller 1983; 1985; see also Chapter 4 of this book). These tend also to undermine rigid dichotomies between subjective and objective, reason and emotion, the natural and the human, and point to non-reductive and more holistic research programmes in science.

An important qualification needs to be spelted out at this point. Neither Hartsock nor Rose is committed to a romantic celebration of women's caring and reproductive work as it is currently institutionalized in patriarchal and capitalist societies. Rose points out the differences between caring for children, for sick or aged dependants, and for husbands or partners, and emphasizes the contradictory character of many of these caring roles when carried out under social and cultural conditions which distort them through coercion, devalue them and fail to resource or reward them. Hartsock makes very similar points, and notes the resistance of the male ruling class to attempts by women of colour and working-class women to overcome the isolation of domestic work by collectivizing it.

So, the standpoint theorists are not arguing that the feminist alternative to established knowledge is already present and fully formed in women's actual life experience. It is, rather, a potential to be realized through practical struggles for new kinds of social relations: new forms of rationality and understanding are seen both as emerging through these struggles and as, in turn, serving as a resource for them. There is, then, an internal relationship between the new forms of knowledge, and the struggle for liberation from oppressive and dis-torting social relationships. In this respect, the standpoint epistemologies can be seen as an extension and deepening of their predecessors in the Hegelian and Marxian traditions. However, that legacy raises serious questions about the relationship between the feminist theorists who identify and elaborate the liberatory potential in women's ordinary lives and the contradictory and distorted common experience of those women. Both Hartsock and Rose are clear in their responses to this issue: the key resource for theorizing must be the forms of knowledge and experience generated through the practice of the wider feminist social movement itself. And the potentials identified by them for a liberatory knowledge can have no basis other than the prefiguring of unalienated experience in the midst of the current contradictions:

> How far is women's caring part of what Hilary Land and I have called compulsory altruism? For caring, whether paid or unpaid, like other forms of labour, exists predominantly in its alienated form but also contains within itself glimpsed moments of an unalienated form. It is important with all forms of labour to insist that the experience of the unalienated form is located – however fleetingly – within the alienated, as otherwise we have no means of conceptualizing – however prefiguratively – the social relations and labour processes of a society which has overcome alienation. (Rose 1994: 40)

The Psychological Dimension: Feminist Object Relations

These social-structural accounts of the different life experiences of men and women, together with their consequences for gendered ways of knowing, are complemented by accounts of gendered personality development derived from the 'object relations' tradition in psychoanalysis (see Craib 1989, esp. chs. 8 to 10). This approach focuses on the process of personality formation from a very early stage – often before birth – and gives a central role to the relationships in reality but also, and often more importantly, in fantasy between the developing personality and the person (or people) who take the primary role in caring. In effect, we are here dealing with the caring work of women which is at the core of Hilary Rose's version of standpoint epistemology, but from the perspective of the infant and child who is the recipient of the care.

In the feminist version of object relations theory (Nancy Chodorow (1978) is the theorist most cited) there is an emphasis on the differences in the inner conflicts which have to be resolved by boys and girls in achieving an independent and (more or less) stable sense of self. Where the primary (or exclusive) carer is the mother, the female infant undergoes a more gradual and less conflictual growth towards adult independence, and learns the feminine identity required for her future mothering role through identification with the mother. By contrast, boys are required at an early stage to renounce their primary identification with the mother as a condition of learning their distinct masculine identity. Moreover, this is itself problematic due to the relative absence of the father, in both physical and emotional senses. Rather than directly learning gender identity in the concrete and practically present domestic sphere, as is possible for girls, boys must learn masculinity in a more conscious way, and on the basis of a more abstract and stereotypical model of the father's external role in the public sphere.

The resulting masculine identity is one which tends to be more fraught with inner contradictions, and which requires strong boundaries between self and other as a defence against lapsing back into an infantile dependency upon, and identification with, the mother. Primarily, this defensive ego defines itself against the mother, and, by implication, against women in general, but, secondarily, against more generalized 'others': different races and cultures, and nature. There is a tendency to avoid strong emotion, and to devalue the concrete practical domestic sphere in favour of an 'abstract' public world.

Both Nancy Hartsock and Jane Flax (1983) draw on this feminist development of object relations theory. Hartsock indicates a certain scepticism, referring to it as an empirical hypothesis, and combining it, as we have seen, with arguments drawn from a materialist social theory. It is more central to Flax's early contribution to the debate. She uses it to explore ways in which the dominant (masculine) traditions of philosophy, including epistemology, pose such problems as the opposition between self and other, nature and culture, subject and object and so on as *universal* problems of human knowledge and being, when in reality they derive from specifically *male* psychological dilemmas.

As with the social-structural versions of standpoint epistemology, there is a problem about overgeneralization. However, the object relations approach differs from more orthodox Freudian psychoanalysis in that it is less deterministic. It uses clinical practice as a basis for characterizing dilemmas and available strategies and resources encountered by individuals in the course of personality development, but it leaves considerable open space for each individual to resolve or deal with problems in unique ways. So, the abstract characterizations of masculine and feminine identity formation are better seen as ideal types, with most individuals located at different points along the continuum between, but with males tending toward the masculine pole, females towards the feminine. In another departure from more orthodox psychoanalysis, the approach recognizes the possibility of different kinds of gendered personality formation if the responsibilities of care were differently allocated, and if, in particular, men played a more central role in caring work, and women had more opportunities in the public sphere beyond the immediate familial context. So, as with the social-structural versions of standpoint epistemology, the psychoanalytic one posits a close relationship between the potential for new kinds of understanding and the struggle to transform social relationships in liberatory directions.

Whatever the specifics of their social or psychological analyses, these versions of standpoint theory yield strikingly convergent views on the character of the alternative, feminist forms of knowledge. They favour concreteness, sensitivity to qualitative difference and complexity as against abstract concern with merely quantitative relations; they anticipate the overcoming of the abstract dualisms of Western, masculine thought (nature and culture, subject and object, reason and emotion, body and mind) in favour of contextualized, holistic understandings of the relatedness of things; and they propose the reintegration of knowledge with everyday life-experience. Finally, they emphasize the relationship between these alternative forms of knowledge and the struggles of subaltern social groups (primarily, but not exclusively, women) against social domination, exclusion and devaluing. In Hartsock's summary:

> The experience of continuity and relation – with others, with the natural world, of mind with body – provides an ontological base for developing a non-problematic social synthesis, a social synthesis that need not operate through the denial of the body, the attack on nature, or the death struggle between the self and other, a social synthesis that does not depend on any of the forms taken by abstract masculinity. (Hartsock 1983b: 246)

In this way the feminist standpoint epistemology offers both an explanation of the social and ecological destructiveness of modern technoscience and posits an alternative form of understanding linked to liberation from social domination, and a new, harmonious relationship with the rest of the natural world. This broad pattern of thought is continuous with the eco-feminist claim that there is a special connection between women's gender interests and the protection of nature (This is deeply contested within the feminist movement; there is a vast literature, but see, in particular, Shiva 1989; Biehl 1991; Mellor 1992, 1997; Mies and Shiva 1993; Plumwood 1993; Salleh 1994; Jackson 1995; Soper 1995: ch. 4; Mellor 1996; Salleh 1996.)

Debating the Feminist Standpoint

But, it might still be asked, what is epistemological about this? We have been presented with some strong reasons for expecting that in virtue of their place in the social division of labour and the way they establish their independent personalities women will tend to understand the world differently from men. We might also be convinced that their alternative mode of understanding is linked to a vision of a more equal, reciprocal and loving society at peace with nature. But does any of this give us reasons for accepting feminist thought as true? Why should it be given more credence as an account of the way the world is than the productions of orthodox science? Surely the very success of science and technology in securing both social domination and the mastery of nature is testimony to the power of its knowledge?

The main contributors to the debate have shifted ground considerably in the way they respond to this set of questions, and there remain important differences of opinion. What we might think of as the 'classic' standpoint answer is that the distinctive women's/feminist viewpoint *of itself* confers the superior view. The standpoint from which the view is generated is what confers on it the right to be accepted as 'true' (or 'more reliable', 'less false'). In Hartsock's original version, for example, the metaphors of 'levels', 'depth' and 'visibility' are used to sustain the privileging of women's standpoint:

> If the reality of class domination only becomes apparent at the epistemological level of production, what epistemological level can allow us to understand the systematic domination of women? I argue that the domination of one gender by the other can only be made visible at a still deeper level, an epistemological level defined by reproduction. Thus, rather than argue, with Marx, that reality must be understood as bi-leveled, I am suggesting that it must be understood as three-tiered. (Hartsock 1993b: 9–10)

These topographical terms go well with the basic standpoint metaphor, though they interestingly invert the location from which one might expect the best view: not from the top of the social structure, but from tunnelling through its foundations. The most common justification for this is that the view from the top is necessarily distorted by the deceptions and self-deceptions made necessary by social domination. There is also an echo of the Renaissance thinker Vico's view that we understand what we have ourselves created. Women and workers are the social groups who make society, and so understand it in ways which the ruling groups, who merely depend upon and appropriate what others create, do not.

This is the 'classic' feminist standpoint approach and is closest to 'classic' Lukács's Marxian standpoint epistemology, with which it shares the same problems. It also stands in the sharpest contrast to the insistence of 'traditional' epistemology (such as the empiricist and Kantian approaches we have considered in earlier chapters of this book) on separating questions of truth and falsity from the identity of the people who make the truth claims. It is worth noting that the motivation for this was precisely to deprive the powerful of their right to dictate what was to count as knowledge (note requirement (c) in the list on p. 140), and so was egalitarian in its intent.

The key difficulty for the classic standpoint, whether Marxian or feminist, is that the theory used to identify the preferred standpoint, to characterize the group which occupies it, and to justify the privileging of their forms of knowledge as better knowledge, *itself* stands in need of justification. Standpoint theorists have to make knowledge-claims about historical change, the sexual division of labour, the formation of gendered identities and so on, *prior to* and as *a means of* establishing the epistemology in terms of which truth claims are to be evaluated. The exercise is, in other words, circular. Standpoint theorists necessarily assume what their theories set out to prove.

This argument is a direct and powerful one. However, perhaps it is too powerful! A critical look at the traditional epistemologies reveals that they, too, rely on assumptions – about the nature of the human mind, the validity of certain forms of reasoning, the relationship of the thinking self to the external world, the reliability of sensory experience and so on. These assumptions, like those of the standpoint epistemology, are open to challenge, and stand in need of independent justification.

So far, then, it seems that standpoint theories are no worse than the more established epistemologies when it comes to the charge of circularity. There are two basic options for dealing with this situation. One of them is to take up a relativist position about epistemologies themselves, and accept that there can be no good reasons for accepting one rather than another, so that choice is merely a matter of subjective preference (based on political values, social interests, the toss of a coin, or whatever). This takes us in the direction of post-modernist criticisms of standpoint epistemology, and, indeed, of epistemology as such. We will return to consider these criticisms a little later.

A second way of dealing with the circularity of attempts to ground approaches to the theory of knowledge in prior assumptions is to see if we can find *good reasons* for preferring one set of assumptions and the epistemology they give rise to as against the alternatives. For this to be possible, there has to be some common ground between the epistemologies, some basis for bringing them into dialogue with each other (that is, they shouldn't be completely incommensurable – see p. 33). There are, in fact, two very basic features which feminist standpoint theorists and traditional epistemologies have in common. One is a commitment to logical consistency, to attempting to construct theory in ways which avoid self-contradiction. The second is a commitment to a non-relativist realism: that is to say, to the view that there is a world independent of our thought about it, that some thoughts about it are more reliable, closer to the truth than others, and that it makes sense to devise ways of telling the difference.

Noting that traditional and standpoint epistemologies have these features in common, we can begin to assess their relative merits. Since both are committed to consistency, we can, for example, consider how well each of them lives up to this commitment. As we saw in Chapters 2 and 3, the empiricist epistemology which is used to defend the rationality of science is inconsistent with what seem to be unavoidable features of scientific explanation – the role of values and interests in theory choice, the theory dependence of empirical evidence, the role of unobservable entities, and so on. By contrast, feminist standpoint epistemology offers a socio-historical account of the gendered processes of knowledge creation which is not obviously inconsistent with its epistemology. This is clearly an area of debate which could be taken much further, but feminist standpoint theories appear to be well placed.

The shared commitment to realism provides another basis for evaluating rival epistemologies. Both traditional epistemologies and feminist standpoint epistemologies offer ways of distinguishing between more and less reliable knowledge-claims, and generally do so in terms of procedures to be followed in order to arrive at more rather than less reliable beliefs. Implicit in either epistemology is a theory of knowledge as a process by which beliefs about reality are generated and evaluated. In Chapters 2 and 3 we discussed the account empiricists have given of this process, and at the beginning of this chapter (p. 140) we summarized in four points the key features shared by all the traditional epistemologies. We can now compare feminist standpoint with traditional epistemologies with respect to their shared commitment to accounting for and providing rules for the creation of reliable knowledge.

What about the proclaimed universality of the concepts of science? This is by no means uncontroversial in contemporary natural science, but in historical and social sciences it is still more problematic, for reasons discussed in Chapters 5 to 7. It is clear that forms of human social life and their cultural practices differ from place to place and time to time. And it follows that the social and historical sciences need to develop theories which are sensitive to specificity and difference. However, in order to detect difference it is necessary to have at least some concepts which span the different cultures under comparison. It is arguable that we need some basic concepts of human universals (birth, death, labour, sex, for example) for us to be able to make any sense at all of other cultures (see Chapter 6, p. 99).

Feminist epistemology posits such human universals (sex differences, mothering, some form of social division of labour and so on), but simultaneously argues that socio-cultural processes combine with them to produce diversity and specificity. By contrast, the central concern in empiricism, rationalism and Kantian epistemology with universality is a part of the explanation of the difficulty the natural sciences have with particularity and difference. Attempts to apply abstract and general scientific and technological knowledge to very different concrete situations (large dam projects and green-revolution agriculture are well-studied examples) often produce unwanted and disastrous social and ecological consequences.

The concern with objectivity is shared between the most influential standpoint epistemologists and traditional epistemology, in the sense that both are committed to the existence of an external world in virtue of whose character our beliefs are either justified or not. However, they differ markedly in the way they describe the conditions most favourable to arriving at reliable or justified beliefs. In the empiricist model, as we saw, value judgements were to be excluded from science. Critics of empiricism doubt whether this is possible. Feminist standpoint epistemologists argue that it is not even *desirable*: political and moral values inspire the social movement struggles which are essential to the growth of knowledge. This point also challenges the traditional epistemologists' commitment to the irrelevance of personal or social identities to science: some things can only be seen from some standpoints, or 'subject positions'.

So, who is right? We saw in Chapter 2 that the focus of empiricism is on devising criteria by which genuine knowledge (justified belief, and so on) can be distinguished from falsehood ('pseudo-science', and so on), and the crucial role of testability by observation and experiment in their account of this. For them, the emphasis is on quality control in science. As we also saw (in Chapter 3, pp. 35–7), this emphasis, together with their very narrow view of rationality, led the empiricists (and Popper) to neglect the rationality involved in the processes of *creation* of new scientific ideas and hypotheses. For empiricists this is a matter of 'psychology', for Popper a matter of imaginative 'conjectures'. However, critics of empiricism have shown how the invention and development of metaphors, the application of criteria of relevance, plausibility and so on are rational processes involved in the creation of scientific theories. Without these processes, there would be no theories or knowledge-claims to test by experiment and observation! The case can be made that they are absolutely central to an understanding of science as a dynamic and creative human activity.

By contrast, feminist standpoint epistemology and related sociological accounts of science expose the limitations of the 'abstract individualism' shared by the traditional epistemologies: the creation of knowledge is a thoroughly social process. Moreover, feminist standpoint epistemologies explain the potential resources, in terms of diverse experiences, perspectives and cultural meanings, available for creative work in science which are excluded or suppressed by the general exclusion of women and other groups from active participation in knowledge creation.

So, feminist epistemology does much better than its traditional rivals in the way it understands and proposes to improve the processes of knowledge *creation* (this is close to the position developed by Sandra Harding (1991: ch.6)). But this still leaves the matter of *evaluation* and *testing* of rival knowledge-claims once they have been produced. Are the traditional epistemologists right in insisting on value-neutrality, universality, impersonality and empirical testing for this aspect of science (sometimes called the 'context of justification' as opposed to the 'context of discovery')?

First, it should be noted that this distinction is not as clear as it is sometimes made out to be: quite a lot of 'testing', often in the form of 'thought experiments', goes on in the creative process of devising a theory or hypothesis (see Darwin's notebooks (Darwin 1987) for an extraordinary example of this long-drawn-out process of mental 'trial and error'). Second, there are important differences between the various scientific disciplines with respect to what should count as 'evidence'. What feminist standpoint epistemology brings out very clearly is the way one and the same society can be seen very differently on the basis of the life experience and social practice of people differently situated within it. The experience of a 'disabled' person attempting to use public transport is not like to the experience of reading a thermometer in a scientific experiment. The latter is one which is in principle replicable by 'standard' observers, irrespective of who they are, or where the experiment is conducted. By contrast, the experience of the disabled in relation to transport access is unavoidably located and particular. The authenticity of its status as a contribution to knowledge about the society derives from the identity and characteristics of that particular subject of the experience. It is precisely this aspect of the role of evidence and experience in historical and social scientific work which feminist standpoint epistemology grasps.

However, not all evidence that social scientists and historians use is like this. Much of it is provided by state bureaucracies, opinion surveys, large-scale quantitative research projects and so on. Moreover its reliability, validity and theoretical significance remains open to debate. Surely classical epistemology has the edge over feminist standpoint epistemology when it comes to providing rules for conducting this debate? There is more to be said about this than we have space for, but if we take, for example, the traditional epistemological demand for anonymity and impersonality, this has good reasons behind it. The justification of these rules (we leave aside here the question whether they are really followed in actual scientific institutions) is that they provide a context for evaluating knowledge-claims in which the quality of evidence and argument can be considered independently of power and status hierarchies among participants to the debate.

However, there is another and more radical way of achieving this aim. It is to re-institutionalize scientific debate in ways which open it up to a more diverse and inclusive range of participants, and at the same time to resist the existing hierarchies of power and status. If the contributions of all are equally valued and respected, then the shield of anonymity and impersonality is no longer so crucial. This is very much in line with the project of increasing women's participation in a reformed practice of science which is shared by the main advocates of both so-called 'feminist empiricism' and standpoint epistemology. It is also an interesting, if only partial, convergence with Habermas's idea of an 'ideal speech situation' (see Chapter 7). A significant difference, of course, is that the idea of 'standpoint' suggests the likelihood that diversity of outlooks will persist through even the most egalitarian dialogue.

The above considerations show at least one way in which the claims of feminist standpoint epistemology can be justified. However, in the process the ground has shifted to some extent. The approach being justified here is not the classic standpoint one, since it is not the standpoint itself which justifies the perspective it gives. Feminist epistemology is not justified simply and solely because it has been arrived at from the perspective of women, or feminists. Rather, the position we have arrived at is that feminist epistemology compares very well with traditional epistemologies, and offers insights and possibilities for reform inconceivable for them. This can be shown by giving reasons and citing evidence (for example, about the actual practice of contemporary science). No one is expected to accept these arguments just because they are uttered by feminists, but, equally, it is not just a coincidence that they have been developed by feminists. Feminist standpoint theory offers (testable) explanations of this fact (in terms of the sexual division of labour, gendered personality development and so on).

This takes us back in the direction of Sandra Harding's 'feminist empiricism' (pp. 145–6). We suggested earlier that the transformations already achieved by feminists working in some social science disciplines seem to be much more far-reaching than this somewhat disparaging term implies (see Holmwood 1995). The implications of the 'revised' standpoint approach just discussed are that the struggle against 'bad science' need not be limited to exposing factual biases and errors, but can extend to a much broader challenge to prevailing research programmes, conceptions of what counts as 'good evidence', methodological procedures, social relations and institutional forms, the relationship of scientific work to popular social movements, and also access on equal terms to scientific work on the part of previously excluded or marginalized groups.

Post-modern Feminism

So far we have discussed the way feminist standpoint epistemology can be justified in terms of what it shares with feminist empiricism and traditional epistemologies. However, the period during which feminist standpoint epistemology was being developed also saw the deluge of anti-Enlightenment thinking known as 'post-modernism'. Some feminists, including several of those involved in the creation of standpoint epistemology, were attracted to some post-modern themes. In a number of cases they drew on what they considered to be important insights offered by feminist versions of post-modernism, while holding on to a (revised) standpoint approach, whereas others identified themselves more closely with post-modernism, understood as incompatible with key commitments of standpoint epistemology. This debate is very complex, and many issues remain unresolved.

Many of the issues posed by post-modernism are shared by its feminist versions, and since we will be dealing in more detail with post-modernism in Chapter 10, this gives us an excuse for the very limited discussion of the feminist post-modern criticisms of standpoint epistemology here. The most significant of these criticisms are two in number. The first starts out from an acknowledgement made by Hartsock in her original presentation of the standpoint approach. This was that emphasizing women's commonality ran the risk of marginalizing or suppressing the important differences between the life experiences of women in different social positions: white and black, heterosexual and lesbian, middle class and working class, colonizer and colonized and so on. This recognition of difference within the category 'woman' assumed greater moral and political significance with the insistence on the part of some groups of women that the feminist movement had come to represent only the interests of educated, white, middle-class Western women. The ensuing concern with diversity of social identities coincided with much more general claims being made by post-modernists about the fragmentation and fluidity of identities, and the necessary failure of language to refer to any fixed or general category – such as 'woman'. Some feminists have responded to the assertion of diversity by proposing a difference-sensitive reworking of feminism, and linked this with wider coalitions of oppressed and exploited groups (Harding 1986, 1991, 1998). Others have opted for a far-reaching 'deconstruction' of the category 'woman' itself, in line with the post-modernist opposition to 'essentialism' (see Sayer 2000: ch. 4 for an excellent critical realist discussion of post-modern anti-essentialism). It is, of course, hard to make any sense of what it might be to remain a feminist having deconstructed the category 'woman'.

The second, closely related, post-modernist theme to be taken up by feminist critics of standpoint epistemology was the rejection of epistemology itself: the abandonment of any attempt to evaluate knowledge-claims, and even of the notion of an independent reality of which knowledge could be gained. In part, as we will see, this form of radical relativism derived from a certain (question-able) reading of the linguistic theory of Ferdinand de Saussure (see Chapter10), and in part from Foucault's treatment of truth claims ('regimes of truth') as unavoidably connected to strategies of power or of domination. For the critics of standpoint theory, it was too close to 'patriarchal' scientific rationality in its acceptance of the Enlightenment heritage of commitment to truth and object-ivity. What was needed was not better science, or more reliable knowledge, since this spelt only yet another 'regime of truth'. Instead, standpoint theory should give way to a positive welcoming of diversity of cultures and understand-ings, without trying to establish the truth of any one. The limitations of this abandonment of realism are spelt out by Hilary Rose:

> What has been called the 'linguistic turn' is a good reason for being grateful to postmodernism which has indeed been feminism's ally in sharpening our ears to hear the construction of knowledge and its coupling with power, but gratitude does not carry with it any necessary commitment to abandon truth claims. While a historian can read natural science as stories, leaving the scientists with their problems of truth-claims subverted but not resolved, a natural scientist and/or a feminist engaged in health struggles has to be a realist, has to care about 'hard facts'. (Rose 1994: 81).

Further Reading

Sandra Harding's *The Science Question in Feminism* (1986) and *Whose Science? Whose Knowledge?* (1991) are now classic statements, along with Hilary Rose's 'Hand, Heart and Brain' (1983) and Nancy Hartsock's *Money, Sex and Power* (1983b). Hilary Rose's more recent *Love, Power and Knowledge* (1994) is an excellent guide to the debates. For further reading on feminist epistemology and post-modernism see Hilary Rose (1994; ch 4), Sandra Harding (1986, 1991: pts 2 and 3), L. J. Nicholson (1990), Kate Soper (1991, 1995), S. Lovibond (1989) and G. McLennan (1995).

Post-script

Harding 2004 is a valuable collection of essays relating to standpoint theory – some classic expositions of the theory, others pursuing divergent lines of argument and criticism. Sandra Harding's introduction (as well as her contribution to Turner and Roth 2003) reviews the development of standpoint theory, presents its main arguments and defends it from a range of familiar criticisms. She goes on to outline the practical prescriptions in it for research practice. Nancy Hartsock's pioneering article advocating a materialist standpoint theory (originally 1983) is included together with a selection of her other essays in feminist theory in Hartsock (1998).

The challenge of post-structuralist modes of thought to feminism, as it had been understood and practiced, has produced a number of responses. Caroline New (1998, 2003) provides a valuable assessment of the issues raised from the standpoint of critical realism. Lawson (1999, 2003b) sparked a lively debate in the journal *Feminist Economics* on the value of critical realism for feminist research. See also Barker (2003), Harding (1999) and Peter (2003) and the comments in my post-script to this edition (Commentary on Recent Developments).

10

Post-structuralism and Post-modernism

Introduction

It is difficult to cut a way through the various approaches and ideas which can be catalogued under the headings of this chapter. 'Post-structuralism' is comparatively straightforward in the sense that it is possible to limit the term to the work of those thinkers who were initially seen as structuralists of one sort or another and/or whose work developed from that position to a more fluid and complex set of arguments. This would include, among others, Foucault, Lacan and Derrida – a historian of ideas, a psychoanalyst and a philosopher. The term 'post-modernism' would include, in addition to the ideas of these thinkers, those of the French sociologists Baudrillard and Lyotard and the American social psychologist Kenneth Gergen, as well as many more less-known social psychologists and sociologists. Post-modernist ideas have been influential across several disciplines – sociology, psychology, social psychology, history, literature and the humanities and cultural studies – and they have to some degree entered popular consciousness, at least through the use of the term 'post-modern', although not many people outside universities would know of the post-structuralists.

It is also unclear exactly to what the term 'post-modern' refers. Is it a style of architecture, of literature and art, a form of contemporary culture, a form of society, a form of personal identity or what? And can we actually talk about post-modern philosophy, or is it a contradiction in terms?

The simplest way into these ideas is to take up some of the ideas of structuralism, the movement which dominated French academia in the 1960s, which we can relate to approaches studied earlier in this book. We can see structuralism as in part developing the school of French epistemology discussed in Chapter 4, out of which critical realism developed (Chapter 8). It cut across different disciplines: anthropology (Lévi-Strauss 1966, 1968), history and the history of ideas (the early Foucault, 1970, 1972), literature (Culler 1975), forms of analysis which would now be known as cultural studies (Barthes 1967), psychoanalysis (Lacan 1968) and (through Althusser's Marxism) sociology (Althusser 1969).

Common to all these writers was an emphasis – often an overemphasis – on underlying structures and an underemphasis on the acting subject, or an even stronger dismissal of the significance of the acting subject. Often the power of agency would be attributed to the structure: people were read by books or spoken by language, not the other way around. This position is the diametric opposite of those discussed in the chapters on the interpretive approaches; the proper object of any social science is not, it is argued, people and their meanings but the underlying structures which generate those meanings and in some sense generate the people themselves. Moreover, it is often argued that a series of major thinkers in fact 'decentred' human beings: Galileo had shown that the earth was not the centre of the universe, Darwin that humanity was not the centre of creation, Marx that people were not the centre of their societies and Freud that individuals were not simple acting subjects but the product of unconscious drives.

The model for this was taken from linguistics, and read back into other theories such as Marxism and psychoanalysis. It was a theory developed by Ferdinand De Saussure (1959), a major figure in the linguistic turn in Western thought. Following the same course, it is argued that Saussure shows that people are not the speakers of their language, rather that there is a sense in which they are spoken by their language. Working during the early years of the twentieth century, Saussure made a series of methodological distinctions which enabled the development of a scientific linguistics, arguing that this could not happen as long as it concerned itself with individual speech acts and the history of language. Individual speech acts ('parole') are simply too variable to enable us to understand or explain anything about the language ('langue') as a whole, and language is not changed by individual speech acts, so we cannot understand its history through focusing on them.

To identify the structure of language, Saussure takes several steps. The first is similar to the phenomenological reduction we discussed in Chapter 5. We drop the common-sense assumption that words are somehow naturally attached to the objects to which they seem to refer: there is no necessary connection between the word 'hand' and the rather spidery fleshy things at the end of my arms that I use to type my manuscript. Rather, the connection is a convention – it's as if native English speakers agree that this is what 'hand' will mean; of course, we don't actually negotiate with anybody – speaking English and using its conventions is an offer we can't refuse if we are born in England and want to talk to those around us. The language we speak exists before we are born and continues to exist after we die, and as individuals we have no effect on its underlying structure.

Separating language from its referents enables Saussure to identify an underlying structure of signs and rules governing the combination of signs. The *sign* is seen as a combination of a *signifier* – a material element, the marks on a piece of paper or the noise one makes when speaking – and a *signified* – the concept or idea to which the marks or sounds are attached. It is important to remember that it is the concept, not the object, which is signified and that the relationship is conventional.

For structuralists, a science becomes a science when it develops a coherent theoretical conceptual framework which identifies underlying structures. The structure of a language consists of signs and the rules which govern the combinations of signs. The meaning of a sign is defined not by external objects to which it refers but by its relationships to other signs.

Saussure suggests that these relationships can be analysed along two dimensions. The first, the *syntagm*, is the horizontal axis and consists of the rules which govern the ways in which signs follow each other. Saussure is talking about the smallest units of a language, so we can say that in English the sound *h* cannot (I think) be followed by the sound *b* but the opposite is possible (for example, in the word 'abhor'). The second is a vertical axis involving signs that can be substituted for each other through similarities in sound or meaning. Thus in the sentence 'my hands are on the table', 'hands' could be replaced by my other extremities, my feet, or, if I possessed some South African money, the 'h' could be replaced by 'r' and my rands would be on the table. The anthropologist Levi-Strauss tried to describe languages and cultures in terms of binary oppositions – hand/feet or h/r – where one term could substitute for another term but the two could not be used together. He suggested that the human brain worked through setting up such oppositions and this was the basic way in which humans organize their world. Although not many people now maintain such an idea, it is worth noting the affinity with dialectical thinking.

We have also come across the notion of language and rules in relation to Peter Winch and Wittgenstein in Chapter 6, but it is by no means clear that the two theoretical systems are compatible, and Saussure is best seen as describing a deeper structure than Winch, below the level of intentional statements with which the latter concerns himself. Both share the implication that there is no absolute definition for any word, or any sign. For Saussure the meaning of a sign lies in its relationship to other signs, in between words and not in the words themselves. We will see the idea of difference becomes increasingly important as we move forward into post-structuralism.

To repeat: most structuralists held a strong sense of 'science', defined as the construction of a 'theoretical object' or theoretical grasp of an underlying structure. The work of the scientist is then to elaborate this structure as rigorously as possible. The criteria of whether a particular theory is scientific or not lies not in the relationship of its concepts to empirical reality (as it does for positivism), nor in the extent to which it grasps individual or cultural meanings (as it does for the interpretive approaches) but in the rigorous rational coherence of its structure. Science is about concepts which identify empirical realities, not about the empirical realities themselves. This again is the idealism of the linguistic turn in philosophy, but here it is not language as such but theory which creates the world.

Such an approach, in its purest form, could not last long. One can construct all sorts of rigorous, rational theories, but it does not follow that they are right because they are rigorous and rational, otherwise many people suffering from paranoia would be regarded as brilliant scientists. The development of critical realism (see Chapter 8) in Britain took the ideas close to a more orthodox philosophy, whereas the French development produced something very different.

Post-structuralism: The Move to the Signifier

Post-structuralism brings together a meld of disciplines, primarily but not only those with language-centred concerns. We can look at Lacan's psychoanalytic development of Saussure to show one way in which this happens. Lacan claims to be returning to the original Freud, just as Althusser claims to be returning to the original Marx, each of them intending to lay bare the foundation of a science – psychoanalysis and Marxism respectively. Remember that the foundation of a science is the moment of the discovery or the creation of the theoretical object of that science – in the case of psychoanalysis the unconscious, in the case of Marxism the mode of production.

This is not the place to present an outline of psychoanalysis, but an idea of what Freud meant by the unconscious is important because many post-structuralist theorists absorb it into their view of the world. For Freud (Freud 1982) the unconscious was made up of unacceptable *ideas*, not feelings or memories, as many seem to think. The ideas are unacceptable either because they entail a personal threat (I might as a child have murderous thoughts about my mother, but it is difficult for me to acknowledge them because I feel I am dependent for my very life on my mother's care) or because they receive strong social disapproval (as in the case of sexual feelings towards my parents). These ideas are repressed into the unconscious where they comprise a strange world, not governed by the laws of logic, not developing over time but constantly associated with each other in all sorts of non-rational ways, including the sorts of associations of meaning and sound that govern relations on the paradigmatic axis in Saussure's theory.

Lacan argues that the unconscious is structured like a language, but in his version of Saussure's theory it is the signifier – the thing which expresses or conveys the meaning – that is important. Freud's theory of dream work and free association can be seen as a theory of endless displacement – there is no one dream interpretation in psychoanalysis but a constant reinterpretation as we move from one signifier to the next, a sliding between different signifiers according to all sorts of non-rational associations some of which can be made sense of through the literary figures of metaphor and metonymy (Lacan 1968).

For those unfamiliar with literature and psychoanalysis this might not make much sense, but it can be roughly translated into more familiar ideas, which then enable the unfamiliar to be emphasized. Lacan is claiming that language defines the world for us – we can not reach out beyond language to external reality. We have discussed other theorists who hold such an opinion, but they have all fallen back on some idea of rationality in accounting for how we can understand cultures and actions. Lacan argues that we cannot do this – that language works not just with the aid of rules but with all sorts of associations and slippages which have their root in the unconscious. The 'natural' state (which is a contradiction in terms) of human language use is the 'word salad' of the schizophrenic (and schizophrenia frequently recurs as a metaphor in post-modern writings). For Lacan, the way in which we escape this extreme form of confusion is through the fixing of our desires, which primarily occurs through the development of sexuality as described by Freud.

This way of thinking about identity has led in particular to a rich vein of feminist work in psychoanalysis, questioning both common-sense and more elaborate theoretical ideas about sexuality and gender identity (for a good account of the various approaches see Minsky 1996) and has led to an emphasis on the fluidity and multiplicity of identity. It is the movement from the rigorous elaboration of structures to emphasizing the power of signifiers that turns structuralism into post-structuralism. However, for the main philosophical input of post-structuralism we have to turn to the work of Michel Foucault, which has led to a more rigid conception of identity, and above all, of Jacques Derrida.

Foucault: The Construction of the Subject

Foucault is clearly influenced by the work of Nietzsche, the late-nineteenth/early-twentieth-century German philosopher who is sometimes listed under the heading 'existentialist'. Though Nietzsche's philosophy does not fit easily beside others found under that label, neither does he fit easily into the mainstream of Western philosophy. He develops a history which he calls a 'genealogy' in which development is seen not as a smooth or dialectical process forward but as a series of discontinuous shifts; Althusser reinterpreted the Marxist version of history in this light (Althusser 1969; Althusser and Balibar 1970) and Foucault developed a structuralist history of ideas (Foucault 1972) in which structures of ideas (*'epistemes'*) were seen as replacing each other when all the available positions within the previous structure have been used up. This has produced a range of studies passing under the name of 'discourse analysis' (although some owe more to linguistics than to Foucault) and another way of thinking about identity and subjectivity. This was first seen in terms of the individual subject being the product of a particular discourse, but it was developed by Foucault and his interpreters into a more complex version in which subjectivity or identity is seen as the point where different discourses come together in a point of 'suture'. The metaphor here is the joining together of the edges of a wound – a surgical analogy which captures both the sense of precision in real surgery and the sense of a gap, the space between words which is vital to the generation of meaning in structuralist linguistics. This inverts the interpretive approaches discussed in earlier chapters – the individual subject is created by being subjected to a particular discourse or particular discourses. In the Althusserian framework the subjection is to modes of production or ideological apparatuses. In both cases the play on the word 'subject' (the person who is the subject of action and the person who is subjected to something) is a favourite strategy for this sort of approach.

A second aspect of Nietzsche's philosophy which is clearly evident in Foucault is the inversion of the conventional, Enlightenment-based conception of the relationship between knowledge, power and freedom. The conventional relationship which is deeply rooted, at least in Western common sense, is that knowledge increases our freedom in relation both to the natural world and to ourselves. The more we know the more we are able to do. We saw this questioned by the Frankfurt School theorists, who suggested that the development of the modern sciences was a dialectical process involving both liberation and domination. For Nietzsche it was primarily a process of domination, and this was taken up by Foucault in a series of studies of the way in which scientific discourses were applied to deviants: the mad, the criminal and those whom we would now call sexual deviants, over the nineteenth and twentieth centuries (Foucault 1973, 1977, 1979).

In these studies, it is not *epistemes*, the grand discourses, that create subjects but the discourses of the social sciences such as criminology and psychology and sociology, theories of mental illness and sexuality. They sort out, classify and define different types of person who in one sense did not exist before. For example, although there were certainly always people who engaged in homosexual acts which would have been punishable in some societies and not in others, it was only with the development of the science of psychology (especially psychoanalysis) and of modern medical discourses on sexuality that the 'homosexual' as a sort of person with a supposed specific character structure and lifestyle emerged.

The development of much knowledge in the social sciences can be seen in this way and Foucault's work is at the origin of many studies under the heading of 'governmentality' which take up issues that were once dealt with under the heading of the sociology of the professions. One book in particular, produced by Foucault and his students, illustrates this well. It is a study of the confession and trial of a nineteenth-century French peasant, Pierre Riviere, who took an axe to a number of his immediate family. What the study draws out is the arguments between the emerging psychiatric profession and the legal profession over whether Riviere was bad or mad. It is not an argument over something that can be established according to some external or absolute standard outside of each of the conflicting discourses and against which both can be measured. Rather one constitutes him as a responsible agent who should be punished for his crimes, while the other constitutes him, from the same material, as an insane man in need of whatever treatment might be available. They then fight out a power struggle about the jurisdiction of each profession – the new profession of psychiatry of course representing a threat to the well-established legal profession (Foucault 1978b).

One way of thinking about Foucault is as being concerned about the relationship between reason and unreason, constantly exploring the way in which the former creates the latter – the way in which the sciences and reason necessarily imply their opposite, 'non-science' and unreason, the way in which the rational implies the 'irrational'. In political terms this is translated into thinking about how the exclusion of social groups takes place, and we often find a juxtaposing of science and reason and those with power – the white races, men – on the one hand, and, on the other, those without power – non-white ethnic groups and women, the arts and emotion. It is as if such thought often sets up a rigidified dialectic – there are two opposites but there is no interpenetration or movement; this is something which will be considered again later. Unlike in the theories of identity and subjectivity which developed from Lacan's work, the emphasis is less on the multiplicity of identities and more on rigid forms of constructed identity – technological metaphors are often used (Craib 1998).

One of Foucault's main themes is the way in which social order in the modern world relies less upon external force and policing and more upon the internal disciplining of individual. We are not made to behave in a particular way, but we make ourselves behave in that way. We are not the more or less free-choosing agents of rational choice theory or any other of the interpretive approaches – rather, these very ideas of choice and freedom ensure our subordination.

Derrida and Deconstruction

The most sophisticated philosopher of post-structuralism is Jacques Derrida. His influence is widespread, clearest of all perhaps in philosophy and literary studies but with an implicit or explicit effect on nearly all the social sciences except economics and cognitive psychology. The spirit of his philosophy is often more apparent than the letter, although the term 'deconstruction' in now fairly common in academic circles.

Derrida is best situated in the tradition of Nietzsche and Heidegger (another German philosopher who is commonly labelled an existentialist). The focus of his work is again language and the way in which language relates to our world and our experience. Our way into this chapter was through Lacan's interpretation of Saussure, and the priority that he gave to the signifier, but it will be remembered that while Lacan was aware of the continual movement through signifiers, along, if you like, the signifying chain, he also argued that there were points where that movement was fixed. For Derrida there is no fixed point: he is the philosopher of absence, and what we suggested was a methodological strategy for Saussure becomes what can only be called a metaphysical assumption for Derrida, although doubtless he would deny that as metaphysics is a crime that only others commit.

The others who commit metaphysics include nearly everybody who has contributed to Western philosophy, and the metaphysical assumption Derrida criticizes is the assumption that there is some final presence which is signified. Again we find the idea we met with Lacan, that when we try to give a final meaning to a word we are embarking on an endless (and circular) task of travelling around the signifiers. As a way of showing this, Derrida puts some concepts 'under erasure', a disturbing habit of writing the concept and putting a large X through it. Meaning is always elsewhere, never in the words we use; it is always absent, but most philosophers have assumed or sought a meaning that was present.

Derrida develops a series of critiques of philosophers he regards as guilty of assuming a presence on two levels (Derrida 1973, 1976, 1978). The first level is a critique of *phonocentrism*, of giving priority to the spoken word rather than the written word – Saussure is seen as guilty of this. Speech can give an impression or illusion of self-identity in a way that writing cannot – when I talk I can think that I am expressing my real self; it is only when I sit down at my desk and try to write that I begin to question what I am saying. If a student in a class asks me what Derrida means by 'phonocentrism', I could give a short answer which I could feel to be sufficient: 'He means giving priority to spoken language over written language.' However, looking at my computer screen and trying to elaborate on the idea I find myself asking whether this is what he really means – it can't be that he says this because written language precedes speech historically, or because it is higher than speech in some conceptual hierarchy, since it is precisely that sort of hierarchy that he is contesting. Or have I found a weak point in his argument? And so on.

The second level is a critique of 'logocentricity', the overarching belief in a presence, something to which the word refers, some firm and finite meaning. Logocentric thought looks for the foundations of knowledge, something Husserl does by means of the phenomenological reduction, or for the goals of knowledge, as did Hegel for example when he argued that the development of thought led to the end of history, a final totalization. And it also looks for a principle around which ideas can be organized in a hierarchy. For Derrida language is metaphorical and we can never break free of metaphor. There is no way out of here.

Deconstruction, a term now in use well beyond the boundaries of post-structuralism, involves a constant questioning and dismantling of implicit or explicit notions of presence and a concentration on the play of metaphors, the play of language. The author becomes a means by which metaphors reproduce and extend themselves. Thus my attempt to explain Derrida's work here cannot possibly achieve its goal, since, strictly speaking, there is no work to explain, no pure meaning out there in his books to which I or anybody can gain access.

All I can do is produce metaphors for his metaphors in the endless play of texts upon one anther. A distinctly Derridean notion in literary criticism is that of 'intertextuality' – literary texts being written about and upon each other with is a constant interpenetration between them. There is no one meaning or even one set of meanings to a novel, or a philosophical system or even a scientific theory. If we wish we can read our computer manual as a poem. The late Madan Sarup sums up all this as well as anybody: with deconstruction there is a shift from 'identities to differences, unities to fragmentations, ontology to philosophy of language, epistemology to rhetoric, presence to absence' (Sarup 1993: 59).

Post-modernism: Losing Philosophy

Post-structuralism leaves us in a strange position: absence, difference, fragmentation and rhetoric. None of this has anything to do with knowledge, the concern of every other philosopher and every philosophical position so far considered in this book. David West suggests however that there was still some ambivalence in the work of Foucault and Derrida. They were still both connected to the traditions they criticize, and Derrida in particular was aware of the impossibility of leaving it behind. West suggests that Derrida is best summed up in an adaptation of a line from Samuel Beckett: Western philosophy 'can't go on, must go on' (West 1996; Beckett 1965) – a paradox which would be appreciated by Adorno and which is perhaps not very far from his own position towards the end of his life.

Post-modernism goes further than this and gives up altogether the attempt to found or establish bases for knowledge, and it is questionable whether we should look at it as a philosophy at all. It is arguable that it should be regarded as a contemporary sociology of knowledge since these positions are developed out of analyses of the rapid social changes that seem part and parcel of late capitalism or late modernity or post-modernity. These three different ways of characterizing contemporary Western societies carry different implications but they are not mutually exclusive. The term 'late capitalism' draws attention to the continuities with societies of the nineteenth century, the way in which contemporary globalization can be understood as the most recent manifestation of capitalist relations of production; in fact one argument is that post-modernism can best be seen as an ideology of late capitalism (Harvey 1990; Jameson 1991), an argument to which I will return later.

There are two significant theorists of post-modernism who have something to say of philosophical import. Both are ex-Marxists and the work of one, Jean Baudrillard, can be understood as a development from Marxism more clearly than the one I am going to deal with first – Jean-Francoise Lyotard (1984). Both work with ideas of radical social change breaking up the world of experience (remember, post-modernism has as much to do with the arts and humanities as with the social sciences), and it is often pointed out that schizophrenia and pastiche are favourite post-modernist metaphors. Nothing is certain, nothing stands still long enough to be identified, there is no such thing as knowledge in any scientific sense, philosophy in any totalizing sense; there may be rational thought but it has no priority over the irrational and it eventually merges into the irrational. As we will see, the attempt to think rationally is often equated with political oppression.

For Lyotard it is the rapid growth of information that brings about this change. Power now derives from the possession of information or knowledge rather than possession of capital, and because there is so much knowledge available, we cannot any longer claim that any one is in possession of the truth. He draws on notions that we came across in the chapters on interpretive sociology – Wittgenstein' s notion of language games and notions of narrative – to portray a world of overlapping games and narratives with a shifting focus in which it is not possible to find one 'grand narrative' or 'meta-narrative' into which all narratives and games can be translated. His main book, *The Postmodern Condition* (1984), portrays a fluid, and linguistic reality thought which we move from one language game to another, not a world of objects or structures. It is as if Marx's description of the effects of the capitalist market – 'everything that is solid turns to air' – now describes the whole of reality. Yet as my reference to Wittgenstein and Marx should indicate, firm declarations of the end of philosophy (or anything else) bring with them a great deal of what has supposedly ended.

Baudrillard (1975) does not carry much with him at all. His roots are in Marxism and the theories of consumer capitalism (replacing production-based capitalism) that were popular in the decades after the Second World War. Now, according to Baudrillard, post-modern society has left production a long way behind. What is important now is reproduction. We have moved from copying the real object (the Renaissance period) to reproducing the real object (consumer capitalism) to reproducing the copying process itself – this brings us to the *hyperreal*, the post-modern proper. We live in a world of images, of copies, which leaves the real – whatever that may be – a long way behind, together with truth and anything else that might hint at stability. There is only the surface appearance left, no underlying reality. Baudrillard is famous, or notorious, for his comment that Gulf War did not really happen. That was certainly a great comfort to those Iraqis who thought they were dead. The psychological equivalent of this is Kenneth Gergen's work (Gergen 1991). He claims that post-modern identities are infinitely fluid, that we can be whatever we want to be.

The Politics of Post-structuralism and Post-modernism

Before trying to examine these approaches in philosophical terms, we will look at the political positions with which they are associated. For theories which emphasize movement, fluidity and the paradoxical complexity of a reality which is seen as largely linguistic or symbolic, it is not surprising that they can be associated with a range of political positions.

Both positions see the Enlightenment, rationality and science as representing hierarchies and oppression. At their most simplistic there is a juxtaposition of science, knowledge, rationality, presence, identity, hierarchy, domination, white European males on the one side, and deconstruction, absence, difference, women, minorities, the former colonized peoples on the other. This is clearly highly simplistic, particularly when it is remembered that the discourses which led to the formation of national liberation movements and often the triumph of the colonized peoples as well as those that generated feminism and campaigns for racial equality were the rational discourses of the Enlightenment.

Post-structuralism, in the form of the celebration of difference, can lead on to a multi-culturalism, a sort of political relativism or a position akin to that which we earlier connected to the work of Peter Winch, but which, in the last analysis, Winch managed to avoid: that we cannot judge between different cultures, but should just enjoy the difference – although whether such enjoyment extends to the culture of National Socialism in Germany or that of those societies which practice female circumcision is another matter. If there is no presence, no truth, no morality which can be argued about, it is difficult to know how we can condemn the Holocaust, or the oppression of women or ethnic minorities. If we adopt post-modernist or post-structuralist conceptions of truth or morality, then the paradoxical result seems to be that we cannot argue that the hierarchies we condemn are worse or more oppressive than the absence of hierarchies we propose: they are just different.

The arguments for celebration of difference can also be interpreted as another version of the left-liberalism which has developed in European politics since the end of Second World War – as being a rather anodyne argument for mutual tolerance – although many postmodernists might not be satisfied with this.

Finally there is a critical post-modernism which can be connected with the Frankfurt School, particularly the later works of Adorno. The constant deconstruction of claims to knowledge and truth can be seen as the critique of the positive, the critique of domination, and the rejection of meta-narratives can be seen as equivalent to Ardorno's rejection of totalizing theories and their association with totalitarianism. But that is only one side of the dialectical reason of critical theory, and this leads us to the philosophical arguments about these positions.

What Do We Do with the Posts?

The most intelligent philosophical critique of post-structuralism and post-modernism comes from Habermas (1990), and most of what we say here is a gloss on his arguments. In Chapter 1 we suggested that both of the main schools of philosophical thought implied a radical democratic reorganization of society – what Habermas would call the emancipatory project of the Enlightenment. Like his Frankfurt predecessors he is aware that this project can turn into its opposite, but the main thrust of his work has been to emphasize the emancipatory project as an *unfinished project* rather than to criticize tendencies towards domination. Whereas Habermas tries to hold the two sides together and see the Enlightenment as an unfinished project, the thinkers discussed in this chapter seem to have abandoned it.

The problem with trying to abandon vast and complex bodies of thought is that it cannot be done. One cannot think new thoughts out of nowhere, and critiques of the Enlightenment can only come from within the Enlightenment and be based upon Enlightenment principles. All the thinkers discussed in this chapter, for example, *argue* for their positions; in other words they employ *reason*, the very reason they are criticizing, and they are thus placed very firmly within the tradition they are criticizing, while the radical politics that some of them uphold – notions of democracy, tolerance, multiculturalism, the equality of the sexes – all of these things can be argued for from within the traditions they criticize and in many cases these ideas were generated from these traditions.

The process of dialectical thought suggests that we cannot think about absence without also thinking about presence, that we cannot dispute the existence of a meta-narrative except by positing a meta-narrative that absurdly denies its own possibility. The very process of thinking moves towards a linking of objects, exploring their relationships to each other, and in the end moves towards grasping a totality of objects. In the context of this book, thinking has led us from the world of external objects, the natural sciences, through to several levels of human consciousness and thought, and to ideas of underlying social structures. The thinkers discussed in this chapter seem to use all this to launch themselves into a space where none of these things have much relevance, but it is possible to look at the point of take-off and bring them back to the whole process.

The point of take-off is the methodological act by which Saussure established language as an object for scientific investigation: the dropping of the idea that language has a referent. Now it is quite possible to accept that signs gain their meaning from their relationships to each other *and* that they also refer to something outside themselves. To deny this is to deny everyday experiences that make life itself possible. That the word 'food' is a conventional label that we attach to things we eat, and that its meaning is defined by the conventional system of signs to which it belongs, is beyond doubt. Also beyond doubt is the fact that it refers to the very real bread and cheese (and other things) in my kitchen without which I would I die. These are not mutually exclusive possibilities.

We seem to be talking here about two (probably two of many) ways of using language: the instrumental and the poetic. The manual that comes with the boiler in my central heating system is written in an instrumental language. It could be re-read as a poem, but I suspect it would not be one of lasting value, and to read it that way would be of no use when the boiler goes wrong. On the other hand, one might read *Romeo and Juliet* as a set of instructions about how to behave when in love, but that is most likely to leave one dead or looking foolish. But the two uses of language are a necessary part of human existence. Some uses of language, and in particular that of some philosophers, combine both in a more equal way.

It is arguable that the post-structuralists and post-modernists do get hold of a particular dimension of contemporary experience in the Western world in their denials of truth, beauty, knowledge and so on. The descriptions of social changes by Lyotard and Baudrillard are not exhaustive, but they produce a sense of falling apart, a sense of vertigo at the speed of change, a sense of falling out of control and a sense of disconnection which is theoretically formulated in their work. What they do not and cannot do is grasp the deeper structural changes in society that produce these experiences. In the sense that they grasp part only of contemporary reality we can regard them as philosophical ideologies.

Further Reading

For structuralism, the best introduction is still Frederic Jameson's *The Prison House of Language* (1972). For the development of post-structuralism and post-modernism, see Madan Sarup's *Introductory Guide to Post-Structuralism and Post-Modernism*. See also David West's *An Introduction to Continental Philosophy* (1996: chs. 6, 7) and Ian Craib's *Modern Social Theory* (1992: chs. 8, 9, 10).

For original structuralist texts, see Saussure, *Course in General Linguistics* (1959); Barthes, *Elements of Semiology* (1967) and Lévi-Strauss's *Structural Anthropology* (1968).

There are no easy post-structuralist or post-modernist texts, but the most accessible include Foucault's *Discipline and Punish* (1977) and the first volume of his *History of Sexuality* (1978a), also Lyotard's *The Postmodern Condition* (1984); if you are feeling brave try Baudrillard's *The Mirror of Production* (1985) also Derrida's *On Grammatology* (Derrida 1973).

Post-script

In recent years, the direct influence of the more extreme versions of post-structuralist and post-modernist scepticism has declined, but their legacy in the form of the research focus on language and culture and the popularity of 'constructionist' approaches to social problems remains strong. An important and still influential strand among the 'posts' was not addressed in our first edition. This is the 'post-Marxism' pioneered by

Laclau and Mouffe (1985). Though presented primarily as a new approach to social theory and substantive research, it clearly had philosophical underpinnings. These were to some extent explored in a debate between Roy Bhaskar and Ernesto Laclau (Laclau and Bhaskar 1998), but have been given a valuable extended treatment in Glynos and Howarth (2007). An appreciation and critical discussion of this is given in the postscript to this book (Commentary on Recent Developments).

11

Conclusion: In Defence of Philosophy

In the course of this book, we have set out a number of different but often related philosophical positions, and we have argued various positions of our own; it is now time to go back over these positions and arguments in a way that (we hope) joins up loose ends and emphasizes the most important points that we would want to get across. Perhaps to begin with it is important to make some very general points about the value of philosophical argument. The contemporary philosopher Charles Taylor, in his work on modern conceptions of the self (Taylor 1991), has pointed to the increasing dominance of instrumental thinking in the modern world, and one thing we can learn from the philosophical arguments that we have presented in this book is that there is more to intellectual life than simple instrumentality. We also argue about things not simply in order to find the most efficient method of doing something, of achieving some practical end. We also argue about values, about what amounts to a 'good' or a desirable way of living. If we take the way of looking at the world that we can find in Adorno or Gadamer or Alisdair MacIntyre and compare it with the stricter versions of rational choice theory it is possible to see what we are talking about.

There are particular values carried by the arguments we have explored here. One is respect for the complexity of scientific and philosophical investigations, whether in the natural or the social sciences. It is too easy to say that the social sciences are in no way like the natural sciences rather than ask what they might have in common and where the differences might be; it is too easy to adopt a conventionalist position on both natural and social sciences, and avoid thinking about backing up our ideas with argument and evidence. It is too easy to adopt an interpretivist or phenomenological position without asking how we interpret, how we understand what people tell us. Do we have to take what they say for granted? Do we have to place their statements in a wider context etc? And it is too easy to adopt an interpretivist position without asking difficult ontological questions about the nature of social reality. The message of this is that there is a value in thinking itself, in recognizing the subtleties, depths and paradoxes of the ideas we use, and of the world

177

we study, in not avoiding difficult issues because there is no clear answer to them.

We have presented a complex picture of the social sciences, certainly collectively, but also, we would argue, individually as well – they work with different methods, different forms of knowledge, and different criteria by which that knowledge is judged. More important, the social world itself is complex, involving a number of different objects which do not fall easily into the province of any one social science – economics, history, sociology, social psychology and psychology all study interactions between human beings, from different perspectives and with different ends in view. Human beings are all also objects of biology and other natural sciences which produce their own knowledge of the social world.

In Chapters 2 and 3 we set out the positivist approach to natural science and examined the way in which such an approach has been used by social scientists – Durkheim being the classic example. It would be difficult to rule out of court the practice of this sort of investigation – it is one of the ways we find out about what is going on in society, although it does not necessarily explain what is going on. Historically, such studies have been important guides to political reform and the amelioration of social problems, and social research organized along positivist lines still has its role to play.

The critiques of positivism we examined in Chapters 3 and 4 do not lead to the conclusion that positivist investigations are pointless or that the knowledge that they produce is somehow wrong. Rather they mean that we have to be careful about explaining the information that they produce. For example, the investigation which reveals a link in British society between sex and mental illness – women are more inclined to depression and men to schizophrenia – should not be regarded as establishing a biological cause for mental illness which is different in men and women. The information is a starting-point. Not all women are depressed and not all men are schizophrenic, so there might be psychological variables which have to be taken into account. There may be cultural differences in the ways in which men and women deal with unhappiness and there may be cultural differences in the way that unhappy men and women are perceived by their families and the medical and other caring professions. In other words, the investigation of what we learn from the positivist-based study leads us to interpretivist theorizing, but without that study we have nothing to think about. And of course we can design other studies which can offer us a guide to the adequacy of our interpretive theorizing.

It is always important to avoid seeing issues in black and white. There is perhaps still a tendency among students and the wider population to think that the natural sciences produce knowledge which is somehow absolutely and definitely true, for all time and all places. Unfortunately, some natural scientists seem to make that assumption, but no natural scientist who is worth listening to would claim such an absolute status for what he or she is proposing: knowledge, whether it is produced by the social or the natural sciences, is always provisional, always there to be questioned and investigated further.

It is usual now, particularly among sociologists, to assume that, because it can be shown that scientific knowledge is not in some sense final or absolute, and that it is influenced by the values of the surrounding culture, it is no different from any other way of looking at the world. Some sophisticated versions of this view were examined in Chapter 4, and we argued there that there is a clear case that we cannot absorb everything into discourse or culture. Our contemporary culture has its own view of the natural world but that natural world has an existence that is independent of our view of it. The laws of gravity existed before Newton, and they would still exist tomorrow even if the whole of humanity were suddenly wiped out by some strange new disease.

We argued that this sort of issue is at the moment best understood in the development of critical realism – in distinctions such as that between transitive and intransitive dimensions of knowledge. The existence of scientific activity implies the existence of an *intransitive* reality, of different levels of a reality independent of our conceptions; and there is also a *transitive* area, a cultural area which, as the conventionalists point out, influences the nature of scientific investigations and explanations. Given what seems to be the increasing dominance of conventionalist and constructionist arguments in social science, perhaps this is one of the most important points we have to make here. Importantly, it is a point that depends on a real philosophical argument – not on the empirical investigation of any one discipline or science, but through reflection on what scientists do.

When in Chapter 5 we moved on to the interpretive traditions, we presented them as holding the position that whatever the adequacies or inadequacies of positivism as a philosophy of the natural sciences, the social sciences were different. This is generally the way they have been presented to students and it is half true, but it should have become apparent from the sort of criticisms that we developed, and the logic of their own arguments, that there is more at work than the cultural or discursive dimensions of understanding. Those theorists we presented as employing an instrumental rationality imply the existence of a real external world, a world that is independent of our concepts, an implication which is there on a common-sense level. For the pragmatists, for example, the validation of our knowledge comes from its effectiveness in achieving our ends in the world, an everyday empirical testing and revision of knowledge. Weber's distinction between meaning and causal adequacy indicates that there is something more at work than the cultural validation and coherence of explanation; the phenomenologists begin with a basic sense experience that is not produced by consciousness but is worked on by it.

When we move on to the more elaborate hermeneutic approaches, which call on the authority of cultures or traditions or communities as a basis for knowledge, we move further away from the concerns of the natural sciences, and it is perhaps easier to see all knowledge as a product of discourse. But even here there are problems with these approaches, or there are implications, which indicate that there is more to be taken into account. For example, Winch's identification of birth, death and sexual relations as points of contact between cultures indicates that it might be possible to construct trans-cultural knowledge areas, and this is even more the case if we add production to his list. If we accept Charles Taylor's argument, and Winch's own implication, for example, that the Azande are better at providing coherent identities to the individual lives of members of their culture while Western societies are better at understanding and controlling the physical world, then there must, in principle, be shared standards by which these judgements can be made. And those shared standards will have to come to grips with all the issues raised in the book.

Gadamer's hermeneutics and dialectical thinking generally indicates that it is possible to argue through to agreements about the nature of the world and of knowledge, and we will return to this shortly. For the moment there is another implication of these positions. We led into them through looking at the individualist arguments of Weber and the pragmatists and rational choice theory, but apart from Weber they all imply the existence of something over and above the individual – the culture or tradition or community in relation to which, in the case of Gadamer, the individual is profoundly unimportant. There is however a third area, which sociologists have worked with since the nineteenth century and which we have already touched on in our discussion of positivism in sociology: there are 'social facts', or in other versions 'society' or 'social structure', something which is, like culture, over and above the individual, but, unlike culture, not a matter of language or ideas. It is perhaps arguable that the positivism of Comte and Durkheim, and the instrumental aspects of Marx's work, were necessary to identify the existence of such an area, and we came across it in Chapter 7, in our examination of critical theory and the later developments of Habermas's work. The latter identifies a contra-diction and a struggle between what we could crudely call the area of culture, of values and ways of thinking about the world that members of a society share and work with together with a degree of freedom, and the social system, the social structure which rests on an instrumental rationality.

In fact, Habermas offers a complex and subtle way of thinking about the relationship between the natural and social sciences, each with their origin in a different cognitive interest, but each overlapping at various points: some aspects of the social sciences will be like the natural sciences, and the natural sciences will of course be related to the same culture as the social sciences, but he assumes the existence of the different realms, building on work that has gone before. The most rigorous philosophical warrant for the idea of a 'society' different from a culture can be found in critical realism.

We have already mentioned the distinction between transitive and intrans-itive dimensions of knowledge; critical realism also talks about there being different types of being in the social world – there is, if you like, a 'variegated' ontology of the social world. It is not made up of one type of thing, and there are a number of different levels; what we see is less than what there is, whereas for most interpretive approaches what we see is what we get.

In Chapter 1, we talked about the intimate link between philosophy and politics. This has emerged at various points in the course of our arguments. Critical theory and critical realism argue that it is possible to provide a basis for moral and political argument, although the basis which each would argue for is different. Critical realism is closer to the radical impetus of the empiricist tradition, arguing that the firmer our knowledge of the social world the firmer the moral and political arguments that we are able to develop. Critical theory uses one form or another of the idea of rationality itself for the basis of moral argument. One might say that the former is more rooted in what is and the latter more in what might be, but they both see the social sciences as being in some way critical.

Another way in which the social sciences have been argued to be political is on the basis of knowledge representing the interests of a particular social group. We saw that the Marxist Georg Lukacs argued that because of its social position and the universality of its interests, the working class was able to develop a superior knowledge, and, also in the first half of twentieth century, the sociologist Karl Mannheim (1936) made the same claim for 'free floating intellectuals'. In this book, in Chapter 9, we have discussed a similar claim by some contemporary feminists. It is clear that the concerns of some groups – women, ethnic and sexual minorities and others – can be hidden or ignored by the social sciences, and that it is important that their experience and knowledge of their lives must be taken in account. Such knowledge cannot be treated as better knowledge simply on the grounds that it comes from a particular group, any more than it can be discounted because it comes from that same group. Experience and ideas from these groups need to be included in our arguments about what we know and how we know it.

The significance of this debate is perhaps the most important message of the book, and takes us on to the ambivalent politics and ambivalent attitude towards philosophy found in post-structuralism and post-modernism. West's description of Derrida's attitude to philosophy – 'It can't go on and it must go on' – seems to us quite precise. Derrida participates in a debate the presuppositions of which he is criticizing; it is rather like somebody walking along the road denying that she had any legs. One of the several paradoxes of post-structuralism is that it has rekindled the interest of many students in philosophical issues and provoked one of the more interesting debates in contemporary philosophy, namely that with Habermas. The attitude of some post-modernists, however, is more disturbing. They tend to be sociologists or social psychologists rather than philosophers and tend to argue that the sort of philosophical argument carried on in this book is no longer relevant. It involves an argument that there is no point to argument, which is a self-refuting position. Whereas the philosopher Derrida is well aware of the paradoxical implications of his position and attempts to grapple with them, the social psychologist Kenneth Gergen or some of the sociologists of scientific knowledge discussed in Chapter 4 seem happy to argue for a position which denies the possibility or usefulness of argument. The attempt to dissolve philosophical issues into sociological analyses confuses what we called in Chapter 2 the context of discovery and the context of justification; the latter takes ideas out of their original context and subjects them to testing, including the testing of argument.

One of the achievements of Habermas is to move the activity of argument back to the centre of the philosophical stage as far as the social sciences are concerned and to put arguments about the good life and the just society back into social theory. The structure of arguments from the dialecticians and the hermeneuticists shows that we cannot avoid meta-narratives, nor can we avoid the complexity of the specific. They both keep alive the idea that can be found in Hellenistic philosophy, that there is something good about argument itself, for the community and the individual, and it is important that the social sciences maintain that insight. None of the arguments we have discussed in the book are finished, and there are replies to our own that we have to go on thinking about. We have therefore concentrated on the larger issues, on ontology and epistemology, ethics and politics rather than the technical nuts and bolts which sometimes pass as philosophy in the empirical disciplines. Given the much-noted fragmentation of experience and argument in the contemporary world, this in itself is a political act which we are happy to be associated with.

12

Commentary on Recent Developments

The pace of change in an ancient discipline such as philosophy is not rapid. However, there have been developments in the philosophy of social science since Ian and I wrote the first edition of this book. In this set of comments, I have selected a small number of new works and topics that either open up further areas of controversy or promise to re-organize the field in some way. Two substantial works seem to me to require more extensive discussion. Hutchinson *et al.*'s (2008) trenchant defence of Peter Winch's attack on the very idea of a social science gives me an opportunity to take the discussion of Winch's crucially important work rather further than we (mainly Ian) were able to do in the first edition. Glynos and Howarth (2007), also influenced by a 'Winchian' emphasis on meaning and interpretation, have provided us with a rigorous development of the philosophical underpinnings of the post-Marxist discourse theory pioneered by Laclau and Mouffe (1985). This is certainly a major new development in social and political analysis, and the philosophical development of it given by Glynos and Howarth demands a more detailed engagement than Ian and I were able to give in our Chapter 10 on the 'posts'.

Since the late 1970s, the development of critical realism has seemed to many (including both co-authors of this work) a promising way of overcoming the rather sterile opposition between hermeneutic and 'scientific' or naturalistic orientations to the study of society. Critical realists drew on newer understandings of the history and explanatory methods of the natural sciences to argue that the social studies could be objective, even scientific, without conceding to a widely criticized 'positivism'. However, it quickly emerged that there was no consensus even among those committed to a critical realist approach on how to take forward this prospect. In the decade or so since the first edition of this book, an extensive literature has developed in which rival versions of critical realism have engaged critically with one another. At the same time, critical realists of various persuasions have been engaging with other traditions in philosophy of social science, and, more substantively, with some of the long-established theoretical issues in social science explanation. I have concluded this set of comments with an overview of some of the main

183

themes and developments in this literature. Unavoidably, this is less detailed than the treatment of the texts by Hutchinson *et al.* and Glynos and Howarth, and is offered as a guide to further reading for those readers who wish to delve at greater depth.

As mentioned in the preface to this edition, I have taken up the suggestion of one of the reviewers of the first. This commentary is somewhat more explicit in the stance it takes than was (and remains) the main body of the book. Nevertheless, my intention, at least, has been to treat positions with which I disagree respectfully and as generously as is feasible. Partly because of its somewhat more 'committed' style, readers may find this new material more demanding in level than is the rest of the book. It might be helpful to read, or re-read the relevant sections of the main part of the book first.

Peter Winch and Hermeneutics

A large section of Ian's contribution to Chapter 6 (Rationality as rule following) is rightly devoted to an engagement with the philosophical arguments of the late Peter Winch. Ian centres his discussion on Winch's iconic book *The Idea of a Social Science* (TISS)(Winch 1958) and his classic paper 'Understanding a primitive society' (UPS)(Winch 1974), together with comments on Winch by Charles Taylor, Alasdair MacIntyre and others. Winch offered some comments of his own in his introduction to the second edition of *The Idea* (1990), and Raimond Gaita added an insightful introduction to a 50th anniversary edition in 2007. Following Winch's death in 1997, there was a renewal of interest in his work, and a particularly valuable outcome of this was Colin Lyas's book, simply titled *Peter Winch* (1999). More recently, the explosive force of Winch's initial foray into the world of social science has been re-ignited by a brief, but trenchantly iconoclastic defence of Winch's arguments against the possibility of a 'science' of social life (Hutchinson *et al.* 2008). Their strongly expressed hostility to over-eager generalization, 'theoreticism', 'scientism' and 'intellectualism' among would-be social scientists is supported by their reading of Winch (and his philosophical mentor, Ludwig Wittgenstein). On their interpretation of Winch, most commentators on his work seem to have been guilty of serious misreadings. I have some reservations both about their own reading of Winch and also about their very sweeping rejection of almost everything that others who see themselves as social scientists have done. However, the sheer force of Winch's critical thinking about the possibility of social science and the depth of his questioning of the possibilities of mutual understanding across wide cultural differences are uniquely challenging. Winch's thought deserves to be encountered by every generation of apprentices to the social sciences. So, despite my reservations about it, this new book is to be welcomed in reminding us of the great challenge posed by Winch's arguments.

Meaning, Action and Explanation

Ian's discussion of Winch in the first edition of our book is a sympathetic one – he accepts the importance of Winch's insistence on the necessity for students of social life to struggle to understand the social meanings of those they study, rather than moving (too quickly?) on to interpreting them in the categories of their favoured social science theory or tradition. Although some of Winch's arguments have seemed to some readers to imply that there could be no such thing as cross-cultural understanding, and, even, no possibility of reasonably grounded social or political criticism of established 'practices' or 'forms of life', Winch himself never countenanced such conclusions. Hutchinson *et al.* are surely right about this. Winch uses the ideas of 'rules' and 'language games' to show that the meaning and identity of social actions must, first and foremost, be understood in terms given by their context of use. Ian acknowledges this point, but he goes on to argue that 'understanding the meaning' of an action is not the only thing that social scientists do. We might want to know who made the rules, how different people are situated in relation to the rules and so on. Moreover, there is an implication in Winch that there is something 'transparent' about meanings as they are embedded in everyday social life, whereas even getting clear about the meanings of actions can be a major challenge. As Ian put it: '... all sorts of things happen to us which we struggle to understand, and for which our ideas often seem inadequate (PSS: 100).

As I return to it, it seems to me that Ian's reading of Winch falls foul of few, if any, of the misunderstandings listed by Hutchinson *et al.*, but he still makes out a case for a more ambitious programme for the social sciences than they will allow. As I would want to go much further than Ian in advocacy of a (non-reductive) naturalistic programme for the social sciences, I'll take the argument on from where Ian left it.

Neither Winch nor Hutchinson *et al.* provide a serious account of natural science. It has been suggested that Winch himself was aware of the limitations of his account of the natural sciences (Lyas 1999: 52). However, since Hutchinson *et al.* appear to reject all generalizing theoretical approaches in the social studies, they may not need to stray far into the territory of philosophy of the natural sciences. Habermas, Bhaskar, Giddens, Bourdieu and, in general, post-modernists are all repeatedly lined up for dismissal, though none of them is subjected to any specific critical attention.

Central to the argument developed by Hutchinson *et al.* is Winch's insistence on the priority, in characterizing social actions, of grasping the meanings present in the practices to which they belong. Sometimes, it seems that they are committed to the strong thesis that this – perspicuous presentation of the meanings of social actions or practices – is all that social studies can justifiably do. So, for example, on p. 95: 'Understanding *what* people are doing obviates the need for a *why* question, or put another way, means that the description of their action answers any *bona fide* why question.' This clearly implies that Ian's points about further questions we might, as social researchers, ask about a practice cannot be '*bona fide*' questions.

However, elsewhere they seem to take a less restrictive position. Sometimes they seem to accept that asking questions about the origins or conditions for practices may be acceptable, so long as we do not 'presuppose some general, unifying theory', and so long as this does not 'displace' the practice itself as explaining someone's action under it (p. 82). But this is potentially quite a large concession. If we can ask questions about origins and conditions of practices that go beyond simply displaying the meanings that are embedded in them, then, surely, something further needs to be said about what kind of answers might legitimately be given, how they might be checked and discussed and so on. And, though a general theory might not be *presupposed*, might it not *emerge* from further investigations of other practices? How can they know, *a priori*, that this would be something 'absurd'? No good reason is given either by Winch or by his latter-day defenders why accounts of social actions in terms of the meanings available to participants in the social practices to which they belong should not be able to co-exist with understandings and explanations which *begin* there but probe deeper, make links with other sorts of practice and even give rise to modest generalizations. Maybe the authors would concede this in their less polemical moments, but it renders their position much more moderate than their prose-style (and title!) leads the reader to suppose, and it opens up the possibility of a substantive dialogue with other approaches in the social sciences which they dismiss out of hand.

But, as Ian fully acknowledges, even if the Winchian claim about the priority of participants' understanding is accepted, it does not at all follow that this settles the question how to grasp and present that understanding. Ian's point about Winch's assumption of the 'transparency' of social practices and forms of life could be developed further. First, there is a gap between understanding a rule in the sense of 'knowing how to go on', and being able to give an explicit account of it. Wittgenstein's conception of philosophy as 'a battle against the bewitchment of the intelligence by means of language' draws attention to this – and social scientists (as well as critically oriented citizens) are often engaged in related battles (Wittgenstein 1958, 1997, paragraph 109 (p. 47)). Part of the problem is that social practices and the meanings embedded in them may have a misleading superficial form (this is what Wittgenstein had in mind), but also the meanings of many social practices are contested by the participants themselves: there is no single set of meanings that can count authoritatively as 'participants' understanding'.

An incident that occurred during a workshop called to discuss the relationship between Wittgenstein's philosophy and Marxism will serve to illustrate this point and another. The event took place in King's College, Cambridge, and there was a certain irony, given the topic (not to mention the political views of a good proportion of the attendees), in the performance of the required mealtime rituals of the College: to stand as the fellows arrived and took their places, to remain standing while a Latin grace was read and, after the meal, to rise again till the fellows had departed. Interestingly, all but one of us meekly complied. Bar one, we all participated in a practice, thus confirming in action the social relations between ourselves as guests and the fellows of the college. Subsequent reflection revealed that this common participation 'expressed' a number of quite different ideas. Some, perhaps, were expressing a desire to be accepted into a community for which they had sincere respect. Others understood themselves to be guests, and thus under an obligation to conform to the expectations of their hosts; yet others conformed so as to avoid embarrassing the college servants who had issued us with our instructions. Others had performed a calculation and considered that the issue was too insignificant for it to be worth making what would be seen as a protest action. Others, no doubt, rose to their feet in time with the others, absent-mindedly staring at the large portraits adorning the walls of the great hall, and with no particular ideas in their heads at all. Ideas, then, are not identical to social actions or relations, and one and the same action or practice can be performed consistently with participating agents expressing, or concealing, a whole range of different ideas about what they are doing – or perhaps having no particular ideas about it at all.

However, Winch would have taken this to be too simple-minded as a response to his argument. The ideas he refers to are not the contents of the heads of participant agents, but, rather, the established social meanings assigned to institutional practices and relations: ideas which have a life, independently of what any particular individual happens to be thinking at some particular moment, in the cultural traditions to which they belong. But there are problems with this, too. What are the ideas 'expressed' by the college mealtime rituals, and the social relations they confirm? Winch's case depends very much on the implied analogy between the meanings of such practices and relations, on the one hand, and the meanings of linguistic performances, on the other. In some cases, non-verbal actions have a more-or-less satisfactory verbal equivalent. In such cases, the extension of Wittgenstein's treatment of linguistic meaning to them is more-or-less unproblematic. However, in cases such as the mealtime ritual, meaning is better understood not by analogy with linguistic practice, but, rather, by reference to a range of forms of interaction through which hierarchical relations of power and subordination or higher and lower status are symbolically acknowledged and confirmed. In interpreting such rituals, we might be involved in more than providing a perspicuous account of the rules being followed. We might be interested in the genealogy of the ritual forms adopted – why just these, and not others, and when did they come together in this particular assemblage, all at once or over an extended period of time, how did the social distinctions being marked and affirmed arise, what patterns of command over what sorts of economic or cultural resources, or what sorts of patronage enabled this particular hierarchical form of relations to emerge and confirm itself in this particular setting? The answers to these questions might or might not be of interest to the participants, and they would almost certainly constitute information or discoveries about their practices, rather than mere 'reminders' of what was already tacitly understood through the practice of participation itself. Indeed, becoming informed in this way might irreversibly alter the attitudes of participants, even to the point where they no longer felt able to continue the practice.

Yet another of Ian's points is worth developing here. When he says '...all sorts of things happen to us which we struggle to understand', he is hinting at his long-running engagement with depth-psychology, and his related sense that the participation of individuals in social life is not a smooth, uncomplicated process of learning to 'follow the rules' (Craib 1989, 1994). Hutchinson *et al.* seem to regard occasions when we need to resort to reflective 'interpretation' as the exception, compared with the more typical 'unreflective' routine, taken-for-granted practical understanding involved in everyday participation in social practices. However, in complex societies (probably, all societies!), individuals have to meet an immense variety of challenges as they negotiate their way through life, dealing with other family members, the complex demands of schooling, finding work, engaging in relationships with sexual partners, forming households, becoming parents or carers and so on. Much of this entails acquiring and testing a stock of 'rule-of-thumb' causal knowledge – often not fully articulated, but nevertheless deployed, often with great skill. At key moments, however, when we face major ethical dilemmas, confront the break-up of a central relationship or face the death of a loved one, we are impelled to question the tacit underpinnings of our lives. At such moments, we are lay 'social theorists', engaging in just the sort of generalizing and causal thinking about our social lives that Hutchinson *et al.* dismiss as a legitimate activity when conducted by those whose profession it is. This is something that the Italian Marxist Antonio Gramsci (indirectly, through, his association with Piero Sraffa, a significant influence on Wittgenstein (see, for example, Monk 1990: 260; Davis 2002)) expressed in the aphorism 'Everyone is a philosopher' (Gramsci 1971).

The essential point here is that if we are to bind our work as students of society closely to the forms of understanding of the participants in the social practices we study, as Hutchinson *et al.* advocate, then this is not nearly so restrictive as they suggest. An example might make this clearer. In a university in the south of England, in the early days of computerization, the management let it be known that in future their communication with employees would be via email. One of the manual employees responded thus to the 'house magazine':

> May I point out that a large proportion of university staff have no access to computer terminals nor email. These include electricians, plumbers, fitters, carpenters, cleaners, porters, technicians, gardeners, groundsmen and me. Are we, the manual brigade, being marginalised by an elitist computerised administration who consider us a lower caste not worthy of information or an opinion? . . . we may be light on computer skills, but we do have real skills, which include the skill to pull the plug.

The distinction between a managerial elite and the 'manual brigade', with the former exercising an exclusive power on the basis of differential access to their favoured means of communication, but with the latter possessing a reciprocal power through their performance of tasks on which the former are dependent, condenses a sophisticated causal account of the university's social structure and the role of technology and access to means of communication in it. And yet, this is still an example of 'participants' understanding' – it seems that in their everyday interpretations of their social lives, at least some participants are able to develop causal generalizations and theoretical ideas that Hutchinson *et al*. would deny to social scientists.

It might be that Hutchinson *et al*. would respond to this by simply rejecting my interpretation of the above statement as embodying causal knowledge-claims. Their argument against the possibility of causal knowledge in the social studies follows that of Winch. It relies on a contrast between the normative regularities involved in human social rule-following and the event-regularities which form the basis of scientific causal laws. However, this contrast, and its frequent use by Hutchinson *et al*., relies on a concept of scientific laws as 'constant conjunctions' that has long been subjected to strong criticism in newer philosophies of science such as critical realism (this work: Chapters 2–4 and 8). But my own justification for thinking of the above-quoted email as embodying causal knowledge is much simpler than this. It relies on tacit recognition of a 'common sense', generic concept of 'cause' as whatever makes the difference between something happening and not happening. My argument here is that this is just an example of the ways in which everyday social participation necessarily presupposes a stock of causal knowledge, in this sense, as well as a complex set of normative orientations. This causal knowledge and the associated normative orientations do, indeed, presuppose that we first 'understand the meanings' embedded in the social practices we engage in. They do not 'displace' it, but neither can they be reduced to it. Rather, they enable us to act with a degree of coherence and autonomy, securing, where appropriate, a degree of critical distance and a capacity to bring about change. True, Hutchinson *et al*. do defend the Winch (and Wittgenstein) from the misunderstanding that their philosophies are necessarily conservative – but they fail to show more positively how deliberate strategies for change might emerge and be reasonably grounded.

Understanding Other Cultures and Criticizing One's Own

A continuing legacy of Winch's philosophy has been a set of deep questions about how it is possible to understand radically different cultures from one's own, or, relatedly, how to interpret and establish a critical relationship to practices and patterns of belief in one's own society. Some of the argumentation in Winch's TISS seems to point towards a relativistic perspective, such than one could neither understand an 'alien' culture nor have culturally neutral grounds for evaluating its practices. This might mean that one would have no justifiable grounds for objecting to practices of genital mutilation, slavery or capital punishment if they formed part of a culture in whose terms they made sense and were unquestioned. It might also mean that one would have no justifiable grounds for disputing religious beliefs about the origin of life, the special creation of species or the providential nature of chance phenomena, on the basis of scientific evidence. These inferences might be – and have been – drawn from Winch's insistence on understanding in the social studies being always tied to participants' understanding, and the inappropriateness of applying the standards of one culture or practice to the interpretation of another.

This line of argument plays a significant part in the argument of TISS and also seems to be at work in Winch's critique (in UPS) of Evans Pritchard's application of the scientific outlook of his own culture in his dismissal of the Zande belief in witchcraft. However, Hutchinson *et al.* argue that this is a misrepresentation Winch's position. First, they argue that Winch (following Wittgenstein) should be read as offering only 'grammatical reminders', and that he does not seek to offer positive guidance for the social studies. Rather, his arguments should be taken in a wholly negative spirit – as therapeutic guidance aimed at helping us to avoid gross *mis*understandings. Of Winch (and Kuhn, too – this work: 58–61), they claim: 'They had, they have, no views, they make no assertions' (Hutchinson *et al.* p. 60). But this will not do – either as a characterization of Winch or of their own practice. They clearly *do* have views – quite strong ones – about what cannot legitimately be done in the social studies, and those views are buttressed by strong substantive claims about the nature of social practices, understanding, language use and meaning. At the core of these substantive claims is a fundamental categorial opposition between 'humans' and 'things' (sometimes 'things' includes other animals, sometimes not). So, for them, a key difference between the students of society and natural scientists is that the former have to understand the subject of their investigations as well as one another, while natural scientists have to understand only one another – the 'object' of natural scientific knowledge has no self-understanding, its behaviour is not 'meaningful' and so on. 'Things' are simply there to be observed, measured, experimented on and theorized about. The following extracts give the flavour of their commitment to this ontological divide:

Perhaps he [Schatzki] would accept that one can and sometimes does learn from others and transform oneself, in the encounter with other cultures, if one lets it be a genuine encounter, rather than being like the encounter of a biologist with a laboratory specimen. (p. 49)

. . . whatever one says about the social world must be responsible to social actors, in a manner having no parallel in the physical sciences. (p. 52)

If we are to risk generalizing at all, we shall say that the production of descriptions or presentations of human action/behaviour which are not interpretations, let alone explanations, is the only way to avoid grossly failing to 'capture' that behaviour, given that such rule-following etc. behaviour is utterly unlike what we call the 'behaviour' of inanimate objects . . . 'Self-understanding' etc. is, again, vital to understanding humans as human animals rather than as material objects or even as (the vast majority of non-human) animals. . . . (p. 61)

This strong ontological anti-naturalism that Hutchinson *et al.* share with Winch is what underlies the tendency towards both cognitive and moral relativism that many of Winch's readers have seen in his writings. For them, we can't measure, manipulate, experiment on, generalize about and even classify or compare different cultures, practices, patterns of belief and so on in the way we can with physical objects and processes, and (most) other animals. Encounters with other humans are different in kind, we must be 'responsible' to them in the way we characterize their activities, we must be open to learning from, and even to being changed by, the encounter.

Now, this is no mere 'grammatical reminder', nor even a piece of methodological or therapeutic advice. It is a substantive ontological claim, and one that is open to empirical evidence. This is hinted at in the phrase in parentheses in the third of the above quotations. We do now have good evidence that some primates have a sense of self, and this seems to be part-acknowledged by Hutchinson *et al.* It is also true that many other species are social. And we could ask many questions about them: Are they social in the sense of organizing their social lives on the basis of conventional rules? Can they be said to interact meaningfully? Could we learn to understand them? Do any of them have what we might call 'culture'? Might scientists 'be responsible' to them, too? All interesting questions simply cut short by the human/nature dualism of their central ontological doctrine.

But what about understanding other cultures? Hutchinson *et al.* (rightly) claim that neither Winch nor Wittgenstein denied the possibility of this. As always, Hutchinson *et al.* agree with Winch and Wittgenstein (on their reading). Contrary to popular misrepresentations, both philosophers did think that cross-cultural understanding was possible, and that it was, after all, legitimate to use standards drawn from one's own culture to criticize the practices and beliefs of others (for example, Hutchinson *et al.*, pp. 119–121). So, it is accepted by them that Winch had no problems with Evans Pritchard's *ethnography*. His critique was, rather, focussed on the application of inappropriate standards from Evans Pritchard's own culture (that is, those of science) in his dismissive *interpretation*. An adequate understanding of Zande witchcraft practices in its own terms would recognize that it is not a merely instrumental method for improving productivity, or revealing the source of an illness. Rather, it should be seen as having greater affinity with ceremonial or religious practices in our own society – and these would be a better source for a critical evaluation than western science. Elsewhere in their book, Hutchinson *et al.* seem to be suggesting the problem of possible 'incommensurability' between cultures is really no problem. The individuation of cultures, along with questions about how much they might differ, and the associated debate between 'relativists' and 'rationalists' cannot be resolved because they arise outside of any specific context that could give them decision-procedures.

It seems that, according to Hutchinson *et al.*, the sorts of questions most readers have understood to be posed by Winch (and Wittgenstein) actually don't arise at all (so we should just avoid playing those 'intellectualist' games), or, alternatively, they do arise but can be resolved so long as we take the trouble to get to grips with serious understanding of what the 'others' are up to. This is a process in which we neither incorporate the other's culture into our own nor abandon our own to take a leap into another cultural world. Rather, it is a process of engagement in which we are changed by the encounter, and our own culture also changed.

The argument that questions as to the 'commensurability' of cultures do not arise because there is no specific context to provide decision-making criteria could be countered by recognizing that there is, after all, such a context. Questions about the identity and difference of cultures, relativism, commensurability and so on *do* get raised and find answers (albeit generally contested ones). The context in which this happens is that formed by the traditions and conceptual practices of philosophy and the social science disciplines! The second option offered by Hutchinson *et al.* is much more promising, but it seems to beg some crucial questions. In countering misreadings of Winch that render him as a 'conservative' and relativist, they succeed rather *too* well. Perhaps what makes Winch's writings interesting and challenging is that his arguments seem to point to conclusions that we and he know *must* be unacceptable – the challenge, then, is to see *how* cross-cultural understanding, rational criticism and so on are possible, notwithstanding some powerful arguments that point in the opposite direction.

It seems to me that Winch was genuinely puzzled about how it was possible to understand a culture as radically different from his own as that of the Azande as 'presented' by Evans Pritchard. Hutchinson *et al.* argue against critics of Winch such as Martin Hollis and Donald Davidson (2001) who attempt to solve Winch's problem. For Hollis (1970), mutual understanding between cultures is possible on condition there is a 'bridgehead' of shared beliefs (shared rationality in this case), while Davidson appeals to 'transcendental' conditions of possible understanding in our common humanity. Hutchinson *et al.* consider this exercise to be absurd, as there is no context or standard for deciding how different cultures are from one another. This is disappointing, as not only did Winch himself clearly think there was a problem, but actually made a very interesting suggestion about what the required 'bridgehead' might be.

'Limiting notions', Human Nature and Social Science Naturalism

In UPS, Winch avoids the relativism implied by notions of incommensurability between radically different cultures by advocating a creative process of re-evaluation of one's own culture in the light of the encounter with the other: 'Seriously to study another way of life is necessarily to seek to extend our own' (Winch, UPS in Wilson (ed.) 1974: 99). But even this seems to beg the question: What if there are no points in common for us to begin this creative process? At first, Winch seems to accept MacIntyre's argument that all cultures have language, and thus some form of rationality. But this, too, begs the question whether their version of rationality is fundamentally incommensurable with ours. In the final, tantalizing pages of UPS, Winch finally gets down to presenting his own version of the 'bridgehead'. This is made up of a trio of what he calls 'limiting notions': birth, sex and death. These are 'inescapably involved in the life of all known human societies in a way which gives us a clue where to look, if we are puzzled about the point of an alien system of institutions' (*ibid*. p. 107). Winch here seem to be offering us an empirical generalization about human societies – oddly, one that Hutchinson *et al.* don't seem to have noticed.

Winch is not entirely clear what he means by 'limiting notions'. He says they refer not to 'events in life', but rather mark life's outer limits or boundaries. This applies fairly straight-forwardly in the case of birth and death, but what about 'sex'? It becomes clear that what Winch means by sex is what we might now call 'gender'. His handling of gender as a 'limiting' notion reads as somewhat traditionalist by the standards of our own culture, as he tells us 'The life of a man is a man's life and the life of a woman is a woman's life: the masculinity and the femininity are not just *components* in the life, they are its *mode* . . .' (*ibid*. p. 110). What, I wonder would he have made of the slogan 'A woman needs a man like a fish needs a bicycle'?

Though this is an intriguing step for Winch to have taken, it has some fairly obvious problems. One is that it risks being read as a form of biological reductionism: most unwelcome given Winch's anti-scientism. However, if we take birth, death and sex/gender as 'notions' that are present in all societies in the sense that they are the source or locus of shared cultural meanings in each society, then the problem of mutual intelligibility arises yet again: 'gender' is lived in all societies and provides ways of giving meaning and experience in people's lives, but it is 'done' differently in different societies (and, often, differently by different groups within each society). To put it in a way that might appeal to Hutchinson *et al.*, what is the context, and where are the criteria by which we can identify practices in different cultures as each doing 'gender'?

If we are to use the 'limiting notions' as a means of rendering intelligible puzzling aspects of other cultures (and, of course, our own!), it seems that we need to be able both to identify birth, death and sex as 'brute', observable, 'natural' facts about us, as well as to recognize that human cultures surround and make sense of these brute facts in very different, but still potentially traceable ways. In other words, we need to be able to *make links between*, rather than a dogmatic *gulf* between, natural facts of life, on the one hand, and the distinctive ways in which they are lived and given meaning by people who inherit and engage with different cultural traditions, on the other.

But, to go some way towards both Winch and Hutchinson *et al.*, there is no need to identify 'natural facts' with what a biologist might tell us (let alone an ultra-Darwinian ideologue: Hutchinson *et al.* deal effectively with the pretensions of evolutionary psychology as a would-be social science). It is true that humanity can rightly be characterized as an evolved primate. However, no more and no less than other primates, we have our own species-specific attributes. Winch and those who think like him put the focus on language-use, and there is much to be said for this, but the peculiar modes of social bonding through which humans reproduce themselves, and the immensely flexible and variable forms of social cooperation through which they interact with the rest of nature in meeting their material and cultural needs also form the context in which we can understand the evolution of language itself and the significance it acquires. These, too, are facts of life, but this is not to concede that biology (or the 'life sciences' generally) has a uniquely authoritative perspective on them.

Having got this far, I can't resist the temptation to push on to a still more provocative naturalism. Considered as 'facts of life', Winch's trio – and some others, too – are not only 'inescapably involved in the life of all known human societies', but are equally inescapably involved in the life of most non-human animal species (sexually reproducing ones, at any rate). In addition to enabling us to make other cultures intelligible, perhaps Winch's 'limiting notions', understood as I've just suggested, might provide 'bridgeheads' through which we make the intelligible the modes of life of the other species with which we share the planet. Perhaps their modes of life, like ours, can be understood as so many different (evolved) ways of resolving the problems of sustaining life in the face of ecological exigencies. And, perhaps, too, the effort of engaging with them might cause us to re-evaluate our own (historically emergent) modes of socio-cultural life in the light of *their* unique modes of life, so extending our horizons and coming to acknowledge a 'responsibility' to them just as Hutchinson *et al.* acknowledge a responsibility to other (human) social actors? Perhaps the natural sciences could be (as they sometimes are) more like a Winchian practice of the social studies than either Winch or his adherents recognize.

A naturalism of this sort is not, after all, so far removed from some of the arguments of Winch's mentor, Wittgenstein. In the *Philosophical Investigations* (PI), Wittgenstein (1958, 1997) asks how one could understand various activities in an unknown country with a strange language. His answer is: 'The common behaviour of mankind is the system of reference by means of which we interpret an unknown language' (PI, para 206). Elsewhere, he refers to linguistic activities such as 'commanding, questioning, recounting, chatting' as being 'as much a part of our natural history as walking, eating, drinking, playing' (PI, para 25). Indeed, the central claim of Wittgenstein's later philosophy of mental life is that the language in which we talk about our 'inner' mental lives could not be taught or learned if there were no natural outward expressions. As Wittgenstein put it: 'If things were quite different from what they actually are – if there were for instance no characteristic expression of pain, of fear, of joy; if rule became exception and exception rule; or if both became phenomena of roughly equal frequency – this would make our normal language games lose their point.' (PI, para 142)

There are places where Wittgenstein countenances just the sort of cross-species naturalism that I indicated above. In explanation of his point about the necessity of natural expressions of pain for us to have a language to talk about pain, Wittgenstein says: 'And now look at a wriggling fly and at once these difficulties vanish and pain seems to be able to get a foothold here' (PI, para 284). And, again, for the concept of intention: 'What is the natural expression of intention? – Look at a cat when it stalks a bird; or a beast when it wants to escape.' (PI, para 647) The value of such an orientation for the social sciences might be new ways of looking at what we share with other species as a setting for new ways of thinking about those traits that mark us out as different. It might also further the process of taking more fully into our account of human social life its necessary embedding in and dependence on the rest of nature – living and non-living (for further discussion of this and related arguments, see Benton 1993, Moog and Stones 2009).

Post-Marxism and Post-Structuralism

While Hutchinson *et al.* vigorously maintain (their version of) Winch's anti-scientism in the social sciences, much research activity in some social sciences – especially in some approaches to political science and economics where conclusions are drawn from the statistical manipulation of large data-sets – is conducted without much 'navel-gazing' about philosophy, or the more fundamental questions of social theory. Often (but certainly not always), this research assumes a loosely positivist account of science. The polarized philosophies of social science – 'hermeneutics' and 'positivism' – still seem to be at work in shaping rival research traditions, with the hermeneutic approach, centring on the understanding of the meanings deployed by participants in social life, prevailing in much of sociology and anthropology. This is especially true of the research conducted by individual scholars with limited resources of time and finance, in contrast to those working in large, externally funded research centres, where collection and analysis of large bodies of empirical data is both practically feasible and normatively required.

However, a large part of the motivation that Ian and I shared when we wrote this book was to move beyond what we saw as a rather sterile and inconclusive opposition between the merits of meaning versus cause, particular versus universal, qualitative versus quantitative methods. One way of transcending these oppositions that became intellectually fashionable in the decade or so before we wrote the book was to declare oneself 'post' whatever tradition or set of debates one saw as definitive of the *status quo* in the social sciences (as well as philosophy, literature and the creative arts generally). This had the strategically satisfying

effect of situating oneself in the vanguard of a historical progress (whose existence, paradoxically, most 'posts' denied!), and simultaneously rendering past
intellectual work and its problems passé. Ian grappled honourably in the limited space we had available with some key intellectual beacons of this movement, finding much of value in their work but ultimately exposing internal
contradictions and partialities in their thought in terms he drew from Habermas's
critique (Chapter 10).

If we were not inclined to follow the 'posts', this left three prominent philosophical approaches to the nature of social reality and our ability to make sense
of it that satisfied two criteria:

1. They were aware of and took into the content of their thinking about the
    social sciences the newer developments in the history and philosophy of
    the *natural* sciences that we considered constituted genuine advances.
2. They took seriously the arguments of Winch and other advocates of a
    meaning-centred practice of the social studies, but looked for ways of
    developing more ambitious and critical research programmes consistently
    with the insights present in those arguments.

These three approaches were the critical rationalism associated with Habermas
and some of his associates (this work: Chapter 7), new work linking various
strands of feminism with philosophy (this work: Chapter 9) and various versions of 'critical realism' associated with the work of Roy Bhaskar, Andrew
Collier and others (this work: Chapter 8).

Although both of us were sympathetic to different aspects of all three of these
approaches, I had a long association with critical realism, and Ian, too, might have
identified with this, though situating himself rather differently within it (closer to
the hermeneutic, subject-centred end of the spectrum). Since we wrote, various
versions of critical realism, and the debates among them, have been a prominent
feature of subsequent work in the philosophy of social science (especially in the
UK context), and have had significant influence in substantive social scientific
research. However, there have also been new developments among some of the
'posts' that deserve serious attention (and, indeed, satisfy the two criteria set out
above). One example is the development of the philosophical aspects of the
'post-Marxism' pioneered by Ernesto Laclau and Chantalle Mouffe (1985).

In their *Logics of Critical Explanation in Social and Political Theory* (2007),
Glynos and Howarth seek to provide philosophical underpinnings for a non-
positivist, but still explanatory and critical approach to social science and politics
that draws on the work of Laclau and Mouffe as well as some of the key post-
structuralist thinkers discussed by Ian in Chapter 10 (especially Derrida, Saussure,
Lacan and Foucault). Although their philosophical arguments are intended to
show a way forward beyond the positivist/hermeneutics impasse, their critical
fire is directed most fiercely against the positivism which they see as still alive
and well in the field of political science. For them, the ideal of explanation

proffered by positivism is the 'subsumption' of particular events (activities, processes and so on) under universal laws, and the attempt to test the truth-claims embodied in such laws by deducing predictions from them.

Their view, which is shared by Winch and other advocates of the centrality of meaning in the social studies, is that the transfer of this model of explanation and theory-testing to the social world is radically misguided. This is because there is an irreducibly hermeneutic dimension in human social action and interaction, and this must be acknowledged and respected in all would-be interpretive and explanatory work that takes such action and interaction as its object. In turn, this derives from the basic ontological 'fact' that humans are ' "meaning produc-ing" or "self-interpreting" animals' (Glynos and Howarth 2007: 23). Since they make the inapplicability of the 'covering law' model of scientific explanation to the social studies a matter of the different kinds of beings, processes, activities and so on that form the topics of these disciplines, Glynos and Howarth are able to sidestep the more basic question whether that model of scientific expla-nation is (generally) applicable even in its original domain of the *natural* sciences. In fact, they do acknowledge the newer non-positivist thinking about the natural sciences, especially in their very interesting discussion of the impor-tance of the form of reasoning known as 'retroduction' (this work: 36). However, their point is that whatever its status as an account of the natural sciences, it still has a powerful, and in their view malign, hold over much social science research. This is particularly so in disciplines such as political science and eco-nomics. That is why it still needs to be criticized. As I'll try to show later, this tendency to avoid philosophical discussion of the natural sciences is at the root of some problems at later stages in their argument.

Though they side with Winch and other hermeneuticists in rejecting the cover-ing law model of explanation in the social sciences, and insisting on the necessity of a hermeneutic aspect to all social scientific explanation, Glynos and Howarth believe it is possible, consistently with these, to provide explanations and critical evaluations of social relations and practices. They recognize (as we have seen in the readings offered by Hutchinson *et al.*) that neither Winch nor Wittgenstein was committed to the abandonment of either explanation or criticism. However, their claim is that the writers they discuss within this tradition leave undeveloped or indeterminate how either aspiration of social research might be met.

In their view, there are only two approaches that might provide philosophical justifications for more ambitious explanatory and critical research programmes in the social sciences. These are, first, their own way of developing some of the insights of post-structuralism and, second, another tradition which they identify with the search for 'causal mechanisms' in social life. Unfortunately, though this suggests an engagement with critical realism, they deal only very briefly and inconclusively with the work of Roy Bhaskar within this tradition, and they reserve most of their critical discussion for the methodological individualist social philosophy of John Elster (it is a justified criticism of our book that we dealt only too briefly with related individualist 'rational choice' theories – but to do this here would be beyond the scope of this set of comments. For those who find rational choice theory plausible and wish to consider it further, a range of critical approaches to it are included in Archer and Tritter 2000).

Glynos and Howarth agree with critical realists that any philosophy for social science must pay attention to questions of ontology – and for them this means not just saying what sorts of things there are in the social world, but also specifying the assumptions that have to be made in accounting for their possibility and devising ways of understanding and explaining them. However, unlike Roy Bhaskar, they do not attempt to derive their ontology by way of a retroductive or transcendental argument from an unproblematic description of some familiar social action (this work: Chapter 4: 57–8 and 8: 123 ff.). Instead, they simply present key 'constitutive' features of the social world that they derive from certain post-structuralist thinkers, often by way of their re-working by Laclau and Mouffe. Against the tendency of much post-structuralist thinking, they endorse the view of Laclau and Mouffe that 'the real' is ultimately irreducible to the 'concept'. In other words, our linguistically constructed conceptual apparatus always and necessarily fails to fully capture external reality. Glynos and Howarth refer to this as a materialist ontology, though I would see it as a rather a minimally realist one. There are many varieties of materialism, but they generally go beyond mere affirmation of an irreducible reality that exceeds our thought, and make substantive claims about what kinds of things go to make up 'the real'. There is a rather technical and inconclusive discussion of what is at issue between critical realism and discourse theory on this question in a debate between Roy Bhaskar and Ernesto Laclau (Laclau and Bhaskar 1998). At its core, the difference turns on whether one can make justified inferences about the world as it is independently of our thought about it. For Bhaskar (and probably most critical realists), we can justifiably infer from the existence of human social and discursive practices what must be the case, 'extra-discursively', for them to be possible. For proponents of discourse theory, the conclusions of any such inference must themselves be discursive in character. It seems that there is some tension within discourse theory between wanting to assert that reality is something independent of our thought about it, and at the same time wanting to incorporate reality into its discursive construction. Still, the two approaches do share a commitment to specifying an underlying ontology for social research.

The content that Glynos and Howarth go on to put into their own ontology for the social studies emphasizes what they call the 'radical contingency of social relations and identities'. They sometimes sum this up as an 'ontology of lack'. A full engagement with the meaning and implications of this ontology for social scientific practice is far beyond my scope here, but at least there is space for me to highlight what seems to me a key difficulty. The notion of 'contingency' as Glynos and Howarth use the phrase is sometimes taken to mean that for any set of social practices (or 'regime') there is always a possible alternative. However, 'radical' contingency means something more than this, in the sense that there is a necessary or 'constitutive' incompleteness in all social practices and also in all subjective identities. For them, it follows that there is an ever-present possibility that moments of 'dislocation' might occur in which the incompleteness of a practice, its inherent 'flaw or crack' may become visible to its subjects, whose response may vary in ways not fully predictable. This is the beginning of the elaboration of a set of carefully worked concepts that Glynos and Howarth develop as an approach to understanding the conditions of possibility for the 'transformation and/or stabilization of regimes and practices' (p. 103).

In large measure, this is a sophisticated philosophical re-working of Gramsci's notion of hegemony and counter-hegemonic struggle, and takes as its broad definition of the research task Gramsci's own theoretical problem. However, this is only partially so. One important theoretical innovation that shapes their ontology is their gloss on the hermeneutic insight that they retain. For them, any social process, even where we may seek to explain it non-intentionally, '*is parasitic upon human practices, in the sense that they are constitutively sustained and mediated by the discursive activity of subjects*' (Glynos and Howarth 2007: 97 – italics in the original). The hermeneutic concepts of 'meaning' and 'interpretation' are transformed under the influence of post-structuralists (notably Saussure and Foucault) into the tricky and contested notion of 'discourse'. For some, this implies that social (and even psychological) processes are always linguistic, or 'language-like'. For others, the notion of discourse can be extended to embodied social practices so long as these in some sense can be said to be meaningful, to be intelligible in terms of culturally provided rules and norms. For Glynos and Howarth, following Laclau and Mouffe, 'all actions, practices and social formations' are discursive in nature. For them, 'an object's identity is conferred by the particular discourses or systems of meaning within which it is constituted', and 'the notion of discourse signals the centrality of meaning to practices' (all on p. 109).

In what ever way we interpret the concept of discourse, it is clear that the contrast between objects of the natural sciences, which are not meaning-producing, or 'self-interpreting' is central to the social ontology advocated by Laclau and Mouffe and their associates.

Interestingly, their position in this respect is very similar to that of the earlier work of Bhaskar, who also works with a very strong ontological contrast between human agents and social structures, on one hand, and the objects of the natural sciences, on the other (this work, Chapter 8: 134 ff, and Benton 1981). One way to call this into question is to note that sometimes human agents are characterised as 'meaning-producing *animals*' (Glynos and Howarth 2007: 23). It is as though the social sciences could proceed as if the meaning-producing attribute alone were the whole of what we needed to take into account for our study of the social life of this very special 'human' animal. Even for their neo-Gramscian problematic of getting clear about the conditions for stabilization or transformation of regimes, there needs to be some acknowledgement of the role of coercion, or the threat of it, including the use of direct physical violence, as well as the role of material compromises. Each of these inescapably involves recognition of human embodiment, material needs and wants, and the availability of physical (chemical, etc.) technologies whose functioning either depends on, or is accountable only through, natural scientific knowledge. More generally, the most fundamental condition for the possibility of social life of any form is the continuous 'metabolism' between human practice and its material means, sources of energy and materials, and waste/pollution sinks.

Not only are discursive practices conducted by humans who are, whatever else they may be, living organisms, but the social relations they establish or transform include many quite central to their form of life which are not simply social relations among human subjects, but relations between them and material objects, physical, chemical or biological processes, living organisms of other species and so on. The causal powers of those 'others' that figure in human social life play their distinctive part in shaping, sustaining or dissipating it, often in ways that are 'mediated' by discourse and subjective recognitions. However, this is by no means the whole story. Many of the causal networks through which physical, chemical and biotic mechanisms have their effects on human practices and individual lives take place 'behind the backs' of conscious actors, unrepresented in discourse. Such have been the effects of CFCs or CO_2 emissions prior to their scientific identification as causes of increased exposure to ultra-violet radiation, or of climatic change. The recurrent outbreaks of cholera and other infectious diseases wrought their terrible effects prior to and quite independently of the scientific understanding of the causal role of micro-organisms.

Interestingly, Glynos and Howarth (drawing on the research of Griggs and Howarth 2007) do use the modern environmental movement as an example of a political mobilization that sets out to change social practices. Despite clear and insightful description of the tactics used and practices challenged, they conclude with an interpretation of the movement as a challenge to the prevailing language:

> Certain signifiers or linguistic expressions – 'sustainable environment', 'health', 'justice for all' and so forth – function as names that stand in for the absent fullness of a dislocated community or life. Though they are metaphors with no corresponding facts – they are moments of naming in a radical sense – they strive to represent the failure of a signifying system or language. (Glynos and Howarth 2007: 122)

First, there is something questionable, given Glynos and Howarth's adherence to the centrality of subject's meaning, about the fact that the interpretation they give runs so strongly counter to what environmental activists take themselves to be doing. Few, I suspect, would agree that their campaigns are attempts to 'represent the failure of a signifying system', and still fewer that health and sustainability are 'empty signifiers' with 'no corresponding facts'. Arguably, this is not just a somewhat idiosyncratic way of interpreting the environmental, or other social movements, but is an effect produced systematically by the ontology adopted in this approach to social explanation. Partly, this may derive from the ways in which post-structuralists who derive their view of language and discourse from Saussure tend to have difficulty with the idea that language might be used to make reference to anything outside itself – language becomes a screen separating us from the world, not a means for (among many other things) thinking, exploring or talking about it. So, political mobilization, it seems, cannot actually be 'about' deforestation, climate change and excessive consumerism (since there are 'no facts' corresponding to these concerns) but can only be a challenge to the *language* of climate change, deforestation and the rest.

The related post-structuralist scepticism in relation to truth claims is also at work in the tendency of Glynos and Howarth to marginalize the role of cognition in such political mobilizations. Consider, for example, the way that challenges to the fairness of the review process in some climate journals has provided 'climate-change sceptics' with powerful ammunition. Social actors, including political activists, are, indeed 'meaning-producers', and they also have a repertoire of emotional dispositions and capacities, fears, desires and so on (rather obliquely acknowledged by Glynos and Howarth in their technical use of the notion of 'enjoyment' derived from the post-structuralist psychoanalyst, Jacques Lacan – this work, Chapter 10: 166–7). However, human agents are not *solely* producers of meaning and subjects of desire (etc.) but are also knowledgeable subjects, and at least some of what they know includes a stock of causal beliefs about the society they live in, its relative openness or resistance to their actual or contemplated interventions, aspirations, life-strategies and so on. But Glynos and Howarth are right to challenge the 'covering law' model of causality in this context. Much of this causal knowledge is tacit, and when articulated is more likely to take the form of 'rule of thumb' generalizations and expectations. They also are on strong ground when they point to the 'mechanistic' connotations of the language typically used by those of us (including critical realists) who advocate causal explanation in the social sciences. More context-sensitive and differentiated ways of thinking about causal processes in social life are certainly required.

Finally, the focus on discursive practices certainly does illuminate key aspects of the processes of stabilization and/or transformation of regimes. However, as I've tried to illustrate above, the rendering of 'community life' and its 'dislocations' in terms of discursive practices alone unjustifiably marginalizes (or even renders unthinkable) the causal role of living organisms such as crop plants, domesticated animals, disease organisms, industrial and consumer technologies, geographical distributions of humans, productive resources, and pollution sinks and so on in obstructing, facilitating or shaping social and cultural change. Of course, many (but certainly not all) of these non-human beings and relations exercise their causal powers by way of the activities of (embodied) humans, their subjective states and discursive strategies. The point, however, is that even where this is so, little sense can be made of these states and strategies unless the wider context of diverse 'materialities' is brought fully into the social scientific analysis.

Critical Realism and Social Science

Although Glynos and Howarth distance themselves from Roy Bhaskar's (early) version of critical realism, their approach shares a great deal with it. In particular, the strong opposition between nature and human society, and their related qualified sympathy for a hermeneutic approach to social scientific research. The account I gave of critical realism in our book (Chapter 8) deliberately gave due weight to Bhaskar's immense contribution to the development of this approach while at the same time recognizing its initial conception as a broad collaborative 'research programme' involving numerous theorists (and activists), many of whom disagreed significantly with Bhaskar on many issues. In part, this was motivated by my feeling at the time that Bhaskar's thinking was moving on in ways that endangered the crucial insights of his earlier work. Initially, critical realists thought of themselves as 'underlabourers' for social science, taking up and trying to clarify conceptual issues arising in substantive research, and providing defences of certain sorts of explanatory and theoretical moves that were ruled out by both positivism and radical hermeneutics. Subsequently, Bhaskar's later work became an ever more elaborate and schematized metaphysical philosophy, and, eventually, a rather over-blown new-age religion. Some of his closest admirers followed him in this 'spiritual turn', but most of those who saw in critical realism a useful resource in helping to clarify and defend 'critical' social science research have continued their work largely without reference to Bhaskar's later sublimation.

Partly as a result of this rather central challenge coming from within critical realism, there has occurred, since Ian and I wrote this book, a flood of new work in which critical realists engage with one another about a great range of issues, but also reach out to consider the relationships between this approach and others formerly seen as incompatible with it. Several of the contributions to these debates, such as Potter (2000), Sayer (2000), Dean *et al.* (2006), Lopez and Potter (2001), Frauley and Pearce (2007) and Cruickshank (2003) have also provided more accessible introductions to CR. I cannot hope to do justice to this new writing in this short introduction, but I can at least draw attention to the key issues that have emerged, and to some of the books and articles in which they have been aired.

The issues that have received the greatest attention through the first decade of this century can be roughly organized into six topics:

1. What should critical realists make of Bhaskar's 'spiritual turn'?
2. Can critical realism help with long-standing issues in methodology and social theory?

3. Can critical realism help span the division between the social and natural sciences?
4. What is the relationship between critical realism and Marxism (and other substantive approaches)?
5. What is 'critical' about critical realism? Critical realism, morality and 'emancipation'.
6. Does critical realism have anything to offer for feminist social science?

What Should Critical Realists Make of Roy Bhaskar's 'Spiritual Turn'?

It has to be admitted that Bhaskar's writings from *Dialectic* onwards are a daunting prospect for the reader, but some realists have done us the service of taking on the task of subjecting them to serious critical scrutiny. One of these is Gary Potter (2007), who patiently takes apart Bhaskar's new arguments for (and definitions of) 'God'. Also, the authors of a collection of very thoughtful essays all engage critically with Bhaskar's newer writings, in particular his arguments for a 'meta-reality' beyond the reach of science, and only accessible by the self-realizing reflection of human individuals (Dean *et al.* 2006). For some, Bhaskar's later work threatens to subvert the valuable role of CR in its earlier role as 'underlabourer' for the social sciences, while for others the threat is deeper, abandoning the earlier notion of critical and emancipatory activity as collective struggle against specific forms of oppression in favour of a 'new-age' spiritualist concern with individual self-realization. However, the authors say they 'soon came to the conclusion that it was not worth engaging in a sustained critique of Roy Bhaskar's latest work' (*ibid.*: 148). More recently, Greg McLennan (2009) has cast doubt on the continuing value of critical realism in the face of its transformation into a religious ideology by Bhaskar and others such as, in his account, the distinguished sociologist Margaret Archer (see also Archer *et al.* 2004).

My own response has been one of dismay at the transformation of critical realism as a pluralistic collaborative effort to sustain explanatory and critical work in the social sciences into its opposite: a metaphysical-religious belief-system. The provisional and fallible, often mundane work of social scientific research might test the patience of one anxious for 'emancipation', and so the temptation to the certainties of religious faith can well be understood. Those who succumb to the temptation are, of course, entitled to their share of its comforts and consolations. My main point is that the shift to metaphysical system-building and theological speculation should not be confused with critical realism in its original incarnation as a critical philosophy of social science. The latter has a crucially important role still to play in illuminating issues in the social sciences, and should not be abandoned simply because one of its most talented and influential originators has done so.

Can Critical Realism Help With Long-Standing Issues in Methodology and Social Theory?

Some of the most fruitful developments of CR have come less from philosophers, more from social theorists reflecting on their own substantive research experience. Examples include Sayer (2000) on the importance of integrating spatial relations in social theory, drawing on his research in urban sociology and political economy, Mellor (1998 and Hutchinson *et al.* 2002), drawing on her research also in local and urban social processes and Stones (2005), reflecting on his own studies of governmental decision-making and media representations. In economics, Tony Lawson has developed a powerful critique of the formal modelling that dominates the 'mainstream' of his discipline, and explained its predictive failures in terms of his own development of critical realist ideas (Lawson 1997, 1999, 2003a). Several of the contributions to Lopez and Potter (2001) reflect on the value of critical realist philosophy for research in specific domains of enquiry – social policy in relation to smoking and health (Ford), literary interpretation (Tew), identity and cyberspace (Higham), gender issues in computing (Clegg), as well as more general reflections on research methods (Porpora). Carter and New (2004) and Danermark *et al.* (2001) provide much-needed insights into the application of critical realist philosophical ideas in substantive research methods.

One of the most perplexing and long-standing questions in social theory – and one spanning both disciplines and rival meta-theoretic traditions – is the nature of social structures and the relation of 'structure' to 'agency' (Lopez and Scott 2001, Scott, 2001). The essays in Dean *et al.* 2006 address this topic in rather different ways, and the book concludes with an interesting debate between the authors in which this becomes a focus. Several contributors accept the usual critical realist view that social structures are real, and should be conceptualized as distinct from the activities of human agents whose actions may be either enabled or constrained by them, but which also (intentionally or not) reproduce or transform them. However, Wight argues that this 'dualism' of structure and agency (Archer 1995) leaves an explanatory 'gap'. His proposal is to draw on Bourdieu's notion of 'habitus' as was way of representing the way socialization into routine performances embeds structural determinants into the non-reflective practice of individuals. However, Dean, also working within a broadly Marxian critical realism, argues against both Archer's and Wight's conception of 'structures' as external to agents. For her, this is specific to capitalist societies, where money and print produce forms of reified social relation in which 'structures' are experienced as extra-human powers, and 'agents' as strongly individuated 'rational' beings.

Archer's insistence on the duality of structure and agency was pitched against what she calls the 'elision' of structure into agency in the most influential alternative view, that of Giddens's 'duality' of structure. For Giddens (as for Dean), social structure enters into the constitution of the agent and thence into the agent's social practice, but is also the outcome of the agent's practice. Structure is thus both the medium and outcome of social practice. Stones (2005) gives a qualified defence and development of structuration theory which places phenomenology and hermeneutics at the centre of the interpretation of social practices, so emphasizing the interdependence of structure and agency that is the strength of the notion of structuration. However, Stones's advocacy of 'strong' structuration also acknowledges the significance of larger scale 'external' social structures. This debate continues! See, for example, Elder-Vass (2007a, b), King (2007), Porpora (2007), Varela (2007).

Can Critical Realism Help Span the Division Between the Social and Natural Sciences?

My own essay (Benton 1981, reprinted in Archer *et al.* 1998) was an early attempt to show how this could be done by indicating the great variety of natural sciences (geology, physical geography, meteorology, physiology, evolutionary biology, biogeography, organic growth and development and so on), each with its own specific methodological approaches and problems, forms of explanation and modes of evaluation. The absolute ontological and methodological division between natural and social science is much harder to defend in the face of this diversity. Numerous writers have drawn in various ways on critical realism to deal with both philosophical and substantive questions concerning the relationship between society and nature. A selection of this huge literature includes: Andrew Collier (1994a, b, 1999, 2003), John O'Neill (1993, 2007), O'Neill *et al.* (2008), Raymond Murphy (2002a, b, 2007), Mary Mellor (1998), Hutchinson *et al.* (2002), Peter Dickens (2004), Dickens and Ormrod (2007), Kate Soper (1995, 2000, 2004, 2009), Soper *et al.* (2009), myself (1989, 1991, 2001). Although a short review cannot do justice to this literature, I can at least give some indication of the range of questions that are being addressed.

Andrew Collier's *Critical Realism* (1994a: ch. 8) argued against nature/society dualism in critical realist social theory, and in his 1994b, he made use of the Marxian distinction between use value and exchange value to explore the relationship between the sorts of rationality involved in market transactions and the degradation of the environment. His *Being and Worth* (1999) argued for an objective environmental philosophy derived from the theology of St. Augustine, and his subsequent *In Defence of Objectivity* (2003), similarly made a case for both a view of nature as real, independently of human experience or knowledge, and a related view of the objectivity of the value of (non-human) nature. In a tribute to Collier's philosophical work Kate Soper and I (Benton 2004, Soper 2004) endorsed Collier's realism about nature, though arguing for the significance of the availability of cultural resources for human recognition of its meaning and value. The question of the objective reality of values will be taken up a little later in this chapter.

Since her brilliant *What is Nature?* (1995), Kate Soper has continued to develop and defend her version of humanist philosophy in the light of strong environmental concerns, as well as conducting both philosophical and empirical investigation of consumerist culture and alternative sources of pleasure and happiness. In contesting the common assumption that abandoning a consumerist lifestyle involves privation, she has introduced the influential and politically important concept of 'alternative hedonism' (see for example, Soper 2000, 2004 and Soper *et al.* 2009). Since his path-breaking *Ecology, Policy and Politics* (1993), John O'Neill has continued to relate his philosophical work to questions of deliberative democracy and the possibility of reasoned judgements in fields such as environmental policy, where qualitatively different considerations have to be weighed against one another. This is contrasted with the way in which capitalist markets reduce such considerations to a single, quantitative dimension (see, for example, O'Neill 2007, O'Neill *et al.* 2008). Peter Dickens, too, since his major contributions in the 1990s has gone on to explore new developments in capitalist political economy (such as the so-called 'knowledge economy') and their consequences for the subjective life of workers and consumers (for example, Dickens 2004). Together with James Ormrod, he has taken critical realist concern with the relation between humans and nature literally into outer space in the very original and timely *Cosmic Society* (2007). Mary Mellor has continued to develop her synthesis of green, feminist and socialist thought, with a focus on the significance of women's work both outside and within the market for both social and natural sustainability, as well as for the envisioning of radical alternatives (Hutchinson *et al.* 2002, Mellor 1998). Her most recent focus is on local communities and sustainability in an urban context, as well as continuing highly original work on the nature of money and finance (Mellor 2010).

In line with the critical realist concern with questions of ontology as prior to epistemology and methods, this exploration of the relation between the social and natural sciences and with environmental issues has highlighted the age-old topic of human nature. Against the tendency of most post-structuralist thinkers and many 'social constructionists' to dismiss questions about 'human nature' as mistakenly 'essentialist', many critical realists have seen such questions as necessary to social science.

My own *Natural Relations* (1993) was in part a response to normative questions about our treatment of non-human animals, but it also included an attempt to develop a naturalistic view of human nature on the basis of a full acknowledgement of our evolutionary kinship with other species (an approach I called 'human/animal continuism'). On the one hand, this insisted on the importance for social science of recognizing human embodiment, our vulnerability to disease and bodily disability, our dependence on continuous interchange with the rest of nature, our distinctive patterns of reproductive behaviour, extended juvenile dependency and so on. On the other, it resisted the reductive tendencies of some biological determinisms (especially 'sociobiology', but also the more sophisticated 'evolutionary psychology') that seek to explain human social and individual life by direct and unmediated application of generalities derived from a gene-centred version of neoDarwinism. My argument was that the emergent properties of culture and language in hominid evolution did, indeed, distinguish us from other species, but that the nature and significance of this difference was best understood through a comparison with those other species. In other words, culture and language might be better seen as evolved ways in which humans meet needs that they share with other species, rather than as '*sui generis*' attributes, to be understood exclusively in their own terms. Of course, this did not rule out the emergence of radically new needs – as well as vulnerability to new kinds of harms and suffering – as a consequence of the emergence of such attributes (for example, what Maslow (1970) called 'self-actualization' needs – that could not arise for a being with no sustained concept of self, and incapable of imagining unactualized possibilities for its further development).

Peter Dickens and Andrew Sayer, among others, have broadly shared this approach, but Kate Soper has argued for a much stronger sense of human uniqueness, partly in order to sustain an environmental politics that would depend on humans uniquely reflecting on and deliberately transforming their relationships to the rest of nature. Andrew Sayer, too, is more inclined to emphasize human distinctiveness than I have tended to do. In part, these differences of view about human nature may be related to differences in the way non-human animals are represented. Kate Soper, for example, refers to animal needs as 'biological requirements', 'instincts' and the like, whereas my comparisons are with species that share with us relatively complex and flexible psychological capacities and learning abilities, various forms of sociability, parental care and so on (see, for more detail on these exchanges, Dickens, Soper, Sayer and Benton in Moog and Stones 2009).

What Is the Relationship Between Critical Realism and Marxism (and Other Substantive Approaches)?

The development of critical realism as a distinct approach in the philosophy of social science took place during the 1970s, a time when Marxian perspectives of various kinds were very influential in sociology and related social science disciplines. However, the early work of Keat and Urry (1975), Roy Bhaskar (1978) and myself (1977) argued for realism in the social sciences independently of our varying commitments to Marxism. My own book was an attempt to show that the actual explanatory strategies used by Weber and Durkheim in their classic works were realist in character, even though the explicit accounts they gave of their methodological principles were often quite different. However, it soon became clear that Marxist historical materialism fitted the critical realist 'model' of explanation particularly well, and it is probably true that Marxists have made the most use of critical realism as a means of guiding and evaluating their research practice.

More recently the increased interest in critical realism, combined with declining commitment to Marxism, has resulted in a wide range of other theoretical approaches being subjected to the CR 'treatment'. Rob Stones (2005) draws on CR in his critical re-working of structuration theory, Frank Pearce and Tony Woodiwiss (2001) and Jon Frauley (2007) read Foucault as a realist, while Frank Pearce has also made a strong case for Durkheim's realism (2001, 2007) as has Ray Murphy with respect to Weber (Murphy 2002a). Chodos *et al.* (2007) argue for a minimally realist reading of Gadamer, but also use Gadamer in a partial critique of CR itself on the concept of truth.

Despite this variety in critical realist readings of non-Marxian theorists, there is a strong tendency for CR to oppose post-structuralist and post-modernist trends in philosophy and social theory in view of their supposed relativism, resistance to ontology and consequent lack of critical orientation. The edited collection by Lopez and Potter (2001) carried the provocative title *After Post-modernism* and was intended as an intervention against the *posts'* anti-enlightenment stance. However, Stones (1996) while distancing himself from the more extreme versions of the 'posts', offered a more sympathetic account of their critique of 'modernist' theory from a critical realist standpoint. Sayer, too, argued for critical realist recognition of the force of some post-modernist themes, but also provided important critiques of what he terms 'defeatist postmodernism', including a very telling defence of some uses of forms of reasoning rejected by post-modernists/post-structuralists as 'essentialism' (Sayer 2000: ch. 4). Day (2007), too, argues for a more nuanced and sympathetic critical encounter between realism and post-structuralism (as evidenced in Pearce, Woodiwiss and Frauley's treatment of Foucault, mentioned above). It is also worth noting that the version of post-Marxism presented by Glynos and Howarth has much in common with critical realism.

While welcoming this flourishing of non-Marxian uses of critical realist philosophy, it seems to me there remain strong reasons for holding on to the 'affinity' between CR and (some versions of) Marxism. The fruitfulness of the link is either argued for or exemplified in many studies, including the chapters by Albritton, Engelskirchen and Ehrbar in Frauley and Pearce (2007), the substantive social scientific work of critical realists including Bob Jessop, Peter Dickens, Mary Mellor and many more. Jonathan Joseph (2001) used critical realism to great effect in evaluating a range of different versions of Marxism and critical theory, and, together with Kathryn Dean, John Roberts and Colin Wight, co-authored an exemplary exploration of theoretical issues arising from the linking of critical realism with Marxism (Dean *et al.* 2006). Sceptical about the value of Bhaskar's later work, they continue to find CR in its 'underlabouring' mode valuable as a means of correcting and resolving conceptual problems in Marxian historical research.

I have elsewhere argued for the continuing importance of the linkage between CR and Marxism for three main reasons. First, the approach to concept-construction and historical explanation pioneered by Marx and Engels was not only broadly consistent with the precepts of CR, but their own philosophical reflections on their approach had much in common with it. Although elements of realist explanation are certainly present in the work of other classic theorists, their development was limited by inappropriate philosophical considerations (Benton 1977). Second, much of the attention of Western Marxism in the twentieth century has been devoted to developing Marxian cultural and political theory, so that the old critique of Marxism as a form of 'economic reductionism' has no serious purchase – if it ever had. In view of this, it is now 'safe' to return to the analysis of the dynamics of capitalist political economy. Capitalism as a socio-economic form of life continues to have overwhelming causal importance in shaping the geographical distribution of economic activity, the life-chances of whole categories of people, the available policy-options for dealing with pressing economic, social and ecological problems and so on. In the wake of the neo-liberal ascendancy and capitalist globalization, this is even more inescapably so. It remains the case that the Marxian legacy offers the most fully developed and theoretically sophisticated critical account of capitalism as a whole system and its dynamics. Third, the commitment to 'naturalism' that has been a consistent theme in CR provides indispensable methodological support for research that investigates in a non-reductionist way the interrelations between human social, economic and personal life and the naturally given conditions and processes that sustain life, health and human flourishing. Arguably, it is current work (some of it mentioned above) enabled by both CR and contemporary Marxism that has taken us further with this aspiration than any other approach. The emergence of an emancipatory politics with any hope of addressing the growing crisis in the relationship between contemporary capitalism and our ecological life-support systems may depend on the kinds of understanding such research can achieve.

But this takes us on to a further set of questions about critical realism – and also, of course, to wider questions about the purposes and significance of social science itself.

What Is 'Critical' About Critical Realism? Critical Realism, Morality and 'Emancipation'

As Ian and I noted in the first edition, one of the reasons critical realism has proved attractive has to do with the adjective 'critical'. This implies that under the guidance of CR, social research can provide justifications for normative (ethical, moral, political) judgements about the states of affairs that are studied, and, through that, justifications for political actions to preserve or change those states of affairs. The concept that has been most used to link the critical realist account of social science explanation with morals and politics is that of 'explanatory critique'. In the work of Bhaskar and Collier, especially, this concept applies to the way some social structures can give rise to false beliefs, and also to the way some of them may give rise to avoidable suffering or deprivation. If social structures can be shown to have these effects, then we can pronounce a negative judgement on them, and justify their removal/transformation. The impression is given that this overcomes the traditional philosopher's claim that moral judgements cannot be deduced from mere statements of fact (to do so is held to fall foul of the 'naturalistic fallacy'). But for the proponents of the notion of explanatory critique, the sense in which a normative judgement follows from a factual statement is not captured by the notion formal deduction. Rather, the point is that to say someone is starving but should not be fed just does not make sense. Of course, it is admitted that there could be exceptional circumstances in which it *would* make sense not to feed someone who is starving (there may be extremely limited food, and many people starving, so hard decisions about priorities would have to be made) – so the connection between starving and feeding has to be qualified by a '*ceteris paribus*' clause – that is, 'other things being equal', we should feed the starving.

One obvious objection to this sort of argument is that descriptions of people's unmet needs, suffering, delusions and so on are themselves implicitly evaluative, so the explanatory critique only derives value-judgements from 'factual' claims that already embody the values that we draw from them. The issue of value-commitment is only pushed a step further back into the question of the concepts we use to describe social structures, states of affairs and so on. There are two main ways this retort can be addressed. The first is to pursue the 'holy grail' of a value-free description of social life, as proclaimed by positivism, while the second is to acknowledge the ineradicably 'valuey' nature of all meaningful characterizations of social life. The first option would, if taken to its limits, deliver descriptions that told us little or nothing intelligible about its topic. This is partly, but not wholly, because the self-understanding of social actors is ineradicably evaluative and as such (partially) constitutive of social life. So, the second option seems to be what is left: acknowledge that any worth-while characterization of social practices, structures and so on will necessarily carry with it value-connotations.

Now, this is a problem for the concept of explanatory critique if it is held to *of itself* justify a value-judgement, or, still further, to provide objective grounds for political action to transform the social structure or practice that is the alleged cause of suffering or delusion. The move to claiming the 'reality' or 'objectivity' of values, as Bhaskar and Collier, especially, are inclined to do, cannot be sustained by appeal to the model of explanatory critique (whether it can be underwritten by theology is a separate question). Of course, there is a sense in which values *are* 'real' and 'objective'. They are really present as part of the substance of social life itself – they are the means by which people and societies make sense of what they do, form their identities, define their hopes and aspirations, make decisions in difficult times and so on. This is part of the substance of Andrew Sayer's eloquent critique of the way much sociology fails to acknowledge the rationality in the 'lay normativity' of everyday life (Sayer 2009).

However, to recognize that values are present in the social practices we study is also to recognize the immense diversity of value-orientations that empirical social science discloses: we seem to be back with the value-relativism and abandonment of independent critical judgements about social life that the hermeneutic tradition has often been thought to imply!

But there are other problems with the idea of explanatory critique (see, especially, Sayer (2000), Benton (this work: 135–40, Benton 2004). It might be, for example, that a causal mechanism that produces suffering or injustice also has other effects that favour human well-being. Even if we accept that the suffering it produces is bad, there would still be an issue about whether it should be abolished in the light of what we know about its countervailing good effects. Tourism might be an example here – we might think its negative effects on environmental sustainability would justify banning or reducing it, but this would have to be weighed against the positive values of contact with other places and cultures, and of individual liberty. This could be addressed by the 'other things being equal' qualification, but the difficulty with this is that other things never are equal. In the complex situations in which difficult choices have to be made, any action is likely to have consequences along more than one axis, and be open to a variety of different, often incommensurable, considerations. How do we weigh the loss of liberty involved in banning a popular activity, or the injustice involved in using market incentives to restrict enjoyment of it to those who can pay, against the benefits of reduced carbon emissions, increased cross-cultural understanding, increased affluence of sections of local communities, or social and ecological degradation and increased social inequality of tourist destinations? It is hard to see that the notion of an explanatory critique would get us very far with untangling these issues.

Sayer (1995, 2000) points out that 'defeatist' post-modernism gives up on the critical project in the face of this, but he argues persuasively for an alternative: give up on the unreflective adoption of a critical standpoint in favour of explicit engagement in normative argument. If the critical social theorist or researcher is at odds with a prevailing social practice and the ideas that sustain it, then she is required to be clear about her initial value position, and to engage in a critical dialogue with the disputed values. This would entail a much more developed normative discourse than critical realism has so far provided. Here, it seems to me, we have to find a way of thinking about normative discourse – concerning value-commitments, the grounds for moral judgements, conceptions of the 'good life' and so on – that avoids two opposite extremes. The moral relativism of 'anything goes' is not only itself morally unacceptable as it dismisses and trivializes a central feature of human life but is also self-refuting, as it is *itself* a moral claim. The contrary position, that there are objective moral truths is both philosophically indefensible (in secular terms) and potentially oppressive or, at least, liable to intolerance.

Between these opposite poles, it can be recognized that we can and do have reasoned arguments about moral questions – about the justification or otherwise of abortion, assisted suicide, same-sex relationships, or the death penalty as well as broader questions to do with the moral ordering of our social relations and relations to non-human nature. People care, often passionately, about these issues, and in practice (if not in some versions of academic social theory) believe themselves to be right and their opponents wrong (even 'evil'). Though actual public debate frequently falls short of mutually respectful reasoned argument, this is nevertheless possible (and desirable!). Actual moral disputes appeal to a variety of sources of evidence – including empirical evidence of a social scientific kind – as well as pragmatic considerations, moral principles, rival interpretations or applications of moral principles, more-or-less consistent or grounded general views of human nature, claims of inconsistency or hypocrisy, reference to widespread human emotions and moral sentiments and so on. Even if we suppose moral dispute conducted under the conditions specified by Habermas's notion of an ideal speech situation (this work, Chapter 7 and also Chapter 8: 159) and continued without limit of time, it is difficult to believe that a society-wide moral consensus could be reached. Irreducible, bedrock moral pluralism is, perhaps, the wisest assumption to make if we are to think seriously about the conditions under which, in a complex and cosmopolitan society, we are to order our relations with one another.

Nevertheless, there remains an important place for reasoned normative dis-course, even if we do not *assume* that consensus will be the end-result. Some-times, indeed, consensus will be reached; sometimes rival parties will gain in respect for one-another's views and so find some form of compromise, or mode of co-existence; sometimes a 'second order' consensus might be reached about a framework within which continuing conflict can be contained, or put to constructive purpose.

The previous two paragraphs take us a step beyond 'critical' social theory and its justification. Many critical realists speak of some versions of social theory as 'emancipatory', and this is one important link between CR and Marxism. However, other orientations to social theory – linked to social movements other than the labour movement, such as feminism, anti-racism and the green movement – also see a link between critical social theory and a wider project of 'emancipation'. As we saw above, the critical realist notion of societies as 'open systems' implies that social life includes numerous interacting structures and practices, such that changing one structural cause of a specific form of injustice or suffering will have consequences that ripple out beyond the point at which intervention is made – and might well undermine whatever good is done, or generate further problems. For example, setting financial targets for health ser-vice trusts to ensure that beneficial new investment is efficiently used may have the unintended effect of distorting medical priorities and harm patient care.

These are well-known problems facing particular policy initiatives conceived and given effect within a broad 'taken-for-granted' framework of power relations, institutional structures and so on. However, the notion of emancipation is generally taken to involve a more profound and extensive transformation of social relations. It is usually taken to be implicit in the overthrow of a regime of domination and subordination that is in some sense at the core of the functioning of a social order. Classically, of course, it was applied to the overthrow of slave-systems, but in its Marxian version, it was applied to the relation between capital and wage-workers. In feminist thought the fundamental oppressive relation is the power wielded by men over the lives of women and in the case of anti-imperialist struggles it is the oppressive and exploitative rule of an imperial power over the people of a subordinated nation or culture. Because the relation of power that is challenged by an emancipatory struggle is viewed as central to the functioning of the established order, emancipatory movements carry, implicitly or explicitly, a vision of a qualitatively different whole mode of social life.

However, Sayer (1995, 2000) takes to task much critical social science, especially as reconstructed by CR, for performing only part of the necessary critical work. To criticize a particular structure, or, even more seriously, a whole pattern of social power relations and associated institutions as a source of suffering, injustice or unmet needs carries weight only if there is an alternative way of ordering society that is both feasible and desirable. That is, a mode of life that can be brought into being, and that can reasonably be expected to ameliorate the negative aspects of the *status quo* without producing ills that are even worse than the ones criticized. In short, our system might be bad, but it might be less bad than any of the alternatives! Sayer is critical of the notion of emancipation often relied on by CR as the replacement of unwanted determinations by wanted and needed ones. Although this does acknowledge that emancipation cannot mean a leap into some absolute, unconditioned 'freedom', it does not adequately address the diversity of needs, aspirations, values and interests that would have to be taken account of and realigned in any fundamental transformation of society. Nor does it seem to recognize the role of the obligations and commitments that flow from human social relations, nor the constraints that follow from a qualitative re-ordering of human and practical relationships to the rest of nature. This is, of course, not a critique of the vision of radical emancipatory change as such. Rather, it is a call for a more complex and nuanced understanding of what would be involved.

Dean *et al.* (2006) take issue especially with aspects of Bhaskar's later work on *Dialectic* and the 'spiritual turn' (Bhaskar 1993, 2002). In their view, emancipation has to be understood as a creative and collective project of social transformation, whereas, for them, Bhaskar's later work reduces the notion to one of individual 'self-emancipation' through contemplative activity. Joseph (2006), especially, comments that emancipatory practice should be understood in terms of the possibilities given by concrete, historically given circumstances, rather than presented in abstract, universalizing concepts. Kathryn Dean, however, recognizes that Bhaskar, as well as Marx, do envision an alternative mode of social life in which distinctively human potentials might be realized. There is, then, a response to the challenge posed by Sayer – an attempt to specify the outlines of a possible form of human society in which the frustrations and 'absences' of our current capitalist way of life would be transcended. Dean argues that humans are instinctually underdetermined, so that it is only through being nurtured in a specific culture that their potentials can be actualized. She draws on Aristotle's conception of 'eudaimonia' – a state of social being in which virtue and practical wisdom ('phronesis') are nurtured by the practices of citizenship. This implies a public sphere in which citizens exercise judgement in their deliberation on the common good. Divested of Aristotle's unjustified exclusions from citizenship of women, slaves and others, this account of the 'good life' provides a contrast with the individualizing and depoliticizing character of the processes through which individual selves are formed under capitalism.

The growing recognition by critical social scientists that criticism is seriously weakened if we can say little or nothing about feasible alternatives has led to a resurgence of interest in utopian thought – whether in the shape of literary fiction, film or philosophical–political speculation. Interestingly, most of the commercially popular representations of the future in literature or film are decidedly dystopian – to the point that it has been said it is easier to imagine the end of the world than the end of capitalism. However, social theorists and philosophers such as Ruth Levitas, Kate Soper, Martin Ryle, Andre Gorz, John O'Neill, Pat Devine, myself and others have persisted in facing up to the challenge of imagining future societies which might enable human potential to be realized on the basis of social justice, conviviality and respect for the non-human world. In this, they can draw on a long history of utopian thought from at least as far back as Aristotle, and including the diggers and levellers of the English Civil War, the artist and mystic William Blake, designer and revolutionary William Morris and many more. All of this heritage of thought about alternative modes of social being does, of course, bear the mark of its time and place, and it is a useful reminder of how difficult it is even for the most imaginative thinker to escape from the prejudices and assumptions of her or his own historical moment. Nevertheless, theoretical imagining, drawing on these past works, as well as study of attempts in practice to 'prefigure' possible futures in social experiments such as cooperative enterprises, communes, local exchange and trading schemes and so on is necessary if the horizons of our own political culture are to be opened to possible alternatives – alternatives so far systematically excluded from our public discourse. While by no means all of this imaginative work is carried out by critical realists, it is arguable that CR has much to offer, both in sustaining the rationality of such work, and in providing criteria by which to assess its outcomes

Does Critical Realism Have Anything to Offer for Feminist Social Sciences?

Feminists influenced by critical realism include Kate Soper and Mary Mellor, whose work has already been mentioned. Caroline New (1998, 2003) has argued for the value of a version of CR in defence of feminist research in the face of some versions of post-structuralism that criticized feminist research and political mobilization based on an assumed common interest among women.

Critical realist economist, Tony Lawson, too, sparked a lively controversy in the journal *Feminist Economics* (1999, 2003b) by arguing that a critical realist turn to social ontology among feminist theorists would have much to offer for the emancipatory potential of that discipline. The ontology he outlines is one of human society as open, structured (in the sense that structures are not reducible to the activities of human individuals), dynamic, or 'processual' and predominantly comprising internal relations. The view of emancipation he offers acknowledges the importance of 'differences' (of gender as well as others) but situates these in the context of a deeper sense in which there are common-alities shared by all humans in the necessary conditions for our flourishing. These include our need to develop species-specific competences such as language. On this account, emancipation would amount to the emergence of a society in which 'the flourishing of each is a condition of the flourishing of all and vice versa' (1999, p. 125). In the course of this argument, he also notes a conver-gence of CR as he interprets it with feminist standpoint epistemology (this work: Ch. 9). If we, following CR, think of society as an open system, it follows there is no single privileged point of access for understanding – the interests or 'standpoint' of the investigator will necessarily shape the specific phenomena and associated causal mechanisms that they select as research topics.

Sandra Harding (1999), Drucilla Barker (2003) and Fabienne Peter (2003) in their responses raise several issues. Barker agrees that CR has important methodological insights into the failings of 'mainstream' economics and notes the convergence between Lawson's version of CR and standpoint epistemol-ogy. However, on the key claim that CR can provide a general account of human nature (a 'philosophical anthropology') that would overcome the divisions of perspective that flow from human difference, she is sceptical. For post-structuralist and post-colonial thinkers (she particularly cites Donna Haraway), knowledge is always 'situated', so that claims to the effect that there is some underlying or potential unity that transcends the differences that we experience should always be treated with scepticism – *Whose* interest does this 'universalizing' claim express? *Who* is to be emancipated by the proposed course of action? And so on. Both Harding and Peter call into question CR's account of science. Since Bhaskar's early transcendental arguments for the social ontology of CR rested on the assumption of successful scientific explana-tion, they argue that the feminist *critique* of science as a social practice driven by power relations, most notably those whereby women's contributions are excluded or marginalized, is something that CR cannot take into account. Like Barker, Peter argues against CR's moral realism, and its claims to know what universal needs humans share.

This is clearly an on-going debate, with a number of unresolved issues, but a few comments can be made here. First, the claim that CR assumes the success of scientific explanation and so cannot effectively criticize its unjust institutionalization has some force, especially against Bhaskar's early use of transcendental arguments in relation to physical science. However, it is also true that Bhaskar's view of science theorized it as a social practice in a way that was absent in earlier 'mainstream' philosophies of science. Unfortunately, he did not take that insight far into a critical enquiry into the history and sociology of scientific practices and institutions of the sort that would meet the requirement of feminist critics. But Lawson's version of CR explicitly draws on a range of familiar experiences, and is not dependent in the way Bhaskar's was on the argument from scientific success.

Lawson's proposal that a 'philosophical anthropology' linked to CR could indicate human commonalities that might transcend the difficulties arising from systematic differences and divisions of interest poses many important but challenging issues. We saw above that serious critical social research – especially where it is held to sustain an 'emancipatory' project – stands in need of a defensible account of an alternative to the *status quo* that would be both feasible and desirable. Since one of the standard conservative responses to utopian visions is that they 'do not take account of human nature', it seems likely that any plausible vision of a future society radically different from today's would have to be backed up by an account of human nature such that our irreducible differences, psychological dispositions, emotional repertoires, learning abilities, primary attachments, organic needs, developmental adaptabilities and so on would find a field for their exercise and satisfaction. So, in this sense, a 'philosophical anthropology' almost certainly would be a necessary element in any fully developed argument for an emancipatory project. However, Peter is surely right to resist the claim for objective truth on behalf of any one version of such a philosophical anthropology. For any such claim to remain uncontested would certainly risk oppressive applications, so all proposed alternative visions should accommodate the 'potential contestedness of needs'(Peter 2003: 99).

This does not mean, however, that the effort to use our imagination, evidence (from a variety of disciplines) and reasoning in constructing accounts of human nature is worthless, or, indeed, that any one of them is as good or bad as any other. The hope is that open and inclusive discussion might take us towards better versions, ones in which the perspectives of hitherto powerless or marginalized life-experiences were represented. This might also play a part in legitimating such accounts, and the alternative social visions they carry, among sufficiently diverse and inclusive coalitions for a broadly based emancipatory struggle. But there are two further provisos. While a shared broad view of a common human flourishing might be necessary to inspire the politics of a movement for change, there is no requirement for such a movement to overcome or down-play internal differences or divisions. Lawson's critics take him to be arguing that mobilizations necessarily depend on a notion of a shared, common interest. In fact, many of the most successful social movements have involved very broad coalitions in which significant participation has come from activists who do not stand to benefit directly from the changes they seek: the world-wide struggle against Apartheid, coalitions in favour of the extension of the franchise to women and other excluded groups, solidarity campaigns on behalf of political prisoners and many other examples could be cited.

My second proviso raises questions about the 'humanist' assumptions of the main advocates of the emancipatory objectives of critical social science. Two examples illustrate the point. One of these is the animal rights movement, a leading pioneer of which saw it as the logical next step beyond the emancipation of women, ethnic minorities and subjected nationalities (Singer 1976). The other is the international campaign in defence of the tropical moist forests. True, these are often presented in terms of the ecosystem services and potential medical resources that lie in the biodiversity of the forests. However, the deepest sources of anxiety and anger stem from a moral and aesthetic love of these unique and irreplaceable natural formations – ones that most activists have never visited – as well as solidarity with their indigenous inhabitants. My suggestion, here, is that the unsustainability of our current global social and economic system has provoked a requirement that our envisioning of alternatives has to put at its centre a qualitatively different social, economic and moral mode of human life in relation to those other species with which we (still) share the planet. Mere 'humanism' is no longer enough.

Ted Benton, May 2010.

Appendix I
Personal Conclusions

Ted Benton

Our initial intention was to write two conclusions, in which we would each comment on the chapters written by the other, and state our own independent 'positions'. I found this difficult, partly because, on reading Ian's chapters, I couldn't find very much to disagree with. Even where I do disagree, I don't think my comments would add greatly to whatever usefulness this book already has. So, instead of a conclusion, we agreed to add more personal, even autobiographical comments on the processes and experiences which got us to thinking the things we now think.

I started my working life as a secondary school teacher of science and maths, but had the opportunity (we had grants in those days!) to pursue my passion for philosophy at university level. This opened up the possibility for me of a teaching career in the university, and I had the incredible good fortune to be given a job teaching Philosophy within a Sociology department. Even more fortunate, the job was at Essex University, and I still can't imagine a better place to be! In those days (early 1970s), the university milieu was highly politicized, and there was unceasing debate among adherents of wildly different versions of Marxist, feminist and libertarian thought. Ian joined the staff (to replace Roy Enfield) soon afterwards, and he and I shared the teaching of philosophy of science in the department. Appropriately enough, we were both interested in the relationship between philosophy and the social sciences, and both thought this was a relationship of great importance for the latter.

We also had in common an attraction to Marxist ideas. However, this was not *so* much in common, since this was the time of intense debate over 'humanist' versus 'structuralist' developments of the Marxian heritage, and we experienced each other as on opposite sides of that debate. I put it like this, because that, indeed, was how it seemed. Ian had a strong interest in the work of Sartre (Craib 1976), and was then, as since, strongly committed to a practice of social science which took seriously the inner life of individual people, and the hermeneutic dimension of social life: his position could fairly be described as humanist and anti-naturalist. By contrast, for reasons I think I can explain, I was attracted to the structuralist end of the great debate. Partly this was because I was already a fairly unorthodox Marxist, and I liked the Althusserian proclamation that Marxism was an open-ended research programme – not some finished body of doctrine that you either had to accept or reject *in toto*. My background in philosophy predisposed me to favour the aspiration to theoretical rigour in the re-working of Marxist ideas. I also found my strong sense of the effects of social structures on people's life-chances confirmed in the Althusserian approach.

However, Ian found within the 'humanist' Marxian tradition concepts with which to express something close to that. His humanism was never bereft of recognitions of how people's lives and possibilities are shaped, constrained or stunted by their position in oppressive social structures. On my side of the debate (Ian remembers it differently – but I can refer to things I wrote at the time!!), I was never tempted by Althusser's tendency to reduce individuals to the status of 'bearers' of the social structures, nor was I convinced by his (in effect) identifying ideology with the ruling ideology. Althusserian Marxism was seriously flawed in its inability to comprehend spontaneous resistance and struggle 'from below'.

Partly as a consequence of our being attracted to different versions of the Marxian theoretical heritage, Ian and I tended to take opposite sides on another cluster of issues. These are at the centre of our concerns in this book. In those days, Ian's commitment to the focus on subjectivity and the psychological aspects of social life, together with the literature he drew on, disposed him to an anti-naturalistic view of social science. The positivist bid to incorporate the social sciences into a basically natural scientific methodology was something that had to be resisted. Human subjects and the meaningful relations they created had to be approached in a quite different spirit. In contrast, I retained my respect for the work of the natural sciences, and thought there were strong reasons for linking the social sciences to at least some of the natural sciences (the life-sciences, especially ecology) both substantively and methodologically.

My commitment to a naturalistic approach had two main sources. The first was my life-long passion for field natural history – for observing and studying the wonderful diversity of animals and plants in their habitats. This was linked to my appreciation of biology as a science (my feelings about that discipline are much more mixed today, given the take-over of its research programmes by agribusiness and pharmaceuticals interests), and also to a growing awareness of the interconnection of ecological damage and human social practices. No one who cared about what is now called 'biological diversity' and lived through that period could fail to be horrified by the devastation of natural and semi-natural habitats wrought by 'development' pressures, but most of all by the industrialization of agriculture. A social science which failed to take seriously the 'material' dimension of what Marx called the 'metabolism' between human society and the rest of nature would have no way of addressing these issues.

The second spur to my 'naturalism' was something which at the time I experienced (amazingly enough, in retrospect) as quite separate. This was my intense involvement in labour-movement politics through the seventies and into the early eighties. To put it crudely, it seemed to me at the time that it was just obvious that the whole system of wage-labour was exploitative and alienating, that people's human potential was suppressed and blighted by the compulsion to perform often mindless and repetitive jobs for the benefit of a rich minority. So, the primary emphasis of the humanist socialists on moral denunciation (as I saw it then) seemed to me misplaced. Rather, what was needed was a rigorous and empirically well-founded scientific understanding of social structures and practices which could provide reliable strategic guidance for oppositional struggles.

In academic terms, my own earlier immersion in the life-sciences and familiarity with anti-positivist (both realist and socio-historical) accounts of the natural sciences made it possible for me to be committed to such a naturalistic approach to social science, while rejecting positivism. So, in fact, Ian and I continued to have considerable philosophical common ground, while disagreeing radically with each other on the issue of naturalism. I remained attracted by a 'heroic' vision of science as overcoming superstitious and authoritarian imposition of belief-systems in favour of a democratic use of our human powers of reason and experience to discover the world around us.

Even as science and technology were manifestly more and more being co-opted by big capital and the state in the service of exploitation, military conquest and social control (this was the period of the US war in South East Asia, and support for dictatorships in South and Central America), I was still resistant to the 'constructionist' view that science was no more than the projection of prevailing social interests and cultural values onto an otherwise amorphous or unknowable 'nature'. The research programmes of science, the questions asked and the ones not asked, the links between research programmes even in 'basic' science and commercial or military interests were undeniable, and their distortion of the scientific enterprise quite clear. For all that, the popularized self-image of science as a heroic struggle to understand all the complexity and beauty of the natural world and to give insights into our place in it was still a source of attraction. I vividly recall reading, as a child, a popular book on evolutionary theory (called, as I remember, *The Reason Why? Evolution*), and later reading Darwin's *Origin of Species*. This was a revelation, but not in the religious sense. This and later reading of popular science certainly profoundly changed my sense of who I was, and how connected to the world around me (most obviously in the case of Darwinism, with its recognition of human kinship with the rest of life). But this transformation was brought about by the appeal to arguments, and to evidence which I could sometimes even check for myself – not by appeal to a sacred text. This was a source of knowledge-claims which respected the intelligence and autonomy of those it addressed. So, whatever the distortions and betrayals of the scientific legacy imposed by current power relations, I never lost the sense that there was something inherently liberatory about the struggle to understand our world and our place in it. At its best, and in some possible future, this was what science was for.

At this point (sometime in the late 1970s), Ian's and my life diverged quite considerably. He became increasingly involved in fatherhood, psychoanalysis and therapy. Meanwhile, for me, too, fatherhood and the 'domestic sphere' provided an excuse for temporary withdrawal from active political engagement. Although I was already strongly influenced by the feminist movement which burgeoned in the early years of the 1970s, I don't think I had taken on its full significance until fatherhood hit me. That, and the detachment from active political engagement which it required gave me time to re-think many former commitments, both in terms of the public sphere of politics and in terms of academic issues. During this period of Thatcherite domination of the political and ideological scene, I could not see any hope that the labour movement as then constituted could resist effectively. For some in the labour movement, this recognition meant abandoning socialist aspirations so as to appeal to a public which was assumed to have largely absorbed Thatcherite values. For me, it meant trying to think about how the left's traditional critical understanding of capitalism could be deepened and broadened in its popular appeal. I think it was only during this time that I grasped the depth and significance of both feminist and green critiques, in the sense that I started to see how much of the traditional left's analyses and visions of possible futures would have to be transformed. Luckily, others have shared this diagnosis, and, working alongside and in dialogue we have established something of an international community of scholars and activists who try to bring together feminist, green, anti-racist and socialist forms of thought into a vision which may eventually challenge the desperate consensus that capitalism is 'the only game in town'. It might be more than a coincidence that alarm about whether we might have a long-term future at all really hit home with becoming a father.

Not everyone who is engaged in this dialogue agrees that 'naturalism' is necessary to it. Kate Soper, in particular, has strongly argued against it. I agree that we should be wary of attempts to make too close a connection between philosophical views and political positions. Nevertheless, it does seem to me that a naturalism which remains consistently anti-reductionist does facilitate new ways of thinking about social and political life. In particular, I've followed some feminist writers in insisting that the (different and similar) ways humans are embodied, their vulnerability to illness, the inevitability of death and so on are of profound importance both for any serious liberatory politics and for any adequate social theory. Similarly with the closely related facts of our necessary metabolism with organic and inorganic nature. It would be disastrous to reduce our understanding of what humans are to their bio-chemical make-up, or their genetic inheritance, as reductionist self-styled 'Darwinists' do. Equally, however, a social theory which doesn't pay due respect to our embodiment, mortality, kinship and interdependence with other living beings won't be able to address some of the central issues facing our 'civilization'.

So, to return to the themes of this book. The marks of the above engagements with feminisms, and with ecological politics will be evident in the chapters I've contributed. Both these streams of thought have deepened both my commitment to naturalism and my commitment to an anti-positivist understanding of the value and importance of science. A non-instrumental science of nature, which respects its objects, accepts some humility in recognition of the unfathomable complexity of its object, and fully acknowledges its own standing as a fallible human social project is a necessary dimension in any worthwhile human society. The vision of Hilary Rose, Evelyn Fox Keller and other feminists who do not abandon the quest for 'objectivity', but rather seek to give it a new meaning, offers a prospect of an 'alternative' science with just these characteristics. There is, too, something for ecological politics. These have been characterized by a somewhat uneasy oscillation between hostility to science and technology, on the one hand, and reliance on them to give authority to environmentalist knowledge-claims, on the other. In their different ways, the non-positivist accounts of science open up a way beyond this dilemma. If scientific work could be freed from its current domination from powerful interests and cultural forces, this might open up quite different possibilities for scientific and technical development and their relationship to social life and the natural world. The ethical intuitions of ecocentric ecologism, which require us to value non-human nature for its own sake find their complement in the 'dynamic objectivity' favoured by feminist epistemology. Critical realist work on the nature of science also converges on this recognition that science can be *both* a social practice *and* one which seeks (fallibly) knowledge of a reality beyond itself.

The chapters I contributed to this book chart a tortuous (in retrospect, perhaps more tortuous than was necessary) route through a whole mountain range of books, articles and 'live' debates. The position I've managed to put together as my provisional way-station is a product of this biography. It has been shaped by my intimate relationships (about which I'll say nothing here!), by continuing creative dialogue with colleagues, including Ian, and students at this university, by my various political engagements, by my continuing passion for nature, by cooperative work with scholars and activists in this country and overseas. In short, while I can produce evidence and reasons for what I currently think, it is nonetheless the outcome of a very peculiar life-history. I have no good reason to expect any reader of this book to agree with me. So, what was mildly surprising to me was how close Ian's path and mine had come after having taken such very different routes through the mountains.

One thing, I now see, is that we have both been resistant to what might be called 'sociological imperialism': this is manifest in some versions of 'social constructivism'. In its more extreme versions, constructivism tends to see the subjective life of individuals as wholly constituted by social processes, or to swallow up the notion of an independent nature in the claim that all we have access to are culturally produced discourses of 'nature'. Ian has been insisting on the need to recognize the psychic life of individuals as a domain with its own specific dynamics and processes, not reducible to what is put there by 'socialization'. There is a parallel between this and my own commitment to a re-working of the social scientific heritage which takes our embodiment and our interdependence with non-human nature seriously. Since historically the social and life-sciences have developed largely in ignorance of one another, the desirable reconciliation between them will require prolonged dialogue in which both groups of disciplines are likely to revise some of their most basic assumptions. Social scientists are right to insist on the indispensability of their perspectives in coming to understand our immensely complex world. Equally, however, they need to be open to, albeit critical, respect for the immense contribution of the life-sciences (see Benton 1991, 1994).

But this leads on to a second area of common ground between us. This is our shared persistence with the now rather unfashionable view that knowledge and understanding are indispensable to human emancipation, or to the betterment of human life. For myself, there are two aspects of this. One is that faced with the scale of destructiveness and social disintegration unleashed by contemporary economic, technical and military power, and the cultural forms which have risen with them, those who still have the will to resist need good, testable theory to provide a strategic resource. Rhetorics of moral denunciation, I now accept, have an important part to play, but they aren't enough. But there is a deeper, and perhaps more widely shared respect in which the struggle for understanding is emancipatory. This takes us back to our introductory chapter, and to the recognition that, as Gramsci used to say, 'everyone is a philosopher'. In order to carry on our lives, none of us can avoid the challenge to make sense of the world we have to negotiate, to locate ourselves somewhere in it, to align ourselves in relation to its contradictory tendencies, and so to adopt values. This aspect of life as a struggle to make sense of the world around us and to establish a relationship to it is part of what it is to be human. I don't know a better statement of this than the one given by the young Marx in his Paris notebooks:

> 'Just as plants, animals, stones, air, light, etc. on the theoretical side form part of human consciousness, partly as objects of natural science, partly as objects of art, just as they are his spiritual inorganic nature, spiritual nourishment which he must first prepare for enjoyment and digestion, so they also form part of human life and of human activity on the practical side. . . . Nature is man's *inorganic body* – nature, that is in so far as it is not itself human body. Man *lives* on nature – means that nature is his *body*, with which he must remain in continuous interchange if he is not to die. That man's physical and spiritual life is linked to nature means simply that nature is linked to itself, for man is a part of nature.' (Marx [1844] 1975, pp. 276. See also A. Collier 1991)

But striving to understand the world and our connectedness to it is intrinsically valuable for yet another reason. This has to do with our belated recognition of the social character of this struggle. Feminist epistemology has provided the clearest demonstration that so far this is a social enterprise which is profoundly compromised by its exclusive character. They show the extent to which it has been monopolized by men, the radical science movement would add its subservience to capital and the military, post-colonial theorists would emphasize its complicity with empire and race, while green critics would denounce its complicity with the destructive modern project of domination of nature. The feminist epistemologists' call for a practice of science in which an inclusive dialogue of equals can be conducted on terms and respecting criteria which are subject to continuous re-negotiation offers a prospect of mutual respect and understanding between rival traditions of thought. This in itself would be a true human good. That it is not utopian is illustrated by pre-figurative experiences of something approaching it in our fleeting opportunities for real dialogue in daily life, and, still, just occasionally, in the seminar rooms and coffee bars of colleges and universities.

However, as with all true human goods, the key question is how to extend it from the elite contexts where it is still enjoyed to make it available to all who can and wish to participate. How to realize a genuine democratization of intellectual life? This certainly means enhancing opportunities for previously excluded and marginalized groups within institutionalized settings. But it also means fighting in the wider culture for an ethic which sets value on curiosity and the search for understanding, and which affords opportunities, time and space for a confident citizenry to pursue these values. It means rejecting postmodern irony and economistic contempt for them, and it means opposing the ever-advancing commercialization and 'corruption' of what is left of our common culture.

Ian Craib

It is with some pleasure that I can reciprocate Ted's response to my chapters: reading through his I find little that I disagree with and nothing that I can *usefully* disagree with. Even though I think we have worked with and still work with different intellectual projects, there has been something of a merging of horizons (in Gadamer's sense) from our arguments and attempts to understand each other. I have no problem with Ted's characterization of my positions, so perhaps I'll start by saying what I have learnt from him.

First, I learnt to tolerate what I regarded as more tedious dimensions of the philosophy of science and social science, arguments about logic and meaning which I now find myself defending to students and colleagues. There are some very basic notions which Ted covers in his contribution to the introduction and his discussion of positivism which are like the essentials of learning to play an instrument – learning to read music, play the scales and arpeggios, for example, without which one can make the philosophical equivalent of a horrible noise. Sociologists often do make a horrible noise when they venture into philosophical areas, and my contribution to our praise of the Essex Department is that it has never been afraid to recruit from other disciplines or from the fringes of sociology (I'm talking about myself here) and so set up extraordinarily creative cross-currents. We work in a department where we cannot find security by theorizing other disciplines out of the way.

Second, the development of non-positivist philosophies of science to which Ted has been a major contributor has opened up a range of possibilities that I had not associated with naturalism, and I now think of the crossovers from natural to social science as an intriguing and sometimes exciting area, and it seems to me that increasingly there are dimensions of the sociological enterprise which can learn much from the natural sciences.

Third and most important in the context of this book is that what I appreciate about Ted's contribution is the passion with which he pursues and defends his ideas, and his love of the natural sciences. I have learnt what little I know of the natural sciences from listening to him and talking to him.

Yet we have different intellectual projects and I have always found it difficult to say exactly of what that difference consists. I could not produce my own intellectual history in the way that Ted has done – I feel I floundered through different theorists, different philosophers, different approaches, experiencing it all in the way Hegel describes it in the introduction to his *Phenomenology of Spirit*, and I paraphrase here: the truth is like a drunken orgy from which occasionally one member will stand out clearly defined before being absorbed back into the melee. My political *views* have not changed so dramatically – I am beginning to realize despite my attempts to be a Serious Marxist in the Socialist Workers Party and later on the left of the Labour Party, I have always been very unserious Marxist – perhaps tending more to anarcho-syndicalism – although I don't know if there are any anarcho-syndicalists out there or even if anybody knows what it is any more. In fact I'm not sure that *I* know what it is any more. What I distil from all this is that what is important is *opposition, argument* and *thought*. All three are under sustained attack in many areas, and I think they have been so as long as I can remember, and perhaps the battles have been with us ever since the Enlightenment. In politics, it is opposition, argument and thought which provide us with what limited freedoms we have, and the advice of one of the heroes of my youth still stands: don't follow leaders.

Believe it or not, this has something to do with the way I approach the ideas in this book. To begin with, I think that all the ideas we consider here should be taken seriously and have relevance across the board in the social sciences. The social sciences as a whole and each one separately are complex animals dealing with multiple objects at multiple levels of analysis. No one approach and no one way of working can ever be *the* way. Many colleagues will acknowledge this and then carry on in their preferred way without any reflection. If progress is possible in the social sciences, it will not be achieved through a narrow focus – there are few if any areas where we can see ourselves as accumulating knowledge until we have it all and can pack up and go home, not least because what we study is continuously changing, often *because* we study it.

What we provide here is I think not *a* meta-narrative but a series of complementary and contradictory meta-narratives which enable a creative and critical debate to take place between approaches at both a theoretical and an empirical level – it is the existence of these debates which take us beyond being collectors of statistics and stories. A science in which there is no opposition or argument is a dead science.

This brings me to what Ted calls my interest in subjectivity and to the point where our projects differ. I was always interested in subjectivity on an intellectual level, but there was a point earlier than Ted dates it – in the late seventies – when desperation set in, when my academic life and the political organizations to which I belonged felt like prisons and my personal life went through a number of upheavals. The desperation drove me to psychoanalysis first as a patient, and by the mid-1980s as a trainee group analytic therapist. The work I do as a therapist provides with me with equivalent sources of wonder to those Ted finds in the natural world. It is not the external world which I find wonder-full but the creativeness of the internal worlds and daily lives of the people who come my way in my work for the NHS. I am privileged by being able to witness the way in which people can survive against the odds and usually go beyond survival in their day-to-day lives through processes that remain mysterious to me. A metaphor which my patients regularly produce without my help is that we are given a hand of cards at birth, and however bad that hand is we have to play it, and we can play it well or badly.

The subjectivity that I am interested in is that implicated in the way that the hands are played. Some people seem to be dealt a worthless hand – perhaps they are subjected to treatment in their childhood which can only be described as sustained torture – yet they are able, often by means of their supposed 'symptoms', to build lives for themselves, sustain long-term loving relationships and bring up their own children in a loving way. They do not do this by concentrating on their victimhood, although of course they are victims, but rather by grasping some internal capacity of agency in a particular way. Other people seem to be dealt an average or even a good hand, yet each card they play takes them into further trouble. They use their internal capacity in a different way.

I would argue that given the complexity of contemporary understandings of science, we could develop scientific or rational explanations and understanding of everything up to the point where the hands are played. Beyond that there is something imponderable. However what I would surmize from my own experience and from my experience as a therapist is that people who survive best, who play their hands in a way that does not cause them or others too much suffering are those who allow themselves to think. Psychoanalysis is often thought of as putting people in touch with feelings but more often is about people learning to think about and articulate feelings. It does not cure anxiety or misery but enables people to be anxious and miserable in more creative ways. We cannot explain or predict why one person might achieve this in one way and another person in another, and there are many more ways of achieving it than there are people to achieve it – we can, if we wish, gain access to an endless range of registers of internal achievements, from our dreams to our mathematical abilities to the pleasure taken in cultivating an allotment.

I think it is here where any type of science or rational understanding ceases, and my dominant intellectual concern is to develop critiques of those ideas, from the natural or the social sciences, which attempt to close down this area for if such ideas feed through into political and social policies, as they often do, they contribute to a closing down of human possibilities. To achieve these possibilities is always a struggle. Those who do best in psychotherapy are those who can learn to think about their inner lives, often think the unthinkable, who can learn to tolerate anxiety, contradiction, paradox and uncertainty and internal conflict and make something out of it all. Exactly the same abilities are needed to produce good social science. Opposition, argument and thought are internal as well as external processes. In this context, bad social science is what tries to explain away that imponderable area of creativity and internal confusion; and which closes down investigation and argument to one particular method and area. A living social science and perhaps a living natural science as well has to think in many different ways.

Appendix II
Obituary for Professor Ian Craib (1945–2002)*

Ian Craib, who has died at the tragically early age of 57, was appointed as a lecturer in Sociology at Essex University in 1973, and was promoted to a chair in 1997. Despite his personal modesty, the continuous stream of books, articles and reviews which he authored over more than 25 years earned great respect both in and well beyond the academy. A mark of his originality was his commitment to asking the large and important questions which necessarily transgress disciplinary boundaries. In Ian's case, philosophy, literature, psychoanalysis and social theory were all called upon in the making of his unique contribution. He saw himself as at the margins of sociology, but perhaps because of this, he had a deeper understanding of both its indispensability and its limitations than most. His early work – most notably his first book, *Existentialism and Sociology* – explored the relationships between philosophy and sociology, a connection to which he remained committed throughout his career. This, together with his long-standing political concerns, was expressed in his long association with the journal *Radical Philosophy*. He wrote extensively for the journal, especially through his reviews, and was a member of the editorial group in the early days. Through the 1970s, his advocacy of a humanist Marxism, inspired by Sartre's existentialism, sustained his political activism, first in the International Socialists, and then (uncomfortably) within the Labour Party. In his work as a sociology teacher and writer, he resisted the tide of structuralist thought which swept the humanities and social science disciplines at that time. In a characteristic critique of one T. Benton, he argued:

> The power of theory is its ability to transform consciousness, to change people not necessarily by intellectual conviction but by enabling them to grasp their own world and their own experience in a radically new way and to become aware of ways of changing the world. If Marxist theory is to do this, then it must be able to live inside everyday representations of the world, to take them as the starting point of its argument, and it must be able to transform those representations into an adequate understanding of the world. (*Radical Philosophy* 10, Spring 1975: 29)

---

* The following by Ted Benton appeared in the journal *Radical Philosophy* in 2003. Reprinted with kind permission.

By the end of the 1970s, a combination of personal difficulties and political despair had provoked a retreat from organized politics into a prolonged personal and intellectual engagement with psychoanalysis.

In the mid-1980s Ian had become a trainee psychotherapist, but still had not abandoned his commitment to social theorizing. The first synthesis of these twin engagements was his *Psychoanalysis and Social Theory* (1989). It was the sub-title of this work – 'the limits of sociology' – that signalled Ian's most abiding sociological argument. The shift from existentialism to psychoanalysis turned out to be a way of bringing new intellectual resources to maintain the central concern of his earlier humanism: the claim of the inner life of individuals to be respected and defended from reductive simplifications. Using an image offered by one of his patients, he acknowledged that we might eventually be able, as sociologists, to explain the 'hand of cards' each of us is dealt in life. But much depends on how that hand is played, and there is something imponderable and wonderful about the creativity individuals show in surviving against the odds. Intellectual approaches which fail to recognize this are to be opposed because they threaten to close down on human possibilities.

The 1980s again saw Ian swimming against powerful currents of thought. In the face of fashionable denunciations of large-scale theorizing and *avant garde* dismissals of the sociological classics, he published extensively on sociological theory. His *Modern Social Theory* (1984) was an outstanding example of Ian's ability to communicate complex and difficult ideas in a direct and accessible way, but still conveying the sense of excitement and bewilderment of never-quite-grasping them. Intended as student texts, they immensely successful and valued as such, but they were also more than is commonly understood by that. Ian both demonstrated and argued for the importance of engaging with the major thinkers of the past if we are to understand both the present and its contemporary thought. His *Classical Social Theory* (1997) made this case eloquently. But these were more than just textbooks in another important sense: they were an extension of Ian's much more central commitment to his role as a teacher. In them, one gets a glimpse of his quite distinctive, challenging but still empathic educational philosophy.

At the same time, the interest in psychoanalysis deepened. He trained as a group psychotherapist, qualifying in 1986, and continuing to work as a psychotherapist in the local NHS alongside his job as university teacher. His counselling skills and devotion were also much valued in his role as senior advisor within the university. His therapeutic practice was also a source of inspiration for his thinking about the relationship between psychoanalysis and social thought, and he began to make distinctive and original contributions both to the specialist psychoanalytic literature, and to the critical interconnections between the two disciplines. Written through the first diagnosis and operation for cancer, *The Importance of Disappointment* (1994) was and remains Ian's deepest and most personal statement.

But this more public presence, significant as it has been, is perhaps not what Ian would most wish to have recalled. He came to Essex University in the mid-1970s, and could hardly have found a more stimulating or congenial environment. He latterly paid tribute to the policy of a department unafraid to recruit staff from its 'fringes' and from other disciplines. He engaged passionately in the political and theoretical debates of the time, and the subsequent retreat from organized politics was not an abandonment of politics as such. He recently recognized that while trying to be a 'serious Marxist' he had always been a 'very unserious Marxist': closer, perhaps, to anarcho-syndicalism (though, typically Ian, he added that he wasn't quite sure what this meant!). True to his early humanism, his politics expressed itself in his later years in his devotion to teaching and to his therapeutic work, as well as in his writing. For him, the insistence on 'opposition, argument and thought' was what had given us such limited freedoms as we enjoy, and it was to evoking and educating these capacities in himself and others that his political values continued to express themselves.

He stressed the importance, in therapy, as well as in the process of becoming a sociologist, of learning to 'tolerate anxiety, contradiction, paradox and uncertainty and inner conflict and to make something of it all'. His teaching was a process of challenging, sometimes disconcerting, exploration of possibilities. He could not have been more at odds with the prevailing ethos of higher education under New Labour, according to which its value is defined in terms of enhanced lifetime earnings, and every course must have its pre-determined aims, objects and outcomes. In a recent discussion of Weber's typologies of rational action, Ian contrasts this instrumental approach to its humanist alternative:

> 'For some people education is a value in itself, something to be sought after because the more educated we are, the more civilized we become. Through education we become better people, more sensitive, able to appreciate the true and the beautiful, able to find sophisticated pleasures in the world; we become better citizens.'

It is impossible to put into words the unique place he has occupied in his department and university, but also in the wider world of radical social thought. His combination of complete integrity, and loving commitment to his students and his colleagues is such that his wife, Fiona, refers to the department as 'the in-laws'. Paradoxically, for one who insisted on the un-achievability of 'identity', Ian was always and inimitably himself, a colleague of unfaltering integrity: implacably rigorous, usually iconoclastic, wickedly insightful, but uniquely honourable, generous and forgiving. His characteristically impish, subversive chuckle never left him, even in the dark days of his final illness. He remains in my memory the same party-goer, leaping to the beat of the Rolling Stones' 'I can't get no satisfaction'. That was in happier times, when his libertarian spirit was more widely shared, and its political vision seemed possible. Of course, he did get satisfaction (if never complacency) in the love of his son, Ben (of whom he was immensely proud) and his wife, Fiona.

Ian Craib, born on 12 December 1945, died on Sunday 22 December 2002.

Glossary

activity dependence For critical realists, social structures are activity-dependent if they exist only by virtue of the activity of individuals.

actor-network theory An approach to understanding scientific practice based on close observation of laboratory practice, emphasizing active participation of objects, instruments, materials and so on in the construction of scientific knowledge.

affective action A Weberian category: action based on emotion – a form of meaningful social action but not fully rational. *See also* **traditional action; value-oriented action; instrumental action**.

bridge principle For positivists, a statement defining a theoretical concept with an observable and measurable phenomenon.

causal adequacy A Weberian category: an explanation is adequate on the level of cause if a similar situation can be found in which the proposed cause is absent, and the suggested effect does not occur. *See also* **meaning adequacy**.

closed system For critical realists, a situation where the operation of a causal mechanism can be studied independently of external influences. Closed systems are rare in nature, and scientific experiments are attempts to create them artificially. *See also* **open system**.

cognitive interest Habermas posits three 'cognitive interests' which human beings share in their search for knowledge: the **technical**, the **practical** and the **emancipatory**.

communicative rationality For Habermas, the sort of rationality involved in open-ended argument where people seek to understand each other rather than persuade each other to do something. It offers a standard by which societies can be judged and criticized. This involves **communicative speech acts**: statements aimed at understanding and being understood. *See also* **functional rationality; ideal speech situation; instrumental rationality; performative speech acts**.

concept dependence For Bhaskar, social structures are concept-dependent if they are maintained only by virtue of agents having some concept of what they are doing. This is viewed by him as an ontological limit to **naturalism**.

confirmation(ism) *See* **testability**.

constructionism, constructivism A range of approaches which treat what are commonly thought of as independent, real objects as social or cultural 'constructs'. Some constructionists extend this approach to the natural world.

conventionalism The view that currently accepted scientific beliefs are the outcome of negotiated decisions and conventions. It is associated with relativism and the **strong programme in the sociology of science**.

consensus theory of ethics The view that ethical judgements are arrived at through **communicative rationality**.

context of discovery The processes, including thought processes, involved in the creation or invention of new scientific ideas or hypotheses. There are arguments about whether these processes are or are not rational.

context of justification The processes involved in testing and evaluating an idea, theory or hypothesis once it has been advanced. *See* **context of discovery**.

critical realism An approach to the philosophy of both natural and social science. It argues that there is a world independent of our beliefs about it, and that both natural and social sciences are concerned with investigating underlying structures.

deconstruction A post-structuralist concept most closely associated with Derrida; it refers to the systematic analysis of texts to show how they 'construct' their object and give the impression that they refer to some definite 'presence' – an external reality, or an unquestionable foundation of knowledge.

deduction Deductive arguments are ones in which the conclusion drawn follows with *necessity* from the premises.

dialectics, the dialectic A way of thinking commonly associated with Hegel and Marx. The Hegelian version suggests that philosophy develops through argument and contradiction towards a totalizing knowledge of the world. For Marx this became a process by which societies develop towards communism.

dualism A tendency to divide the world into binary opposites: reason and emotion, culture and nature, body and mind and so on.

eco-feminism A feminist position which argues that women, because of their biological nature, psychological development or place in the division of labour are closer to nature, and better placed than men to defend it from patriarchal exploitation. It is closely related to feminist **standpoint epistemology**.

emancipatory interest The third of Habermas's **cognitive interests**. This is the human interest in clearing away misunderstandings and systematic distortions in our knowledge of the world and our relations with each other.

emergence, emergent power, emergent property When elements are combined together into more complex entities, the latter often have properties which are qualitatively distinct from those of the original elements. This is known as 'emergence', and the properties which 'emerge' in this way are 'emergent properties', or 'powers' – a new level of organization.

empiricism A very broad term, designating those approaches to **epistemology** which give a central place to experience in the acquisition and testing of knowledge.

Enlightenment, the The period roughly covering the eighteenth century in Western Europe during which modern philosophy and science – including the social sciences – emerged.

epistemes A Foucauldian concept: an *episteme* is the underlying structure of a discourse, the fundamental concepts within which all thinking in particular period is determined.

epistemological break A term used in the French tradition of historical epistemology to refer to the process of radical transformation of the conceptual framework of a discipline or field of knowledge through which it first emerges as a science. *See also* **scientific revolutions**.

epistemology The philosophical enquiry into the nature and scope of human knowledge, concerned with distinguishing knowledge from belief, prejudice and so on. It is characteristically concerned with developing criteria by which to distinguish genuine knowledge from mere belief, prejudice or faith. *See also* **standpoint epistemology**.

explanatory critique A concept used by some critical realists to emphasize the close logical connection between some forms of social explanation and the adoption of a critical, normative standpoint in relation to the phenomenon explained.

explanatory and observational understanding Weberian categories: observational understanding refers to the immediate grasp of what the observed person is doing, and explanatory understanding grasps the reasons and or intentions involved in the action.

falsification(ism) *See* **testability**.

functionalism A view of society as a collection of parts, the existence of each of which supports the others; extreme forms of functionalist explanation would explain the existence of a social institution by the function it fulfils for other institutions. Functionalism is a form of **holism**.

functional rationality A concept from Habermas, referring to a form of **instrumental rationality** which works to maintain the social system and colonize the **life-world**, that area of life where decisions are reached through **communicative rationality**.

hermeneutics/hermeneutic circle Hermeneutics is the science of interpretation and understanding, originating in the interpretation of sacred text. As with **dialectial thought**, the *whole* is important and the process of thinking is seen as moving from the part to the whole and back again.

holism The explanation of social phenomena by means of the social whole rather than the individual.

hyperreality Baudrillard's description of the post-modern world, where, he argues, reality and we are subjected to increasingly rapid copies of copies of copies.

idealism In philosophy it usually refers to a position in **ontology**, according to which the (ultimate) nature of reality is held to be 'ideal', or 'spiritual', the material world being a misleading set of 'appearances'. There is an extended use in social theory to refer to those approaches which give the primary role in explaining social life to consciousness, culture or 'discourse'.

ideal speech situation Habermas's ideal of a rational, democratic society where everybody has equal access to democratic debate and relevant information and everybody is listened to. A utopian standard by which existing societies can be judged.

ideal type Weber's central methodological concept: a rational reconstruction of a social phenomena or process which can then be compared with the empirical reality.

ideology In its contemporary usage, 'ideology' refers to a systematically distorted set of ideas about reality; the ideas are distorted to favour a particular social class or group. Althusser employs the term as an opposite to 'science'. Predominantly used in Marxist traditions.

individualism The attempt to explain social phenomena by the actions of individuals – usually opposed to **holism**.

induction A form of argument which assumes from past evidence of regular associations that such associations will continue into the future. This is not logically necessary, although we tend to assume that it is.

instrumentalism *See* **theory**.

instrumental rationality/action A way of describing Weber's 'rational action oriented to practical goals'. An important idea in the development of economics. It is used critically by the Frankfurt School theorists to point to that dimension of Enlightenment thought which entails the domination of nature and human beings.

interpretivism A name given to those approaches that concentrate on the interpretation of human actions and cultural products.

intertextuality A concept originating with Derrida. It refers to the way texts constantly rely on and draw on each other, and points to the absence of any 'original' or 'definitive' text.

intransitive dimension A technical term in critical realist philosophy, used to refer to the real objects of scientific knowledge, which are held to exist and act independently of our beliefs about them.

language game A concept developed from Wittgenstein's work describing a language (and by extension a culture) as a game governed by a set of rules. The metaphor has been employed by sociologists and anthropologists.

langue/parole The linguist Ferdinand de Saussure distinguished between the 'langue', the underlying structure of a language, which was the object of the science of linguistics, and 'parole' – individual speech acts which are too variable to be studied by a science. *See also* **structuralism.**

laws (scientific) For empiricism, laws are regular event sequences, or 'constant conjunctions'. Difficulties with this view led to Bhaskar's critical realist account of scientific laws as 'tendencies' of causal mechanisms – which may or may not be expressed in the form of observable regularities.

life world A term used by phenomenologists to describe the flow of experience out of which consciousness constructs identifiable objects; a term taken over by Habermas to describe the area of life dominated by **communicative rationality** as opposed to that dominated by the social system and **functional rationality**.

logic In philosophy, this is the study and classification of the argument-forms through which valid inferences can be made from premises. Logic is not concerned directly with the truth or falsity of statements, but rather with the relationships between them. One way of summarizing this is to say that logic is about the rules for the correct use of the word 'therefore'. *See also* **deduction; induction; retroduction; transcendental arguments**.

logocentrism A term coined by the post-modernist philosopher Derrida to describe the reliance of Western philosophy on Logos – the power of logical, rational argument. *See also* **phonocentrism.**

materialism In philosophy materialism is a position in **ontology**, according to which the (ultimate) nature of the world is physical, or material; mental life is understood as an **emergent property** arising from matter in complex combinations.

meaningful action/meaningful social action For Weber, the proper object of sociology: meaningful action is action to which the actor attaches a meaning. Meaningful *social* action is meaningful action directed to other individuals.

meaning adequacy For Weber, an explanation is adequate if it makes sense – if it is rational according to the standards of the culture in which it takes place, if it is a believable story.

meta-narrative A term employed by Lyotard to identify totalizing or general theories which he believes are no longer possible in the post-modern world, where modern information technology means that all accounts of the world are challenged and relative.

metaphysics The most ambitious branch of philosophy, concerned with giving a systematic reconstruction of the totality of human knowledge, on firm foundations.

narratives The idea that human beings are story-telling animals and make sense of their lives in narrative form has long been present in the interpretive traditions; in this text we find it emphasized in the work of the philosopher Alisdair MacIntyre and the psychologist Jerome Bruner.

naturalism There are, in philosophy, (at least!) three quite distinct meanings given to this term. First, in moral philosophy, naturalism means that a moral judgement can be deduced from factual statements (*see* **explanatory critique**). The most common philosophical view is, on this issue, anti-naturalist. Second, the term can be used to refer to those approaches to the social sciences that model themselves on the natural sciences. The third philosophical use of the term is to characterize views of human nature and society which situate them within 'nature', broadly understood, rather than in opposition to it. Darwinian evolutionary views, for example, represent humans as one evolved primate mammalian species among many.

normal science *See* **scientific revolution**.

object relations psychology A psychoanalytic approach which gives priority to the internalization of early social relations rather than drives such as sexuality.

ontology A general theory about what kinds of things or substances there are in the world, usually presented as one aspect of a metaphysical system. A more modest use of the term refers to the range of entities and relations acknowledged within a particular field of knowledge or scientific specialism.

ontological individualism The position, held by Max Weber, that only individuals exist in the world, not societies or social classes or other collective entities. Weber held that if people believed that societies existed and acted accordingly then we could treat them as if they existed, but not all ontological individualists would go this far.

open system In critical realist philosophy, used to characterize the (usual) state of affairs when a plurality of causal mechanisms interact with each other. *See also* **closed system**.

paradigm For Thomas Kuhn, the framework of a shared scientific theory and shared common-sense beliefs about scientific practice that is necessary for a science to come into existence. *See also* **scientific revolution**.

paradigm/syntagm The axis along which de Ferdinand Saussure analysed the structure of language. The sytagm refers to the rules which stipulate which sign can follow which – the syntagmatic chain. The paradigm or paradigmatic chain refers to rules which govern which signs can substitute for which in the same place in the syntagmatic chain. *See also* **sign; structuralism**.

perfect market A model posited by economists which assumes that everybody on the market has a perfect knowledge of market conditions, a scale of personal preferences, and can make rational decisions to realize those preferences.

performative speech acts Habermas opposes performative speech acts intended to persuade somebody to do something to **communicative speech acts** which aim to achieve understanding.

phenomenological reduction From Husserl – the act of 'bracketing off' what we know about something and describing the acts of consciousness by means of which we come to know it.

phonocentrism From Derrida – used to describe the priority given to the spoken as opposed to the written in Western philosophy. *See also* **logocentrism**.

post-modernism A label originating from the arts; some would claim that it is a form of contemporary society, and it is debatable whether there could be a post-modern philosophy since post-modernists deny the possibility or usefulness of **meta-narratives**. Post-modernism emphasizes difference, fragmentation, change, pastiche, the irrational.

post-structuralism In terms of emphasis on fragmentation, difference and so on, post-structuralism is similar to **post-modernism**, but it has a rather firmer philosophical background in that it develops from a critique of Western philosophy, and therefore despite itself, shares its concerns. It condemns the **logocentrism** and **phonocentrism** of Western philosophy – the search for firm foundations to knowledge.

pragmatism A philosophy developed in America in which knowledge-claims are seen as attached to actions – crudely, what is right is what works.

problematic Term used in historical epistemology to characterize the way the concepts making up a scientific approach or tradition are interlinked with one another, and define what questions can be asked, what objects can be seen, and which rendered unaskable or 'invisible'. *See also* **epistemological break; epistemological obstacle**.

rational choice theory A social theory that assumes that social phenomena can be understood through the rational choices of individuals. *See also* **ontological individualism; instrumental rationality; perfect market**.

rationalism An epistemological position which argues that knowledge can be established through the use of human reason.

realism This term has an immensely complex array of common-sense and philosophical uses. In this book we mean the view that (some of) the things about which we have beliefs are independent of those beliefs and are, in principle, knowable.

reflexivity Arguably a characteristic of all conscious beings, the ability to take oneself as an object of knowledge, or 'reflection'.

relativism At its crudest, the belief that all points of view are context-dependent and of equal worth – there are no context-independent criteria by means of which we can judge between different points of view.

retroduction A form of inferential argument which starts with some phenomenon, or pattern, and poses the question 'What sort of process, mechanism, agency, and so on, if it existed, would have this phenomenon as its consequence?' The conclusions are not logically necessary, but it offers a rational process for devising candidate explanations. *See also* **induction**.

rules, rule-following Peter Winch takes Wittgenstein's philosophy of language as the basis of his argument that cultures, like languages, can be seen as sets of rules and that the social scientist's job is to elaborate these rules and the ways in which they are followed. The notion of implicit rules is also central to ethnomethodology, and the sociology of Anthony Giddens. Wittgenstein is a major figure in the linguistic turn of twentieth-century philosophy.

scientific revolution Thomas Kuhn uses the term to refer to a fundamental transformation in accepted scientific belief and theory (*see* **paradigm**). This becomes the framework for future research, setting the issues to be investigated. Kuhn calls this 'normal science' and sees it as a form of puzzle-solving. The failure to solve puzzles can lead to another revolution and a new paradigm.

sign; signifier/signified Saussure analysed language as a structure of signs. A sign consists of a signifier – the noise or mark on a piece of paper, a physical element, and a *concept* – to which the physical element is attacked. The sign does *not* refer to an object but to an idea, and gains its meaning from its relationship to other signs. Saussure is a major figure in the linguistic turn of twentieth-century philosophy.

standpoint epistemology The argument that some social positions can produce a more adequate form of knowledge than others. Used by Marxists about the proletariat and more recently by feminists. *See also* **epistemology**.

strong programme in the sociology of science An approach which seeks sociological explanations of beliefs quite independently of their supposed truth or falsity.

structuralism A movement which arose across the social sciences and philosophy during the 1960s. Science was seen in terms of identifying the underlying structures of the phenomena under study.

symbolic interactionism An approach on the borders of sociology and social psychology which is based on pragmatic philosophy. *See also* **pragmatism**.

tacit knowledge Implicit knowledge of the rules of social life. This knowledge cannot always be made explicit. *See also* **rules, rule-following**.

testability The various empiricist and most realist approaches to epistemology share the view that knowledge-claims should be open to correction. Many see rational argument as part of this, but some put greater emphasis on empirical testability. Some emphasize supporting evidence (the confirmationists), but the truth of a statement can never be established conclusively this way (*see* **induction**). This gave rise to the falsificationist argument: we can't prove conclusively that something is right, but we can prove that it is wrong. A scientific statement is defined by its testability.

theory The attempt to explain phenomena by going beyond our common-sense, everyday explanations, and beyond our immediate sense experience.

traditional action One of Weber's categories of rational action – action based on tradition. In fact it is not a very rational form of action.

transcendental argument A deductive argument in which the premises are the description of some activity and the conclusion is a statement about what must be the case for the activity to take place. A form of argument used by critical realists. *See also* **deduction**.

transitive dimension In critical realist philosophy, those features of human agents, their social practices and conceptual means which are involved in the production of knowledge, by contrast with the 'objects' about which knowledge is sought. *See also* **intransitive dimension**.

transformational model of social action Bhaskar's view that social structures and individual agency are mutually dependent, but should not be confused with each other, or run together. Social action is possible only by virtue of the existence of social structures, but social structures likewise persist only by virtue of the actions of individuals. In general, individual actors reproduce or transform social structures, but this is not necessarily, or even usually, their purpose in acting.

understanding, observational and explanatory understanding Weber's concepts – social scientists should aim at an explanatory understanding of human action; an observational understanding is a grasp of what the actor is doing, while the explanatory understanding grasps why the actor is doing it.

value freedom Weber argued that a value-free sociology was possible, but only within certain limits. The social scientist is bound by the values of his or her culture and historical period and by his or her commitment to the values of social science. *See also* **value-oriented action**.

value-oriented action Another of Weber's types of rational action. The value choice itself is not rational, but once the choice is made the actions taken in pursuit of the value are rational.

verstehen The German word for understanding; sometimes mistakenly translated as empathy; it involves a grasp of the language and culture of the actor being studied.

Bibliography

Abel, P. (ed.) (1991) *Rational Choice Theory*. Aldershot: Edward Elgar.

Adorno, T. W., Frenkel Brunswik, E., Levinson, D. J. and Sanford A. N. (1950) *The Authoritarian Personality*. New York: Harper.

Adorno, T. W. (1967) *Prisms*. London: Neville Spearman.

Adorno, T. W. (1973) *Negative Dialectics*. New York: Seabury Press.

Adorno, T. W. (1974) *Minima Moralia*. London: New Left Books.

Adorno, T. W. and Horkheimer, M. (1969) *Dialectic of Enlightenment*. New York: Seabury Press.

Althusser, L. (1969) *For Marx*. London: Allen Lane.

Althusser, L. and Balibar, E. (1970) *Reading Capital*. London: New Left Books.

Andreski, S. (1974) *The Essential Comte*. London: Croom Helm.

Andrews, M., Sclater, S. D., Squire, C. and Treacher, A. (forthcoming) *Lines of Narrative*. London: Sage.

Atherton, M. (ed.) (1999) *The Empiricists*. Maryland: Rowman & Littlefield.

Archer, M. (1995) *Realist Social Theory: The Morphogenic Approach*. Cambridge: Cambridge University.

Archer, M. S. (2000) *Being Human: The Problem of Agency*. Cambridge: Cambridge University.

Archer, M., Bhaskar, R., Collier, A., Lawson, T. and Norrie, A. (eds) (1998) *Critical Realism: Essential Readings*. London and New York: Routledge.

Archer, M. S., Collier, A. and Porpora, D. (2004) *Transcendence: Critical Realism and God*. London: Routledge.

Archer, M. S. and Outhwaite, W. (eds) (2004) *Defending Objectivity: Essays in Honour of Andrew Collier*. London and New York: Routledge.

Archer, M. S and Tritter, J. Q. (eds) (2000) *Rational Choice Theory: Resisting Colonization*. London and New York: Routledge.

Ayer, A. J. (1946) *Language Truth and Logic*. London: Gollancz.

Bachelard, G. (1964) *The Psychoanalysis of Fire*. Boston, MA: Beacon Press.

Bachelard, G. (1968) *The Philosophy of No*. New York: Orion.

Barker, D. K. (2003) Emancipatory for whom? A comment on critical realism. *Feminist Economics* 9(1): 103–8.

Barthes, R. (1967) *Elements of Semiology*. London: Jonathan Cape.

Barnes, B. (1974) *Scientific Knowledge and Sociological Theory*. London: Routledge & Kegan Paul.

Barnes, B. (1982) *T. S. Kuhn and Social Science*. London: Macmillan.

Barnes, B. and Bloor, D. (1982) 'Relativism, Rationalism and the Sociology of Knowledge', in M. Hollis and S. Lukes (eds), *Rationality and Relativism*. Oxford: Blackwell, 21–47.

Barnes, B. and Shapin, S. (eds) (1979) *Natural Order: Historical Studies in Scientific Culture*. London: Sage.

Baudrillard, J. (1985) *The Mirror of Production*. St Louis, MO: Telos Press.

Beck, U. (1992) *Risk Society: Towards a New Modernity*. London: Sage.

Beckett, S. (1965) 'The Unnamable' in *Three Novels by Samuel Beckett*. New York: Grove Press.

Beer, G. (1983) *Darwin's Plots: Evolutionary Narrative in Darwin, George Elliot and Nineteenth Century Fiction*. London: Routledge & Kegan Paul.

Benton, T. (1977) *The Philosophical Foundations of the Three Sociologies*. London: Routledge & Kegan Paul.

Benton, T. (1980) 'Lecourt: The Case of Lysenko', *Radical Philosophy* 24, 30–42.

Benton, T. (1981) 'Realism and Social Science', *Radical Philosophy* 27, 13–21. (Reprinted in M. Archer *et al.* (eds) (1998) *Critical Realism: Essential Readings*. London and New York: Routledge).

Benton, T. (1984) *The Rise and Fall of Structural Marxism*. Basingstoke: Macmillan.

Benton, T. (1989) Marxism and natural limits: an ecological critique and reconstruction. *New Left Review* 178: 51–86.

Benton, T. (1991) Biology and social science: why the return of the repressed should be given a (cautious) welcome. *Sociology* 25(1): 1–29.

Benton, T. (1993) *Natural Relations: Ecology, Animal Rights and Social Justice*. London and New York: Verso.

Benton, T. (1995) 'Science, Ideology and Culture: Malthus and *The Origin of Species*' in Amigoni, D. and Wallance, J. (eds) *Charles Darwin's Origin of Species: New Interdisciplinary Essays*. Manchester: Manchester University.

Benton, T. (2001) Why are sociologists naturephobes? In Lopez and Potter (eds) *op. cit.*: 133–45.

Benton, T. (2002) 'Wittgenstein, Winch and Marx' in Kitching and Pleasants (eds) *op. cit.*: 147–59.

Benton, T. (2004) Realism about the value of nature? Andrew Collier's environmental philosophy. In Archer and Outhwaite (eds) *op. cit.*: 239–50.

Berger, P. and Luckmann, T. (1967) *The Social Construction of Reality*. London: Allen Lane.

Bernal, J. D. (1939) *The Social Function of Science*. London: Routledge & Sons.

Bhaskar, R. (1975, 1997) *A Realist Theory of Science*. London: Verso.

Bhaskar, R. (1978) *The Possibility of Naturalism*. Hemel Hempstead: Harvester Wheatsheaf.

Bhaskar, R. (1979, 1998) *The Possibility of Naturalism*. Hemel Hempstead: Harvester Wheatsheaf.

Bhaskar, R. (1986) *Scientific Realism and Human Emancipation*. London: Verso.

Bhaskar, R. (1989) *Reclaiming Reality*. London and New York: Verso.

Bhaskar, R. (1993) *Dialectic: The Pulse of Freedom*. London: Verso.

Bhaskar, R. (2002) *Meta Reality. The Philosophy of Meta Reality*. Delhi: New Sage.

Biehl, J. (1991) *Rethinking Ecofeminist Politics*. Boston, MA: South End.

Birke, L. (1986) *Women, Feminism and Biology*. Brighton: Harvester Wheatsheaf.

Birke, L. (1994) *Feminism, Animals and Science: The Naming of the Shrew*. Buckingham: Open University Press.

Bloor, D. (1991) *Knowledge and Social Imagery*. University of Chicago Press.

Blumer, H. (1969) *Symbolic Interactionism: Perspectives and Methods*. Englewood Cliffs, NJ: Prentice-Hall.

Brown, J. R. (1994) *Smoke and Mirrors: How Science Reflects Reality*. London and New York: Routledge.

Brown, A., Fleetwood, S. and Roberts, M. (2002) *Critical Theory and Marxism*. London: Routledge.

Bruner, J. (1987) 'Life as Narrative', *Social Research* 34(1), 11–34.

Bryant, G. A. and Jarry, D. (eds) (1997) *Anthony Giddens: Critical Assessments*. London: Routledge.

Bynum, W. F., Browne, E. J. and Porter, R. (1981) *Dictionary of the History of Science*. London and Basingstoke: Macmillan.

Callon, M. (1986) 'Some Elements of a Sociology of Translation: Domestication of the Scallops and the Fishermen of St Brieuc Bay', in Law, J. (ed.), *Power, Action and Belief: A New Sociology of Knowledge?* London: Routledge & Kegan Paul, 196–233.

Callon, M. and Latour, B. (1992) 'Don't Throw the Baby out with the Bath School!', in A. Pickering (ed.) *Constructing Quarks: A Sociological History of Particle Physics*. University of Chicago Press, 343–68.

Caplan, A. (ed.) (1978) *The Sociobiology Debate*. New York: Harper Row.

Carling, A. (1986) 'Rational Choice Marxism', *New Left Review* 186: 24–62.

Carnap, R. (1966) *Philosophical Foundations of Physics*. New York and London: Basic Books.

Carson, R. (1962) *Silent Spring*. Boston, MA: Houghton Mifflin.

Carter, B. and New, C. (2004) *Making Realism Work: Realist Social Theory and Empirical Research*. London: Routledge.

Castree, N. (2002) False antitheses? Marxism, nature and actor-networks. *Antipode* 34(1): 111–46.

Chalmers, A. F. (1999) (3rd edn) *What is this Thing Called Science?* Buckingham: Open University Press.

Chodorow, N. (1978) *The Reproduction of Mothering*. Berkeley: University of California Press.

Chodos, H., Curtis, B., Hunt, A. and Manwaring, J. (2007) Gadamer's minimal realism. In Frauley, J. and Pearce, F. (eds) *op. cit.*: 296–315.

Cioffi, F. and Borger, R. (1970) 'Freud and the Idea of a Psuedo-Science', in Borger, R. and Cioffi, F., *Explanation in the Behavioural Sciences*. Cambridge University Press.

Collier, A. (1989) *Scientific Realism and Socialist Thought*. Hemel Hempstead: Harvester Wheatsheaf.

Collier, A. (1991) 'The Inorganic Body and the Ambiguity of Freedom', in *Radical Philosophy* 57, 3–9.

Collier, A. (1994a) *Critical Realism*. London: Verso.

——— (1994b) Value, rationality and the environment. *Radical Philosophy* 66: 3–9.

—— (1999) *Being and Worth*. London and New York: Routledge.

Collier, A. (2003) *In Defence of Objectivity*. London: Routledge.

Collin, F. (1997) *Social Reality*. London and New York: Routledge.

Collins H. M. (1985) *Changing Order: Replication and Induction in Scientific Practice*. Beverly Hills: Sage.

Collins, H. M. (1996) 'Theory Dopes: A Critique of Murphy', in *Sociology* 30(2), 367–73.

Collins, H. M. and Yearley, S. (1992a) 'Epistemological Chicken', in Pickering, A. (ed.), *Constructing Quarks: A Sociological History of Particle Physics*. University of Chicago Press, 301–26.

Collins, H. M. and Yearley, S. (1992b) 'Journey into Space', in Pickering, A. (ed.), *Constructing Quarks: A Sociological History of Particle Physics*. University of Chicago Press, 369–89.

Collins, P. H. (1991) *Black Feminist Thought: Knowledge, Consciousness, and the Politics of Empowerment*. London and New York: Routledge.

Couvalis, G. (1997) *The Philosophy of Science: Science and Objectivity*. London: Sage.

Craib, I. (1976) *Existentialism and Sociology*. Cambridge University Press.

Craib, I. (1989) *Psychoanalysis and social Theory: the Limits of Sociology*. Hemel Hempstead: Harvester.

Craib, I. (1992) *Modern Social Theory*. Hemel Hempstead: Harvester Wheatsheaf.

—— (1994) *The Importance of Disappointment*. London and New York: Routledge.

Craib, I. (1997) *Classical Social Theory*. Oxford University Press.

Craib, I. (1998) *Experiencing Identity*. London: Sage.

Cruickshank, J. (2003) *Realism and Sociology: Anti-foundationalism, Ontology and Social Research*. London and New York: Routledge.

—— (ed.) (2003) *Critical Realism: The Difference it Makes*. London and New York: Routledge.

Culler, J. (1975) *Structuralist Poetics: Linguistics and the Study of Literature*. London: Routledge & Kegan Paul.

Danermark, B., Ekström, M., Jakobsen, L. and Karlsson, J. C. (2001) *Explaining Society: Critical Realism in the Social Sciences*. London: Routledge.

Darwin, C. (1987) *Charles Darwin's Notebooks 1836–1846*. Ed. Barrett, P. H., Gautrey, P. J., Herbert, S., Kohn, D. and Smith, S. London and Cambridge: BM (NH) and Cambridge University.

Davidson, D. (2001) *Inquiries into Truth and Interpretation*. Oxford: Oxford University Press.

Davis, J. B. (2002) 'A Marxist influence on Wittgenstein via Sraffa'. In Kitching and Pleasants (eds) *op. cit.*: 131–43.

Day, R. (2007) More than straw figures in straw houses: towards a revaluation of critical realism's conception of post-structuralist theory. In Frauley and Pearce (eds) *op. cit.*: 117–41.

Dean, K. (2006) Agency and dialectics: what critical realism can learn from Althusser's Marxism. In Dean *et al. op. cit.*: 123–47.

Dean, K., Joseph, J., Roberts, J. M. and Wight, C. (2006) *Realism, Philosophy and Social Science*. Basingstoke and New York: Palgrave Macmillan.

Delanty, G. (1997) *Social Science: Beyond Costructivism and Realism*. Buckingham: Open University Press.

Derrida, J. (1973) *Speech and Phenomena and Other Essays on Husserl's Theory of Signs*. Evanston, IL: Northwestern University Press.

Derrida, J. (1976) *Of Grammatology*. Baltimore, MD: Johns Hopkins University Press.

Derrida, J. (1978) *Writing and Difference*. London: Routledge & Kegan Paul.

De Saussure, F. (1974) *Course in General Linguistics*. London: Fontana/Collins.

Descartes, R. (1641, 1931) 'Meditations on First Philosophy', in *The Philosophical Works of Descartes*, vol. 1. London: Dover.

Desmond, A. and Moore, J. (1992) *Darwin*. Harmondsworth: Penguin.

Dewey, J. (1939) *Intelligence in the Modern World: John Dewey's Philosophy* (ed. J. Ruttner). New York: Modern Library.

Dews, P. (1987) *Logics of Disintegration: Post-Structuralist Thought and the Claims of Critical Theory*. London: Verso.

Dickens, P. (1992) *Society and Nature*. Hemel Hempstead: Harvester Wheatsheaf.

Dickens, P. (1996) *Reconstructing Nature: Alienation, Emancipation and the Division of Labour*. London and New York: Routledge.

Dickens, P. (2004) *Society and Nature: Changing our Environment, Changing Ourselves*. Oxford: Polity.

Dickens, P. and Ormrod, J. (2007) *Cosmic Society. Towards a Sociology of the Universe*. London: Routledge.

Dilthey, W. (1961) *Meaning in History: W. Dilthey's thoughts on history and society*. Edited and introduced by H. P. Pickman. London: Allen & Unwin.

Dunlap, R., Buttel, F., Dickens, P. and Gijwijt, A. (eds) (2002) *Sociological Theory and the Environment*. New York: Rowman and Littlefield.

Durkheim, E. (1895, 1982) *The Rules of Sociological Method*. London: Macmillan.

Durkheim, E. (1896, 1952) *Suicide*. London: Routledge & Kegan Paul.

Durkheim, E. (1912, 1982) *The Elementary Forms of the Religious Life*. London: Allen & Unwin.

Easlea, B. (1980) *Witch-hunting, Magic and the New Philosophy*. Brighton: Harvester.

Easlea, B. (1983) *Fathering the Unthinkable: Masculinity, Scientists and the Nuclear Arms Race*. London: Pluto.

Elder-Vass, D. (2007a) For emergence: refining Archer's account of social structure. *Journal for the Theory of Social Behaviour* 37: 25–44.

Elder-Vass, D. (2007b) Social structure and social relations. *Journal for the Theory of Social Behaviour* 37: 463–77.

Elliott, G. (ed.) (1994) *Louis Althusser: A Critical Reader*. Oxford and Cambridge, MA: Blackwell.

Engels, F. (1949) *Dialectics of Nature*. London: Lawrence & Wishart.

Etsioni, A. (1995) *The Spirit of Community*. London: Fontana.

Evans Pritchard, E. (1937) *Witchcraft, Oracles and Magic among the Azande*. Oxford University Press.

Eyerman, R. and Jamison, A. (1991) *Social Movements: A Cognitive Approach.* Cambridge: Polity Press.

Feyerabend, P. K. (1975) *Against Method: Outline of an Anarchistic Theory of Knowledge.* London: New Left Books.

Feyerabend, P. K. (1978) *Science in a Free Society.* London: New Left Books.

Feyerabend, P. K. (1981) *Problems of Empiricism. Philosophical Papers*, vol. 2. Cambridge University Press.

Flax, J. (1983) 'Political Philosophy and the Patriarchal Unconscious', in S. Harding and M. Hintikka (eds), *Discovering Reality.* Dordrecht: Reidel.

Flax, J. (1990) *Thinking Fragments: Psychoanalysis, Feminism and Postmodernism in the Contemporary West.* Berkeley: University of California Press.

Foucault, M. (1970) *The Order of Things.* London: Tavistock.

Foucault, M. (1972) *The Archaeology of Knowledge.* London: Tavistock.

Foucault, M. (1973) *The Birth of the Clinic.* London: Tavistock.

Foucault, M. (1977) *Discipline and Punish.* London: Allen Lane.

Foucault, M. (1978a) *The History of Sexuality*, vol. 1. London: Allen Lane.

Foucault, M. (ed.) (1978b) *I, Pierre Riviere . . . A Case of Parricide in the Nineteenth Century.* London: Sage.

Frauley, J. (2007) The expulsion of Foucault from governmentality studies: toward an archaeological-realist retrieval. In Frauley and Pearce (eds) *op. cit.*: 258–72.

Frauley, J. and Pearce, F. (eds) (2007) *Critical Realism and the Social Sciences; Heterodox Elaborations.* Toronto: University of Toronto.

Freud, S. (1982) *The Interpretation of Dreams.* Harmondsworth: Penguin.

Freundlieb, D., Hudson, W. and Rundell, J. (eds) (2004) *Critical Theory after Habermas: Encounters and Departures.* Leiden and Boston: Brill.

Fuller, S. (1993) *The Philosophy of Science and its Discontents*, 2nd edn. New York: Guilford.

Gadamer, H-G. (1989) *Truth and Method.* London: Sheed & Ward.

Garfinkel, H. (1967) *Studies in Ethnomethodology.* Englewood Cliffs, NJ: Prentice-Hall.

Gelsthorpe, L. (1992) 'Response to Martyn Hammersley's Paper "On Feminist Methodolgy"', *Sociology* 26(2), 213–18.

Gergen, K. (1991) *The Saturated Self.* New York: Basic Books.

Giddens, A. (1976) *New Rules of Sociological Method.* London: Hutchinson.

Giddens, A. (1984) *The Constitution of Society.* Cambridge: Polity Press.

Gilbert, N. and Mulkay, M. (eds) (1984) *Opening Pandora's Box: A Sociological Study of Scientists' Discourse.* Cambridge University Press.

Gilligan, C. (1982) *In a Different Voice: Psychological Theory and Women's Development.* Cambridge, MA: Harvard University Press.

Glynos, J. and Howarth, D. (2007) *Logics of Critical Explanation in Social and Political Theory.* London and New York: Routledge.

Goffman, E. (1968) *The Presentation of Self in Everyday Life.* Harmondsworth: Penguin.

Goldberg, S. (1974) *The Inevitability of Patriarchy.* New York: Morrow.

Gramsci, A. (1971) *Selections from the Prison Notebooks.* London: Lawrence & Wishart.

Greenfield, S. (1997) *The Human Brain: A Guided Tour.* London: Weidenfeld & Nicolson.

Griggs, S and Howarth, D. (2007) Protest movements, environmental activism and environmentalism in the United Kingdom. In J. Pretty *et al.* (eds) *The Sage Handbook of Environment and Society*. London: Sage: 314–24.

Grint, K. and Woolgar, S. (1997) *The Machine at Work*. Cambridge: Polity Press.

Groff, R. (ed.) (2008) *Revitalising Causality in Philosophy and Social Science*. London and New York: Routledge.

Gutting, G. (1989) *Michel Foucault's Archaeology and Scientific Reason*. Cambridge University Press.

Habermas, J. (1984) *Theory of Communicative Action*, vol. 1. London: Heinneman.

Habermas, J. (1986) *Knowledge and Human Interests*. Cambridge: Polity Press.

Habermas, J. (1987) *Theory of Communicative Action*, vol. 2. Cambridge: Polity Press.

Habermas, J. (1990) *Philosophical Discourse of Modernity*. Cambridge: Polity Press.

Hacking, I. (1983) *Representing and Intervening*. Cambridge University Press.

Haeckel, E. (1883) *The Pedigree of Man and other Essays*. London: Freethought.

Halfpenny, P. (1982) *Positivism and Sociology*. London: Allen & Unwin.

Hall, S. and Du Gay, P. (1996) 'Introduction: Who Needs Identity?' in Hall and Du Gay (eds), *Questions of Cultural Identity*. London: Sage.

Hammersley, M. (1992) 'On Feminist Methodology', *Sociology* 26, 187–206.

Hammersley, M. (1994) 'On Feminist Methodology: A Response', *Sociology* 28, 293–300.

Hanson, N. R. (1965) *Patterns of Discovery*. Cambridge University Press.

Haraway, D. (1991) *Simians, Cyborgs and Women: The Reinvention of Nature*. London: Free Associations.

Haraway, D. (1992) *Primate Visions: Gender, Race and Nature in the World of Modern Science*. London: Verso.

Harding, S. (1986) *The Science Question in Feminism*. Ithaca: Cornell University Press.

Harding, S. (1991) *Whose Science? Whose Knowledge?* Buckingham: Open University Press.

Harding, S. (1998) *Is Science Multi-Cultural?* Bloomington and Indianapolis: Indiana University Press.

Harding, S. (1999) The case for strategic realism: a response to Lawson. *Feminist Economics* 5(3): 127–33.

Harding, S. (2003) How standpoint methodology informs philosophy of social science. In Turner, S. and Roth, P. A. (eds) *The Blackwell Guide to the Philosophy of the Social Sciences*. Malden, MA and Oxford: Blackwell.

———— (ed.) (2004) *The Feminist Standpoint Theory Reader: Intellectual and Political Controversies*. London and New York: Routledge.

Harding, S. and Hintikka, M. (eds) (1983) *Discovering Reality*. Dordrecht: Reidel.

Harré, R. (1970) *The Principles of Scientific Thinking*. London: Macmillan.

Harré, R. (1972) *The Philosophies of Science*. Oxford University Press.

Harré, R. (1986) *Varieties of Realism*. Oxford: Blackwell.

Harré, R. and Madden, E. H. (1975) *Causal Powers*. Oxford: Blackwell.

Harrison, B. (1978) *Separate Spheres*. London: Croom Helm.

Harrison, B. and Lyon, E. S. (1993) 'A Note on Ethical Issues in the Use of Autobiography in Sociological Research', in *Sociology* 27(1), 101–9.

Hartsock, N. (1983a) The feminist standpoint: developing the ground for a specifically feminist historical materialism. In Harding, S. and Hintikka, M. B. (eds) *Discovering Reality*. Dordrecht: Reidel. (reprinted in Hartsock (1998) *op. cit.*)

Hartsock, N. C. M. (1983b) *Money, Sex, and Power: Toward a Feminist Historical Materialism*. London: Longman.

Hartsock, N. C. M. (1998) The feminist standpoint revisited. In Hartsock, N. C. M. (ed.) *The Feminist Standpoint Revisited and other Essays*. Boulder, Colorado and Oxford: Westview.

Harvey, D. (1990) *The Condition of Postmodernity: An Inquiry into the Origins of Cultural Change*. Oxford: Blackwell.

Hayek, F. A. (1949) *Individualism and Economic Order*. London: Routledge & Kegan Paul.

Hegel, G. W. F. (1807, 1977) *The Phenomenology of Spirit*. Oxford University Press.

Held, D. (1980) *Introduction to Critical Theory*. London: Hutchinson.

Hammersley, M. (1992) 'On Feminist Methodology', in *Sociology* 26(2), 187–206.

Hempel, C. G. (1966) *Philosophy of Natural Science*. Englewood Cliffs, NJ: Prentice-Hall.

Hesse, M. (1966) *Models and Analogies in Science*. South Bend, IN: University of Notre Dame Press.

Hoffe, O. (1994) *Immanuel Kant*. New York: State University of New York.

Hollis, M. (1970) Reason and ritual. In B. R. Wilson (ed.) *op. cit.*: 221–39 (originally In *Philosophy* XLIII, (1967), 165: 231–47).

Hollis, M. and Lukes, S. (1982) *Rationality and Relativism*. Oxford: Blackwell.

Holmwood, J. (1995) 'Feminism and Epistemology: What Kind of Successor Science?', *Sociology* 29: 411–28.

Honderich, T. (ed.) (1999) *The Philosophers*. Oxford University Press.

Honneth, A. (1996) *The Struggle for Recognition: the Moral Grammar of Social Conflicts*. Tr. J. Anderson. Cambridge, Mass.: MIT.

——— (2009) *Pathologies of Reason: on the Legacy of Critical Theory*. Tr. J. Ingram and others. New York: Columbia University.

hooks, b. (1981) *Ain't I a Woman? Black Women and Feminism*. Boston, MA: South End Press.

Horkheimer, M. (1972) *Critical Theory*. New York: Herder & Herder.

How, A. (1995) *The Habermas–Gadamer Debate and the Nature of the Social*. Aldershot: Avebury.

How, A. (1998) 'That's Classic! A Gadamerian Defence of the Classic Text in Sociology', *Sociological Review* 46(4), 828–48.

Husserl, E. (1930–39, 1965) *Phenomenology and the Crisis of Philosophy*. New York: Harper Torchbooks.

Hutchinson, W. F., Mellor, M and Olsen, W. (2002) *The Politics of Money: Towards Sustainability and Economic Democracy*. London: Pluto.

Hutchinson, P., Read, R. and Sharrock, W. (2008) *There is No Such Thing as a Social Science*. Aldershot and Burlington, USA: Ashgate.

Hutchinson, W. F., Mellor, M. and Olsen, W. (2002) *The Politics of Money: Towards Sustainability and Economic Democracy.* London: Pluto.

Irwin, A. (1994) 'Sociology Row Erupts at BA', *The Times Higher*, 16 September, 44.

Irwin, A. (1995) *Citizen Science.* London: Routledge.

Irwin, A. and Wynne, B. (eds) (1996) *Misunderstanding Science?* Cambridge University Press.

James, W. (1975) *The Meaning of Truth.* Cambridge, MA: Harvard University Press.

Jackson, C. (1995) 'Radical Environmental Myths: A Gender Perspective', *New Left Review* 210, 124–40.

Jackson, C. (1996) 'Still Stirred by the Promise of Modernity', *New Left Review* 217, 148–54.

Jameson, F. (1972) *The Prison House of Language.* Princeton University Press.

Jameson, F. (1991) *Postmodernism or the Cultural Logic of Late Capitalism.* London: Verso.

Jasanoff, S., Markle, G. E., Petersen, J. C. and Pinch, T. (eds) (1994) *Handbook of Science and Technology Studies.* Beverley Hills and London: Sage.

Jessop, B. (1982) *The Capitalist State.* Oxford: Martin Robertson.

—— (1990) *State Theory.* Cambridge: Polity.

—— (2002) *The Future of the Capitalist State.* Cambridge: Polity.

Joseph, J. (2001) *Marxism and Social Theory.* Basingstoke and New York: Palgrave Macmillan.

—— (2002) *Hegemony: A Realist Analysis.* London and New York: Routledge.

—— (2006) Marxism: The dialectic of freedom and emancipation. In Dean *et al. op. cit.*: 99–122.

Kant, I. (1953) *Prolegomena to any Future Metaphysics.* Manchester University Press.

Keat, R. (1971) 'Positivism, Naturalism and Anti-Naturalism in the Social Sciences', *The Journal for the Theory of Social Behaviour* 1, 3–17.

Keat, R. and Urry, J. (1975) *Social Theory as Science.* London: Routledge and Kegan Paul.

King, A. (2007) Why I am not an individualist. *Journal for the Theory of Social Behaviour* 37: 221–19.

Kitching, G. and Pleasants, N. (2002) *Marx and Wittgenstein: Knowledge, Morality and Politics.* London and New York: Routledge.

Keller, E. F. (1983) *A Feeling for the Organism: The Life and Work of Barbara Mclintock.* New York: Freeman.

Keller, E. F. (1985) *Reflections on Gender and Science.* New Haven, CT and London: Yale University Press.

Körner, S. (1990) *Kant.* Harmondsworth: Penguin.

Kuhn, T. S. (1959) *The Copernican Revolution*, New York: Random House.

Kuhn, T. S. (1970) *The Structure of Scientific Revolutions.* University of Chicago Press.

Lacan, J. (1968) *Speech and Language in Psychoanalysis.* Baltimore, MD: Johns Hopkins University Press.

Laclau, E. and Bhaskar, R. (1998) Discourse theory versus critical realism. *Alethia* 1(2): 9–14.

Laclau, E. and Mouffe, C. (1985) *Hegemony and Socialist Strategy*. London: Verso.

Lakatos, I. (1970) 'Falsification and the Methodology of Scientific Research Programmes', in Lakatos, I. and Musgrave, A. (eds), *Criticism and the Growth of Knowledge*. Cambridge University Press.

Lakatos, I. and Musgrave, A. (eds) (1970) *Criticism and the Growth of Knowledge*. Cambridge University Press.

Lash, S., Szerszynski, B. and Wynne, B. (1996) *Risk, Environment and Modernity*. London: Sage.

Latour, B. (1987) *Science in Action*. Cambridge, MA: Harvard University Press.

Latour, B. (1988) *The Pasteurization of France*. Cambridge, MA: Harvard University Press.

Latour, B. (1993) *We Have Never Been Modern*. Hemel Hempstead: Harvester Wheatsheaf.

Latour, B. and Woolgar, S. (1979) *Laboratory Life*. Princeton University Press.

Lassman, P. (1974) 'Phenomenological Perspectives in Sociology', in Rex, J. (ed.), *Approaches to Sociology*. London: Routledge & Kegan Paul, 125–44.

Laudan, L. (1996) *Beyond Positivism and Relativism*. Boulder, CO: Westview.

Law, J. (ed.) (1986) *Power, Action and Belief: A New Sociology of Knowledge?* London: Routledge & Kegan Paul.

Law, J. (ed.) (1992) *A Sociology of Monsters: Essays on Power, Technology and Domination*. London: Routledge.

Law, J. (2004) *After Method: Mess in Social Science Research*. London: Routledge.

—— (2007) Making a mess with method. In Outhwaite, W. and Turner, S. P. (eds) *Handbook of Social Science Methodology*. London and Beverley Hill: Sage.

—— (2009) Actor network theory and material semiotics. In Turner, B. S. (ed.) *The New Blackwell Companion to Social Theory*. Oxford and Malden: Blackwell and John Wiley & Sons.

Law, J. and Hassard (eds) (1999) *Actor Network Theory and After*. Oxford and Keele: Blackwell and Sociological Review.

Lawson, T. (1997) *Economics and Reality*. London and New York: Routledge.

—— (1999) Feminism, realism and universalism. *Feminist Economics* 5(2): 25–60.

—— (2003a) *Reorienting Economics*. London and New York: Routledge.

—— (2003b) Ontology and feminist theorizing. *Feminist Economics* 9(1): 119–50.

Leat, D. (1972) 'Misunderstanding *Verstehen*'. *Sociological Review* 20, 29–38.

Lecourt, D. (1975) *Marxism and Epistemology: Bachelard, Canguilhem and Foucault*. London: New Left Books.

Lecourt, D. (1977) *Proletarian Science? The Case of Lysenko*. London: New Left Books.

Lefebvre, H. (1968) *Dialectical Materialism*. London: Jonathan Cape.

Lenin Academy of Agricultural Sciences of the USSR (1949) *The Situation in Biological Science* (*Proceedings for 1948*). Moscow: Foreign Languages Publishing House.

Lévi-Strauss, C. (1966) *The Savage Mind*. Chicago University Press.

Lévi-Strauss, C. (1968) *Structural Anthropology*. Harmondsworth: Penguin.

Levitas, R. and Guy, W. (eds) (1996) *Interpreting Official Statistics*. London: Routledge.

Lewis, D. J. and Smith, R. L. (1980) *American Sociology and Pragmatism: Mead, Chicago Sociology and Symbolic Intreraction*. University of Chicago Press.

Lewontin, R. and Levins, R. (1976) 'The Problem of Lysenkoism' in Rose and Rose (eds) 1976b, op. cit., 32–64.

Little, D. (1991) *Varieties of Social Explanation*. Boulder, CO: Westview.

Longino, H. E. (1990) *Science as Social Knowledge*. Princeton, N.J.: Princeton University.

Lopez, J. (1999) *The Discursive Exigencies of Enunciating the Concept of Social Strucure: Five Case Studies*. Unpublished PhD thesis, University of Essex.

Lopez, J. and Scott, J. (2001) *Social Structure*. Buckingham and Philadelphia: Open University.

Lopez, J. and Potter, G. (eds) (2001) *After Postmodernism: An Introduction to Critical Realism*. London and New York: Athlone.

Lovibond, S. (1989) 'Feminism and Postmodernism', *New Left Review* 178, 5–50.

Lukács, G. (1971) *History and Class Consciousness*. Cambridge, MA: MIT Press.

Lukes, S. (1973) *Durkheim*. Harmondsworth: Penguin.

Lyas, C. (1999) *Peter Winch*. Teddington: Acumen.

Lyons, J. (1977) *Chomsky*. London: Fontana.

Lyotard, J.-F. (1984) *The Postmodern Condition*. Manchester University Press.

MacAdams, D. P. (1993) *Stories We Live By: Personal Myths and the Making of the Self*. New York: Morrow.

MacIntyre, A. (1974) 'The Idea of a Social Science', in B. R. Wilson (ed.), *Rationality*. Oxford: Blackwell, 112–30.

MacIntyre, A. (1981) *After Virtue: A Study in Moral Theory*. London: Duckworth.

MacKenzie, D. (1990) *Inventing Accuracy*. Cambridge, MA: MIT Press.

Mannheim, K. (1936) *Ideology and Utopia*. London: Routledge & Kegan Paul.

Marcuse, H. (1960) *Reason and Revolution*. Boston: Beacon Press.

Marcuse, H. (1964) *One Dimensional Man*. London: Routledge & Kegan Paul.

Marcuse, H. (1968) *Negations: Essays in Critical Theory*. Boston: Beacon Press.

Marcuse, H. (1969) *Eros and Civilisation*. London: Sphere Books.

Marcuse, H. (1970) *Five Lectures*. New York: Beacon Press.

Maslow, A. H. (1970) *Motivation and Personality*. New York and London.

Marx, K. and Engels, F. (1975) *Collected Works, Vol. 3*. Moscow: Progress.

Marshall, G. (1997) *Repositioning Class: Social Inequality in Industrial Societies*. London: Sage.

Marx, K. (1970) *Capital, Volume 1*. London: Lawrence & Wishart.

May, T. and Williams, M. (eds) (1998) *Knowing the Social World*. Buckingham: Open University Press.

McCormack, C. and Strathern, M. (eds) (1980) *Nature, Culture and Gender*. Cambridge University Press.

McLellan, G. (1995) 'Feminism, Epistemology and Postmodernism', *Sociology* 29, 391–409.

McLennan, G. (2009) 'FOR science in the social sciences': the end of the road for critical realism? In Moog and Stones (eds) *op. cit.*: 47–64.

McMylor, P. (1994) *Alisdair MacIntyre: Critic of Modernity*. London: Routledge.

Mead, G. H. (1938) *Mind, Self and Society*. Chicago University Press.

Mellor, M. (1992) *Breaking the Boundaries.* London: Virago.

Mellor, M. (1996) 'Myths and Realities: A Reply to Cecile Jackson', *New Left Review* 217, 132–7.

Mellor, M. (1997) *Feminism and Ecology.* Cambridge: Polity.

Mellor, M. (1998) *Feminism and Ecology.* Cambridge: Polity.

———— (2010) *The Future of Money: Financial Crisis to Public Resource.* London: Pluto.

Merchant, C. (1980) *The Death of Nature.* London: Wildwood, Morgan & Stanley.

Merleau-Ponty, M. (1974) *The Prose of the World.* London: Heinnemann.

Merton, R. K. (1938/1970) *Science, Technology and Society in Seventeenth Century England.* New York: H. Fertig.

Merton, R. K. (1968) *Social Theory and Social Structure.* Glencoe, NJ: Free Press.

Merton, R. K. (1973) *The Sociology of Science.* University of Chicago Press.

Mies, M. and Shiva, V. (1993) *Ecofeminism.* London and New Jersey: Zed.

Minsky, R. (1996) *Psychoanalysis and Gender: An Introductory Reader.* London: Routledge.

Monk, R. (1990) *Ludwig Wittgenstein: The Duty of Genius.* London: Jonathan Cape.

Moog, S. and Stones, R. (eds) (2009) *Nature, Social Relations and Human Needs: Essays in Honour of Ted Benton.* Basingstoke: Palgrave Macmillan.

Morgan, D. and Stanley, L. (1993) *Debates in Sociology.* Manchester and New York: Manchester University.

Mulkay, M. (1979) *Science and the Sociology of Knowledge.* London: Allen & Unwin.

Murphy, R. (1994) 'The Sociological Construction of Science Without Nature', *Sociology* 28: 957–74.

Murphy, R. (1997) 'On Methodological Relativism and Parochial Empiricism: A Reply to Collins', *Sociology* 31, 801–6.

Murphy, R. (2002a) Ecological materialism and the sociology of Max Weber. In Dunlap *et al.* (eds) *op. cit.*

———— (2002b) The internalization of autonomous nature into society. *Sociological Review* 50: 313–33.

———— (2007) Thinking across the culture/nature divide. In Frauley and Pearce (eds) *op. cit.*: 141–62.

New, C. (1994) 'Structure, Agency and Social Transformation', *Journal for the Theory of Social Behaviour* 24: 187–205.

New, C. (1996) *Agency, Health and Social Survival.* London and Bristol: Taylor & Francis.

New, C. (1998) Realism, deconstruction and feminism. *Journal for the Theory of Social Behaviour* 28(4): 350–72.

———— (2003) Feminism, deconstruction and difference. In Cruickshank (ed.) *op. cit.*

Newton-Smith, W. (1981) *The Rationality of Science.* London: Routledge & Kegan Paul.

Nicholson, L. J. (ed.) (1990) *Feminism/Postmodernism.* London: Routledge.

Oakley, A. (1998) 'Gender, Methodology and People's Ways of Knowing', *Sociology* 32, 707–37.

O'Hear, A. (1989) *An Introduction to the Philosophy of Science.* Oxford: Clarendon.

Oldroyd, D. R. (1986) *The Arch of Knowledge.* London: Methuen.

O'Neill, J. (1993) *Ecology, Policy and Politics*. London: Routledge.

O'Neill, J. (1998) *The Market: Ethics, Knowledge and Politics*. London: Routledge.

—— (2007) *Markets, Deliberation and Environment*. London: Routledge.

O'Neill, J., Light, A. and Holland, A. (2008) *Environmental Values*. London: Routledge.

Outhwaite, W. (1987) *New Philosophies of Social Science: Realism, Hermeneutics and Critical Theory*. London: Macmillan.

Outhwaite, W. (1994) *Habermas: A Critical Introduction*. Cambridge: Polity Press.

Pearce, F. (1989) *The Radical Durkheim*. London: Unwin Hyman.

Pearce, F. (2001) *The Radical Durkheim*. Toronto: Canadian Scholars.

—— (2007) Bhaskar's critical realism: an appreciative introduction and a friendly critique. In Frauley and Pearce (eds) *op. cit.*: 30–63.

Pearce, F. and Woodiwiss, T. (2001) Reading Foucault as a realist. In Lopez and Potter (eds) *op. cit.*: 51–62.

Peter, F. (2003) Critical realism, feminist epistemology, and the emancipatory potential of science: a comment on Lawson and Harding. *Feminist Economics* 9(1): 93–100.

Pharies, D. A. (1985) *Charles S. Peirce and the Linguistic Sign*. Philadelphia: J. Benjamins.

Pickering, A. (1984) *Constructing Quarks: A Sociological History of Particle Physics*. University of Chicago Press.

Pickering, A. (ed.) (1992) *Science as Practice and Culture*. University of Chicago.

Pinch, T. (1986) *Confronting Nature: The Sociology of Neutrino Detection*. Dordrecht: Reidel.

Pinker, S. (1997) *How the Mind Works*. Harmondsworth: Penguin.

Plumwood, V. (1993) *Feminism and the Mastery of Nature*. London: Routledge.

Popper, K. (1957) *The Poverty of Historicism*. London: Routledge & Kegan Paul.

Popper, K. (1963) *Conjectures and Refutations*. London: Routledge & Kegan Paul.

Popper, K. (1968) *The Logic of Scientific Discovery*. London: Hutchinson.

Porpora, D. (2007) On Elder-Vass: refining a refinement. *Journal for the Theory of Social Behaviour* 37: 195–200.

Potter, G. (2000) *The Philosophy of Social Science: New Perspectives*. Harlow: Pearson.

Potter, G. (2002) Politics, pedagogy and the 'reluctant student' (review of Benton and Craib (2001) *Philosophy of Social Science*). In *Alethia* (*Journal of Critical Realism*). 5(1): 79–83.

Potter, G. (2007) Critical realism and God. In Frauley and Pearce (eds) *op. cit.*: 74–96.

Putnam, H. (1990) *Realism with a Human Face*. Cambridge, MA: Harvard University Press.

Quine, W. V. O. (1980) *From a Logical Point of View*. Cambridge, MA: Harvard University Press.

Radder, H. (1998) 'The Politics of S. T. S.', *Social Studies of Science* 28, 338–44.

Radical Science Journal (1974–83) London.

Ramazanoglu, C. (1992) 'On Feminist Methodology: Male Reason Versus Female Empowerment', *Sociology* 26, 207–12.

Ramsey, M. (1992) *Human Needs and the Market*. Aldershot: Avebury.

Red–Green Study Group (1995) *What on Earth is to be Done?* Manchester: Red-Green Study Group.

Rees, R. (1960) 'Wittgenstein's Builders', *Proceedings of the Aristotelian Society* 20, 171–86.

Rex. J. and Moore, R. (1967) *Race, Community and Conflict.* Oxford: Institute of Race Relations and Oxford University Press.

Rickert, H. (1962) *Science and History: A Critique of Positivist Epistemology.* New York: Van Nostrand.

Rock, P. (1979) *The Making of Symbolic Interactionism.* Totowa, NJ: Rowman & Littlefield.

Rorty, R. (1982) *Consequences of Pragmatism.* Minneapolis: University of Minnesota Press.

Rose, H. (1983) 'Hand, Brain and Heart: A Feminist Epistemology for the Natural Sciences'. *Signs* 9(1), 73–90.

Rose, H. (1994) *Love, Power and Knowledge.* Cambridge: Polity Press.

Rose, H. and Rose, S. (1969) *Science and Society.* Harmondsworth: Penguin.

Rose, H. and Rose, S. (1976a) *The Political Economy of Science.* London: Macmillan.

Rose, H. and Rose, S. (1976b) *The Radicalisation of Science.* London: Macmillan.

Rose, H. and Rose, S. (eds) (2000) *Alas, Poor Darwin.* London and New York: Harmony, Jonathan Cape.

Rose, S. (1997) *Lifelines: Biology, Freedom, Determinism.* Harmondsowrth: Penguin.

Rose, S., Kamin, L. J. and Lewontin, R. C. (1984) *Not in our Genes: Biology, Ideology and Human Nature.* Harmondsworth: Penguin.

Runciman, W. G. (1972) *A Critique of Max Weber's Philosophy of Social Science.* Cambridge University Press.

Rundell, J., Petherbridge, D., Bryant, J., Hewitt, J. and Smith, J. (eds) (2005) *Contemporary Perspectives in Critical and Social Philosophy.* Leiden: Brill.

Rustin, M. (1994) 'Incomplete Modernity: Ulrich Beck's Risk Society', *Radical Philosophy* 67, 3–12.

Ryle, G. (1963) *The Concept of Mind.* Harmondsworth: Penguin.

Ryle, M. (1988) *Ecology and Socialism.* London: Radius.

Sacks, O. (1986) *The Man Who Mistook his Wife for a Hat.* London: Pan. Ital. Title.

Salleh, A. (1994) 'Nature, Woman, Labour, Capital: Living the Deepest Contradiction', in M. O'Connor (ed.), *Is Capitalism Sustainable?* New York: Guilford.

Salleh, A. (1996) 'An Ecofeminist Bioethic and What Post-Humanism Really Means', *New Left Review* 217, 138–47.

Sarup, M. (1993) *An Introductory Guide to Post-Structuralim and Post-Modernism.* Hemel Hempstead: Harvester Wheatsheaf.

Sayer, A. (1992) *Method in Social Science.* London: Routledge.

Sayer, A. (1995) *Radical Political Economy: A Critique.* Oxford: Blackwell.

Sayer, A. (2000) *Realism and Social Science.* London: Sage.

Sayer, A. (2009) Understanding lay normativity. In Moog and Stones (eds) *op. cit.*: 128–45.

Sayers, J. (1982) *Biological Politics: Feminist and Anti-Feminist Perspectives.* London: Tavistock.

Shapin, S. and Schaffer, S. (1985) *Leviathan and the Air Pump.* Princeton University Press.

Schutz, A. (1962–6) *Collected Papers* (2 vols). The Hague: Martinus Nijhoff.

Schutz, A. (1972) *The Phenomenology of the Social World*. London: Heinnemann.

Scott, J. (2001) Where is social structure? In Lopez and Potter (eds) *op. cit.*: 77–85.

Science as Culture (1987–) London.

Sen, A. (1977) 'Rational Fools: a critique of the behavioural foundations of economic theory', *Philosophy and Public Affairs* 6, 317–44.

Shiva, V. (1989) *Staying Alive*. London and New Jersey: Zed.

Singer, P. (1975) *Animal Liberation*. London: Jonathan Cape.

Soper, K. (1981) *On Human Needs*. Brighton: Harvester.

Soper, K. (1989) 'Feminism as Critique', *New Left Review* 176, 91–112.

Soper, K. (1990a) *Troubled Pleasures*. London: Verso.

Soper, K. (1990b) 'Feminism, Humanism and Postmodernism', *Radical Philosophy* 55, 11–17.

Soper, K. (1995) *What is Nature?* Oxford: Blackwell.

Soper, K. (1998) 'An Alternative Hedonism' (interview with T. Benton), *Radical Philosophy* 92, 28–38.

Soper, K. (2000) Future culture: realism, humanism and the politics of nature. *Radical Philosophy* 102: 17–26.

———— (2004) Objectivity, experience and the aesthetic of nature. In Archer and Outhwaite (eds) *op. cit.*: 251–60.

———— (2009) Realism, naturalism and the red-green nexus. In Moog and Stones (eds) *op. cit.*: 170–84.

Soper, K, Ryle, M. and Thomas, L. (2009) *The Politics and Pleasures of Consuming Differently*. Basingstoke and New York: Palgrave Macmillan.

Stanley, L. and Wise, S. (1983) *Breaking Out: Feminist Consciousness and Feminist Research*. London: Routledge & Kegan Paul.

Stanley, L. and Wise, S. (1992) *Breaking out Again: Feminist Epistemology and Ontology*. Manchester: Manchester University Press.

Stones, R. (1996) *Sociological Reasoning: Towards a Past-modern Sociology*. London: Palgrave Macmillan.

———— (2005) *Structuration Theory*. Basingstoke and New York: Palgrave Macmillan.

Strathern, M. (1988) *The Gender of the Gift*. Berkeley: University of California Press.

Strawson, P. F. (1966) *The Bounds of Sense: An Essay on Kant's Critique of Pure Reason*. London: Methuen.

Tanesini, A. (1998) *An Introduction to Feminist Epistemologies*. Oxford: Blackwell.

Taylor, C. (1985) 'Rationality' in *Philosophy and the Human Sciences*. Cambridge University Press.

Taylor, C. (1991) *The Ethics of Authenticity*. Cambridge, MA: Harvard University Press.

Varela, C. (2007) Elder-Vass's move and Giddens's call. *Journal for the Theory of Social Behaviour* 37: 201–10.

Wainwright, H. (1994) *Arguments for a New Left*. Oxford: Blackwell.

Weber, M. (1904–5, 1930) *The Protestant Ethic and the Spirit of Capitalism*. London: Allen & Unwin.

Weber, M. (1922, 1947) *The Theory of Social and Economic Organisation*. New York: Oxford University Press.

Weber, M. (1915, 1951) *The Religion of China*. New York: Free Press.

Weber, M. (1921, 1952) *Ancient Judaism*. New York: Free Press.

Weber, M. (1921, 1958) *The Religion of India*. New York: Free Press.

Weber, M. (1949) *The Methodology of the Social Sciences*. New York: Free Press.

Webster, A. (1994) 'University–Corporate Ties and the Construction of Research Agendas'. *Sociology* 28, 123–42.

Werskey, G (1978) *The Visible College*. London: Allen Lane.

West, D. (1996) *Introduction to Continental Philosophy*. Cambridge: Polity Press.

White, S. K. (1988) *The Recent Work of Jurgen Habermas: Reason, Justice and Modernity*. Cambridge: Cambridge University.

—— (ed.) (1995) *The Cambridge Companion to Habermas*. Cambridge: Cambridge University.

Wilson, B. (ed.) (1970) *Rationality*. Oxford: Blackwell.

Wilson, B. R. (ed.) (1974) *Rationality*. Oxford: Blackwell.

Winch, P. (1958) *The Idea of a Social Science*. London: Routledge & Kegan Paul.

Winch, P. (1970) 'Understanding a Primitive Society', in B. Wilson (ed.), *Rationality* Oxford: Blackwell.

Winch, P. (1974) 'Understanding a primitive society'. In Wilson, B. R. (ed.) *Rationality* (first published in *American Philosophical Quarterly* 1(4): 307–24.)

Winch, P. (1990) *The Idea of a Social Science*, 2nd edition. London: Routledge.

Wittgenstein, L. (1958, 1997) *Philosophical Investigations*. Oxford: Blackwell.

Wolff, K. H. (1978) 'Phenomenology and Sociology', in Bottomore, T. B. and Nisbet, R. (eds) *A History of Sociological Analysis*. London: Heinemann, 499–556.

Wynne, B. (1996) 'SSK's Identity Parade: Signing-up, Off-and-On', *Social Studies of Science* (special issue on the politics of SSK) 26, 357–91.

Yearley, S. (1995) 'The Environmental Challenge to Science Studies', in Jasanoff, S., Markle, G. E., Petersen, J. C. and Pinch, T. (eds) (1994) *Handbook of Science and Technology Studies*. London: Sage.

Index

255